Keyboard Shortcuts

F1	Switches screen display from text to graphics
F6	Turns coordinate readout on or off
F7	Turns grid on or off
F8	Turns Ortho on or off
F9	Turns Snap on or off
F10	Turns tablet mode on or off
HOME	Cursor appears on-screen
END	Cursor control returns to mouse/puck
INS	Moves cursor into menu area
PG UP	Increases step distance of cursor by factor of 10, then 100
PG DN	Decreases step distance of cursor
CTRL C	Cancels commands

Computer users are not all alike.
Neither are SYBEX books.

We know our customers have a variety of needs. They've told us so. And because we've listened, we've developed several distinct types of books to meet the needs of each of our customers. What are you looking for in computer help?

If you're looking for the basics, try the **ABC's** series. You'll find short, unintimidating tutorials and helpful illustrations. For a more visual approach, select **Teach Yourself**, featuring screen-by-screen illustrations of how to use your latest software purchase.

Mastering and **Understanding** titles offer you a step-by-step introduction, plus an in-depth examination of intermediate-level features, to use as you progress.

Our **Up & Running** series is designed for computer-literate consumers who want a no-nonsense overview of new programs. Just 20 basic lessons, and you're on your way.

We also publish two types of reference books. Our **Instant References** provide quick access to each of a program's commands and functions. SYBEX **Encyclopedias** provide a *comprehensive reference* and explanation of all of the commands, features and functions of the subject software.

Sometimes a subject requires a special treatment that our standard series doesn't provide. So you'll find we have titles like **Advanced Techniques, Handbooks, Tips & Tricks**, and others that are specifically tailored to satisfy a unique need.

We carefully select our authors for their in-depth understanding of the software they're writing about, as well as their ability to write clearly and communicate effectively. Each manuscript is thoroughly reviewed by our technical staff to ensure its complete accuracy. Our production department makes sure it's easy to use. All of this adds up to the highest quality books available, consistently appearing on best-seller charts worldwide.

You'll find SYBEX publishes a variety of books on every popular software package. Looking for computer help? Help Yourself to SYBEX.

For a complete catalog of our publications:

SYBEX Inc.
2021 Challenger Drive, Alameda, CA 94501
Tel: (415) 523-8233/(800) 227-2346 Telex: 336311
Fax: (415) 523-2373

SYBEX is committed to using natural resources wisely to preserve and improve our environment. As a leader in the computer book publishing industry, we are aware that over 40% of America's solid waste is paper. This is why we have been printing the text of books like this one on recycled paper since 1982.

This year our use of recycled paper will result in the saving of more than 15,300 trees. We will lower air pollution effluents by 54,000 pounds, save 6,300,000 gallons of water, and reduce landfill by 2,700 cubic yards.

In choosing a SYBEX book you are not only making a choice for the best in skills and information, you are also choosing to enhance the quality of life for all of us.

TEACH YOURSELF AUTOCAD
RELEASE 11

TEACH YOURSELF AUTOCAD®
RELEASE 11

Genevieve Katz

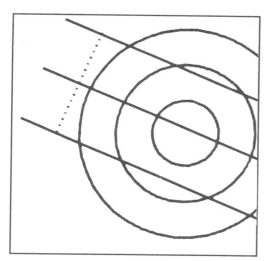 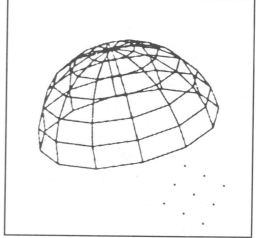

SYBEX®

San Francisco . Paris . Düsseldorf . Soest

Acquisitions Editor: Dianne King
Editor: Richard Mills
Technical Editor: Maryann Brown
Word Processors: Ann Dunn and Susan Trybull
Book Designer: Ingrid Owen
Chapter Art: Ingrid Owen
Screen Graphics: Cuong Le
Desktop Publishing Specialists: Len Gilbert and Dan Brodnitz
Proofreader: Dina F. Quan
Production Assistant: Thomas Goudie
Indexer: Ted Laux
Cover Designer: Archer Design
Cover Photographer: David Bishop

Library of Congress Card Number: 91-65019
ISBN: 0-89588-627-8

Manufactured in the United States of America
10 9 8 7 6 5 4 3 2 1

◆ To my husband, Lou, who introduced me to the magic of computers, and to my son, Steven, who continues in it.

ACKNOWLEDGMENTS

My thanks to the people at SYBEX:

To Rudy Langer and Dianne King, who enthusiastically put their forces behind "something new and different."

To Richard, who could see both forest and trees and restored my faith in editors and in all the wondrous things they can do.

To the many others at SYBEX who helped create what you hold in your hands: Maryann Brown, technical editor; Ingrid Owen, book designer; Len Gilbert and Dan Brodnitz, desktop publishing specialists; and Dina Quan, proofreader.

To David Yost for his Grand Editor, years ahead of its time.

And to the people at Autodesk:

To Patrica Pepper for smoothing out the interfaces, to Gloria Bastides for her understanding of a writer's dilemma, and to the unnamed heroes of tech support who provided answers beyond the manual.

And to my students at California College of Arts and Crafts who, by their learning, taught the teacher.

CONTENTS AT A GLANCE

TABLE OF CONTENTS

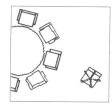

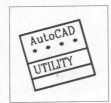
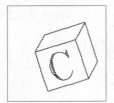
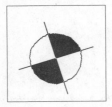

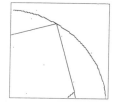

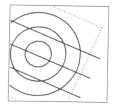

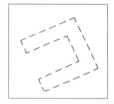

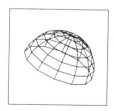

INTRODUCTION

This book is written for those who, when words aren't enough, pick up a pencil to draw.

This book is written for those who still work out designs on the backs of envelopes and napkins, and for those who still find the feel of pencil on paper sensuous.

This book is written for those who see the world in pictures, explain things with a sketch, find a drawing infinitely superior to pages of text, and are intrigued by this thing called "CAD."

✦ How to Use This Book

Teach Yourself AutoCAD started out when I tried to understand why my students didn't read manuals. It became clear to me that the people learning CAD are those who are engaged in the drawing process—and for those people, a picture conveys the concept much more effectively than words. And so the focus of this book is to explain AutoCAD through drawings.

Teach Yourself AutoCAD can be used as a beginning guide or as a quick pictorial reference to help you remember how the AutoCAD commands work. Because one of the difficulties beginners often experience is not knowing where to find the commands they need to use, a Command Finder picture box appears under each command heading, showing at a glance where the command can be found.

My approach is to get you up and drawing as quickly as possible. Because it is a basic book, some advanced commands and the more complex and less used options of some commands are not covered. Nevertheless, you will find all the commands necessary to complete the layout and design of an office space, which you will work on throughout the course of the book. (When you are ready for more complex and advanced concepts, I recommend reading George Omura's *Mastering AutoCAD Release 11*, SYBEX, 1991.)

Teach Yourself AutoCAD uses architectural examples for the tutorials, because I have found that they are more easily understood by people in a wide variety of professions. Although this book covers Release 11, users of earlier releases will find most of the explanations applicable. I make specific mention of those places where Release 11 departs from earlier releases.

The book is organized into chapters that cluster related groups of AutoCAD commands. Most chapters are divided into two parts: The first part contains individual descriptions of AutoCAD commands, and the second part has a tutorial that makes use of the commands introduced in the first part.

Each command description includes

- A Command Finder graphic, which illustrates how to find the command on the pull-down, tablet, and side menus
- A list of command options (if applicable)
- A "Using the Command" section, which uses actual AutoCAD drawings and screen captures, accompanied by text, to show you how to use the command options
- Helpful notes and tips

The tutorial at the end of the chapters step you through some aspect of the office plan that you work on throughout the book. I have attempted to use only commands in the tutorials that have already been covered, but it is difficult to do any AutoCAD drawing without a minimum palette of commands, so the early tutorials include some commands covered in later chapters. When this happens, however, I have made the instructions specific so that you can follow through and complete the tutorial. Of course, you can always look up the material on these commands later in the book (check the inside of the front cover for a list of all the commands in the book and the page numbers on which they can be found).

While the "Using" sections can be used as a quick reference, the tutorials have been designed to be followed sequentially. As you progress through the tutorials and become more familiar with AutoCAD commands, you will create an office space, place windows and doors, design and lay out furniture, dimension the plan, label it, produce 3-D views of it, and insert a title block and plot the plan (if you have access to a plotter or printer).

Instructions are very specific at the beginning. As the book progresses, they become less specific, as you become accustomed to the rhythm and feel of the program.

If you ever need help, AutoCAD's Help command accesses what amounts to a condensed version of the AutoCAD manual. You can either name a specific command or select one from a list. If you are in a command and need information on it, pick Help from the screen or tablet menu. If you select it this way, the command is *transparent*—that is, it can be accessed without interfering with the command you are using. If you enter *Help* from the keyboard, you must type an apostrophe (') before the command for it to be transparent.

✦ Conventions Used in the Book

I have used some conventions in the book to help you use it. In the tutorials, instructions to the user are explained by the use of text, drawings, and special program lines that combine AutoCAD prompts and user responses.

- AutoCAD prompts are in program font.
- User keyboard actions are in **boldface.**
- Other actions that the user is required to carry out, usually with the mouse or puck (such as picking a point), are in *italics*.
- Additional information on what a prompt or instruction means is in parentheses.

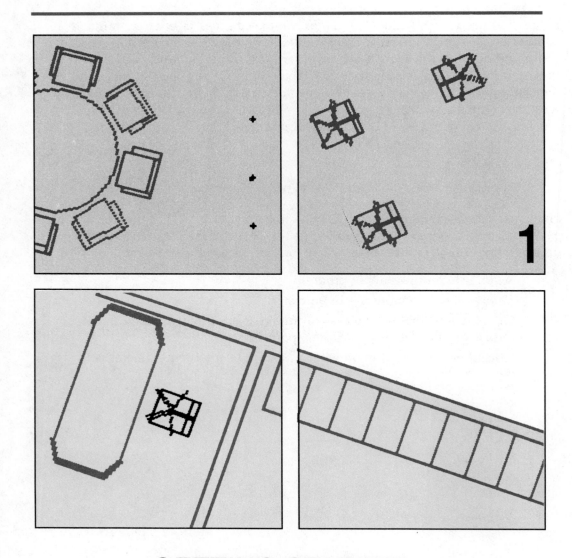

GETTING STARTED

Before you can start creating drawings in AutoCAD, you need to learn some of the basics. By now you should have AutoCAD installed (if you haven't done so already, refer to Appendix A for instructions) and be seated at your computer, ready to go. But first, a few words about your equipment.

✦ The Computer and Disk Drives

Your computer has an On/Off switch, which is probably on the side, toward the back. The On position is 1 and Off is 0. The floppy-disk drives are located in the front. The most common drive is for 1.2MB 5¼" double-sided, high-density floppy disks, although the drive for 1.44MB 3½" disks is rapidly becoming popular.

To insert a 5¼" floppy disk, hold it by the side opposite from the oval cutout with your thumb on the top (the bottom has seams), and gently insert it in the disk slot. Then push the lever down. The magnetic coating on the disk is fragile, so you should not place your fingers on the open portion showing through the oval slot. The sleeves that come with the disks protect them and should be used when the disks are not in the computer.

The 3½" disk has a hard case and a metal slide on one edge and is not as fragile. You insert it by pushing the disk into the drive slot, metal edge first. There is a small arrow pointing forward that is embossed into the upper-left corner of the disk to aid you; the upper-right corner is beveled. You will know the 3½" disk is wrong-side-up if you can see the metal circle in the center of the disk.

✦ Input Devices

You will be communicating with AutoCAD with two input devices, the keyboard and your mouse or tablet.

The Keyboard

The keyboard works pretty much like a typewriter, but it has some keys that are special to computers. In AutoCAD, the function keys **F1** and **F6** through **F10** are used to turn some often-used functions on and off. If you have one of the older keyboards, the function keys may be on the left side instead of across the top. (Figure 1 shows two common keyboard layouts.)

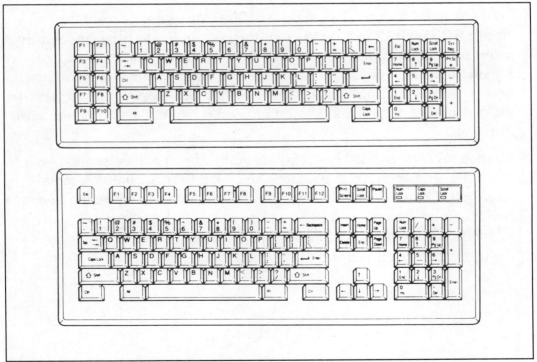

Figure 1: Common computer keyboards

All commands that you enter from the keyboard have to be followed by ⏎. The spacebar can also be used to end commands. You can type uppercase or lower-case letters.

Some keyboard functions require that two or more keys be pressed simultane-ously. You can cancel most commands by holding down CTRL (the Control key) while pressing the C key. Occasionally your computer will "hang up," which is the phrase used when the computer seems to be stuck and doesn't respond to you. At that point you have to reset the machine. I recommend that you do a *warm boot*. Hold down CTRL while pressing ALT and DEL. It takes two hands to prevent you from doing it accidentally. (Some computers have a reset button that provides the same function.) Using the warm boot or the reset button will throw away any work done after your last Save. I do not recommend turning your computer off and on manually, except as a last resort.

Although it is most common to use a mouse or tablet as an input device, you can use the keyboard for pointing and selecting. The arrow keys move the cursor about the screen. Using PG UP and PG DN increases or decreases the increment by which the cursor moves by a factor of 10 the first time you press either key and by 100 the second time. You select a point on the screen by pressing ⏎ or the spacebar. The INS key moves the cursor to the side menu. The pull-down menus cannot be accessed from the keyboard. Once you have activated the arrow keys, any other pointing device you may be using becomes inoperable until you press END. Using the keyboard this way is useful when you have a job to get out and your mouse dies.

The Tablet and Puck

A *tablet* is a drawing surface with an electronic grid that is used with a *puck* (see Figure 2). A plastic overlay on the tablet aids both command selection and the use of cursor functions. A puck can have from three to ten buttons on it; four is the most common. The button assignments for the four-button puck are as fol-lows: Button number 1 is the pick button (used most often), button 2 functions as the Enter key, button 3 calls up the drawing tool called Osnap, and button 4 can-cels the current command.

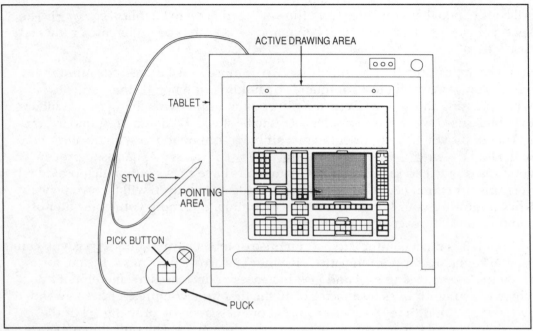

Figure 2: The tablet and puck

The Mouse

Most PC mice used with AutoCAD have three buttons (see Figure 3). The assignment of functions to the buttons is the same as for the puck, except that there is no fourth button on the mouse.

✦ Starting AutoCAD

Most programs, not just AutoCAD, are started by typing in the name of the program's executable file and then pressing ⏎. You type **ACAD** to start AutoCAD. The first thing you see is the Main Menu (see Figure 4).

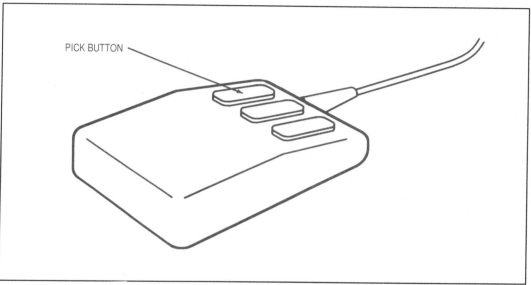

PICK BUTTON

Figure 3: The mouse

Most of the time you will be using the first three functions on the Main Menu. Remember that you must press ⏎ after making a selection.

0. Exit AutoCAD After you finish a drawing session, you still have to get out of AutoCAD by pressing 0 and ⏎. AutoCAD opens temporary files to save your drawings when you start a drawing session, and these files can only be closed and removed when you exit AutoCAD properly.

1. Begin a NEW drawing When you want to start a new drawing, press 1 and ⏎. When prompted for the name of the drawing, type the name of the new drawing and press ⏎. When you start a drawing, AutoCAD loads a default drawing that has certain commands and variables already set. These can be easily changed to fit your drawing needs. (Appendix B lists all the default settings in the prototype drawing named *ACAD*.)

```
                  A U T O C A D  (R)
Copyright (c) 1982-90 Autodesk, Inc.  All Rights Reserved.
Release 11 (10/17/90) 386 DOS Extender
Serial Number:  100-10000000
Licensed to:    Genevieve Katz, Metron Studios
Obtained from:  Autodesk, Inc. - 332 2344 Fax 331 8093
Current drawing:  PLAN

Main Menu

   0.  Exit AutoCAD
   1.  Begin a NEW drawing
   2.  Edit an EXISTING drawing
   3.  Plot a drawing
   4.  Printer Plot a drawing

   5.  Configure AutoCAD
   6.  File Utilities
   7.  Compile shape/font description file
   8.  Convert old drawing file
   9.  Recover damaged drawing

Enter selection:
```

Figure 4: The Main Menu

✦ **Note**

Drawing names cannot be longer than eight alphanumeric characters. Special characters, such as the dollar sign ($), hyphen (-), and underline are also allowed, and there cannot be any spaces in the name.

Files can have extensions, although they don't necessarily have to. An extension is made up of the three letters that follow the period in the drawing name and is something like a last name. The extension gives you a clue as to what kind of file it is—.DWG is a drawing file, .BAK is a backup file, and .LSP is a LISP file. You should not include the .DWG extension when working in AutoCAD; AutoCAD automatically adds it to your drawing name. When working with a file outside of AutoCAD, you must give its full name, including the extension.

---

2. Edit an EXISTING drawing When you go back into a drawing to do more work on it, AutoCAD refers to this as *editing* the drawing. AutoCAD capitalizes *EXIST-ING* to prevent you from confusing this option with beginning a new drawing. A file (drawings are saved as files) must have a unique name. If you give a new file the same name as an existing file, AutoCAD warns you that a drawing with that name already exists. If you select OK, the new file will overwrite the old file.

3. Plot a drawing This option gives you the choice of plotting a drawing without opening the drawing file. It saves time if you have a very large drawing, because it takes time for the drawing to appear on the screen. (In this book, you will plot from inside the drawing editor. You are inside the editor when the drawing area and menus appear on your screen.)

4. Printer Plot a drawing This is the same as the Plot option, except you use it if you have a non-PostScript printer as your output device instead of a plotter.

5. Configure AutoCAD With this option you tell AutoCAD what kind of equipment you have. You generally have to do this only once, unless you add or substitute new equipment. Details on configuring your system are in Appendix A, along with the information on installing AutoCAD.

6. File Utilities If you have forgotten the name of the drawing you want to work on, you can select this option, then *1. List Drawing Files* to get a list of drawings. You can also do some file management with the options provided here. The File Utilities option is also available inside the drawing editor and is explained under the Files command entry in Chapter 3.

7. Compile shape/font description file This option is generally used for designing new fonts and is beyond the scope of this book.

8. Convert old drawing file This option is used with AutoCAD drawings created in versions of AutoCAD previous to version 2.0. AutoCAD automatically makes use of drawings created in versions 2.0 and later; in other words, these files are *up-wardly compatible*. Once these drawings are converted, however, they will no longer work in the older version—you can't go home again.

9. Recover damaged drawings If your drawing editor crashes—an earthquake happens, or someone turns off your computer in the middle of a drawing session—you will get a message of the sort "Fatal Error" or "Internal Error" when you try to use that drawing later. When you select this option, AutoCAD will try to restore your drawing from its drawing database. Just follow the prompts; AutoCAD does the rest.

◆ Inside the Drawing Editor

After you select either option 1 or option 2 on the Main Menu, you go to the drawing editor (see Figure 5).

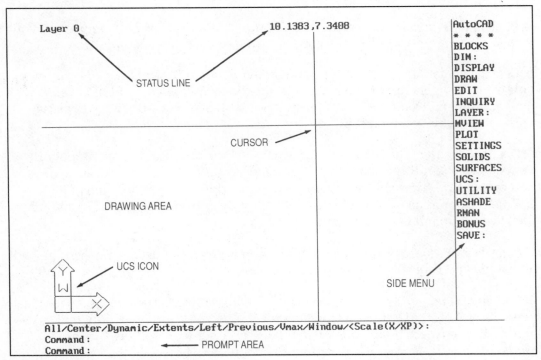

Figure 5: The drawing editor screen

The Root Menu and Status Line

To the right of your screen is the *root menu*. It is the top level of the menu hierarchy, from which you can access all other commands. On the top of your screen is the *status line*. This line gives you information about the current status of your drawing:

- What layer you are on
- Whether you have activated the Snap or Ortho modes
- The coordinates of your cursor

The Prompt Area

At the bottom of the screen is the *prompt area,* where you will see three lines of text. The first two contain prompts and responses already done; the last one is the prompt line you respond to. AutoCAD is very verbose; it always seems to be talking to you. Beginners freeze up because they don't know how to tell AutoCAD what they want it to do. To use AutoCAD, you have to learn to "Autospeak"; here are some helpful tips:

- Don't let all the text on the bottom of the screen confuse you; read and respond to the last line.
- When you see the *Command:* prompt, AutoCAD is waiting for you to issue a command. Enter Move, Copy, or any of the 155 other commands. AutoCAD will laze around until you do.
- If nothing happens, and you have responded to the Command prompt, press ⏎ or button 2 on your mouse or puck. It is unbelievable how many ⏎/button 2 responses are required to operate AutoCAD.
- An "Invalid" response from AutoCAD means that you did not give it the answer it wanted. It could be a simple thing, such as omitting a comma or entering feet when only decimals are allowed. Reread the prompt and try again.

The Menu Bar

When you move your mouse or puck, the cursor moves around on the screen. The cursor is made up of cross hairs that extend to the edges of the drawing area. If you move the cursor to the top of the screen, you will see the *menu bar,* which has nine command options on it (see Figure 6). Pressing the pick button on your

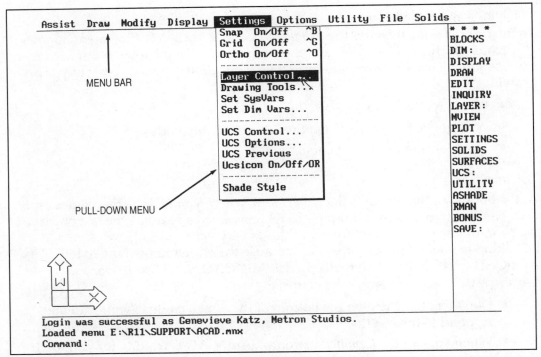

Figure 6: The menu bar and Settings pull-down menu

mouse or puck while the cursor is on an option pulls down a menu with additional options.

✦ Command Organization in the Menus

If you are a new user, AutoCAD's command organization may seem somewhat arbitrary and artificial. Autodesk has attempted to break down the complex and integrated activity of creating a drawing into discrete sets of commands that can be organized into a computer-aided design and drafting (CADD) system.

When you draw by hand, drawing a line, erasing a line, and copying a line are all part of doing the drawing—they are not discrete actions. In AutoCAD, drawing a line is in the drawing section, and erasing and copying it are in the editing/ modifying section. In addition, there are whole sets of commands to let you move about the screen, file your drawings away, make symbols, and do many more things.

Take a look at how the commands are organized under their respective groups. There are some inconsistencies between the pull-down menus and the side menu. For instance, although Draw contains the same commands in both menus, the commands listed under Modify in the pull-down menus are listed under Edit on the side menu. This book attempts to ease this confusion with the Command Finder box, which shows you where to find a command in whatever menu system you choose to use.

♦ Accessing Commands

Try all the methods of accessing commands, then pick one and get comfortable with it. There are all sorts of opinions as to which method works best. Typing in commands is the most direct, and if you are a fast typist, the fastest. The pull-down menus are more graphic and provide dialog boxes. The root menu is the most complete menu; you can access all the AutoCAD commands through it. The tablet menu provides visual clues for the commands, although some feel that glancing back and forth between tablet and screen is tiring.

♦ Tip

A word about getting out of commands when you have picked something you don't want. From the keyboard, pressing CTRL C always works. You can access Cancel in the Tools pull-down menu and under the four stars (****) in the side menu. Dialog boxes always have a Cancel box you can click on. You can also press button 3 on your puck.

If you haven't chosen a command, you can get out of a pull-down menu by moving your cursor to the screen and picking an empty spot or making another menu selection, either from the menu bar or the side menu. Remember, pressing CTRL C always works.

Pull-Down Menus

When you move the cursor to the top of the screen, the menu bar appears. To select commands, follow these steps:

- Move the arrow using your puck or mouse to the left or right until it is over the heading you want.
- Select the heading by pressing the pick button.
- Move your mouse or puck down until the command you want is highlighted.
- Select the command by pressing the pick button again; the command is executed.

The modifying commands on the pull-down menus activate different forms of selections. Erase immediately erases each object selected and uses the Auto mode (see "Entity Selection Sets" in this chapter). Trim and Extend also use the Auto mode but allow you to build a selection set.

For some commands, the pull-down menu triggers the side menu for options related to the command.

Dialog Boxes

A *dialog box* appears after you select certain menu options and contains check boxes, command buttons, and text boxes. Figure 7 shows the Layer Control dialog box.

To change or specify new values in a dialog box, move the arrow into the editing area. When the area is highlighted, enter the new value from the keyboard. Check marks are used to turn modes on or off or to make selections. You move the arrow into the small rectangular area, and use the pick button on your mouse or puck as a toggle switch to turn them on or off. When you are finished, pressing ⏎ activates the OK command button and removes the dialog box.

When a list is longer than the ten lines appearing in the dialog box, *scroll bars* are used to move up and down the list. Picking the head of the arrow moves you up or down through the list one line at a time, depending upon which arrowhead you have picked. Picking the square slider box (the *scroll box*) and moving it to a

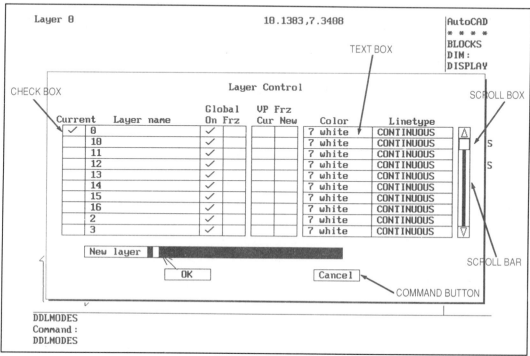

Figure 7: An example of a dialog box

new place moves you to the relative location in the list. Picking the line above or below the box moves you up or down through the list a page at a time.

The Root Menu

The root menu is organized hierarchically. The main groups are contained in the list that starts with Block and ends with Save. All commands branch out from these. For instance, when you pick Draw, the menu page changes to list the drawing commands (see Figure 8).

The commands are arranged alphabetically; when there are too many commands to fit on one page, they continue on the next page. To get to the next page, highlight the word *next* that appears at the end of the list and press the pick button on your mouse or puck. Commands are selected the same way: Move the cursor to highlight the command you want and press the pick button to select it.

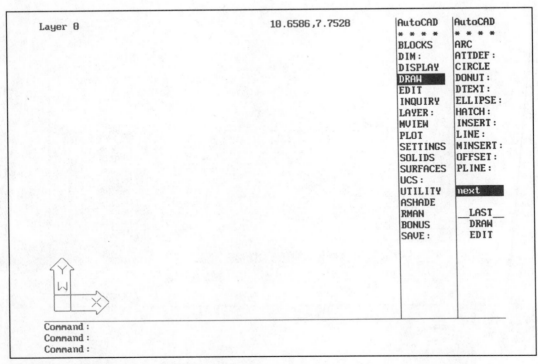

Figure 8: The root menu and Draw side menu

Here are a few tips on how to use the side menu:

- Picking the word *AutoCAD* always brings back the root menu.
- The four stars (****) have goodies hidden under them, such as Help, Cancel, Undo, and Redraw.
- Picking *LAST* returns you to the previous menu.
- Because they are used so often, Draw and Edit appear at the bottom of most of the pages.
- A colon (:) after a command means that it will be executed as soon as you pick it. Commands that have no colon, such as Arc and Circle, are activated as soon as you pick one of the options on the side menu.

The Tablet Menu

AutoCAD comes with an overlay menu for the tablet (see Figure 9). You enter a command by placing the cross hairs of the puck over the box illustrating the desired command and pressing the pick button. For the tablet overlay to work, it first has to be configured by using the Tablet command. (You must have a pointing device that supports the tablet.)

Keyboard Entry

You can always type in a command directly, without regard to the hierarchy imposed by the screen menus; for example, Line can be accessed directly without first going through Draw. Text can be entered either in upper- or lowercase. To cut down on typing, you can abbreviate options in commands. AutoCAD indicates this by capitalization—for example, Window can be specified by *W* and MIDpoint can be specified by *MID*. In addition, in Release 11 there are one- and two-letter aliases for some of the more frequently used commands. These have to be followed by ↵, like all keyboard input.

Alias	Command
A	Arc
C	Circle
CP	Copy
DV	Dview
E	Erase
L	Line
LA	Layer
M	Move
MS	Mspace
P	Pan
PS	Pspace
PL	Pline

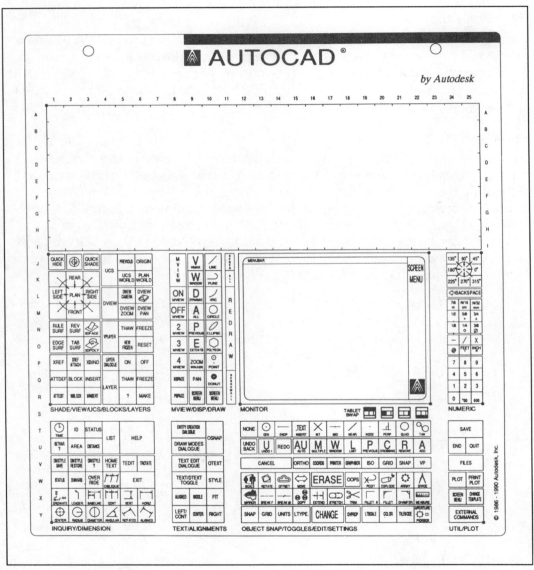

Figure 9: The AutoCAD tablet menu (courtesy of Autodesk, Inc.)

Alias	Command
R	Redraw
Z	Zoom

✦ Transparent Commands

Some commands can work within other commands. These are called *transparent* commands and allow you to do things like zooming in close to get a better view when in the middle of drawing a line from one point to another. Help, Pan, Redraw, View, Setvar, and Zoom (but not Zoom, All or Zoom, Extents) are some of the more useful transparent commands. If you use these commands from the keyboard, they have to be preceded with an apostrophe to be used transparently. The dialog boxes Layer Control and Drawing Tools (which are accessed from the Settings pull-down menu) can also be used transparently.

A command can be repeated by pressing ⏎ or button 2 on your mouse or puck.

The default value for an option is enclosed in angle brackets (< >). This is what you will get if you respond by pressing ⏎, unless you specify something else.

✦ Entity Selection Sets

How do you show AutoCAD what objects or entities you want it to work on? (The terms *entities* and *objects* are used interchangeably in this book; they refer to single items, such as a line segment—not to a series of lines—a circle, or a line of text.) Say you select Copy…copy what? AutoCAD provides many ways to make this selection; the group you select is called a *selection set*. The options are the following:

Point   Selects one object at a time by placing the pick box (the small square that replaces your cursor) over the object

Window   Selects objects totally within a window specified by a box defined by the endpoints of a diagonal

Last   Selects the last *visible* object drawn

Add	Allows the addition of objects to the set
Delete	Allows the removal of objects from the set
Previous	Recalls the last selection set made
AUto	Selection depends upon how you handle the cursor

In Auto mode, if your pick box is on an object, you will get only that object. If your pick box is on a blank portion of the screen, and you move the cursor to the right, the *window* selection mode takes effect; if you move it to the left, the *crossing* selection mode takes effect.

◆ **Note**

When you have finished making your selection, you must indicate it by pressing ⏎ or pressing button 2 on your mouse or puck. Most beginners forget this and sit for long periods of time looking at the prompt *Select objects:*. AutoCAD always waits for you to tell it that you have finished with your selection.

◆ Entering Coordinates

Many times you will place points and draw lines simply by looking at the screen and using your pointing device. But sometimes you will want to draw a line with an exact length or move something a specific distance; you can enter coordinates to do these things. There are several methods, which can all be used interchangeably.

Absolute Coordinates

The absolute coordinates for points on the screen are the x-coordinate, the y-coordinate, and if you are working in 3-D, the z-coordinate. Assuming that 0,0 is the lower-left point on your screen, the x-axis runs along the bottom of the screen in a positive direction from 0,0 toward the right, and the y-axis goes in a positive direction toward the top of the screen. The positive direction for the z-axis is from 0,0 straight out at you.

For the most part in this book, we will be using only the x and y coordinates. The convention for entering coordinates is to enter *x* first, a comma, then *y*, such as *3,4*. This indicates a point located 3 inches in the x direction and 4 inches in the y direction. When entering inches, it is not necessary to affix the inch symbol, ". However, you must indicate feet with an apostrophe ('). Negative x is to the left of 0,0 and negative y is below 0,0. Specifying absolute coordinates is similar to giving a street location, such as 14th Street and Third Avenue.

Relative Coordinates

More generally, it is not the absolute coordinates that are useful to know so much as distances from existing points, which are described by *relative coordinates*. These are distances or directions from the last point that AutoCAD has stored in its memory. This last point can be accessed by the @ (at) symbol. (You would need to know relative coordinates if you were moving a desk 5 feet from a wall or placing a door 4 inches from the corner of a room.)

There are two common ways to enter relative coordinates. One way is to use the regular Cartesian coordinates, which are the x and y values, such as *@2,3*. Another way is to use polar coordinates, which require a distance and an angle in the x-y plane. The symbol for the angle is the less-than sign, <. A point 2 inches to the left of a previous point would be entered as *@2<180*.

The value of this last point, which is accessed by using @, can be controlled by using the ID command and picking a point. This becomes the last point and relative coordinates work off the point you specified with the ID command.

If you have an AutoCAD tablet-menu overlay, the section on the middle of the right edge provides a numeric keypad for entering numbers and angles. The most commonly used angles can be entered by placing your puck over the angle designation and pressing the pick button.

And now on to drawing. Remember to press ⏎ after typing command or option names and to press button 2 on your mouse or puck when you have finished with *Select objects:*.

✦ TUTORIAL:
STARTING YOUR OFFICE PLAN

In this lesson, you start your office plan, which you will work on the rest of the book. You will draw the perimeter first and then offset this line to give the wall thickness. The commands used in the lesson—Units, Pline, Offset, Zoom, and End—are explained fully in later chapters, but you will use them now, along with coordinate entry, to begin drawing.

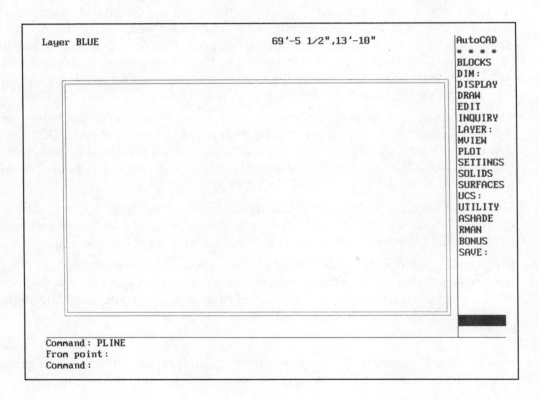

✦1   Type **ACAD** to start AutoCAD if you haven't done so already. (If you are already in the drawing editor, you can exit it by typing **QUIT**, pressing ⏎, and then pressing Y; press ⏎ to discard all changes.)

✦2   When the Main Menu appears, press 1 to begin a new drawing.

✦3   Type **PLAN** as the name of the drawing.

✦4   If you look at the numbers in the upper-right corner of the screen, you will notice that the units are in decimal format. Change them to architectural, and set the denominator of the smallest fraction to 1 to get only whole numbers.

    Command: **UNITS**
    Systems of units: (AutoCAD shows examples)
    Enter choice, 1 to 5 <2>: **4**
    Denominator of smallest fraction to display
    (1, 2, 4, 8, 16, 32, or 64) <16>: **1**

✦5   Press ⏎ after each of the next four prompts to accept the default values. These deal with options for angle measurement, which are more appropriate to surveying techniques than architecture.

    System of angle measurement <Decimal>: ⏎
    Number of fractional places for display of angles (0 to 8) <0>: ⏎
    Direction for angle 0 <0>: ⏎
    Do you want angles measured clockwise? <N>: ⏎

✦ **6**   You will be using absolute coordinates to specify the perimeter walls. The Pline command is used instead of the Line command because it can be offset as a single unit.

> Command: **PLINE**
> From point: **12′,17′**
> Current line-width is 0′-0"
> Arc/Close/Halfwidth/Length/Undo/Width/<Endpoint of line>: **68′6,17′**
> Arc/Close/Halfwidth/Length/Undo/Width/<Endpoint of line>: **68′6,52′6**
> Arc/Close/Halfwidth/Length/Undo/Width/<Endpoint of line>: **12′,52′6**
> Arc/Close/Halfwidth/Length/Undo/Width/<Endpoint of line>: **C,** ⏎

✦ **7**   To see the outline, use the Zoom, All command.

> Command: **ZOOM**
> All/Center/Dynamic/Extents/Left/Previous/Window/<Scale(X)>:**A**

✦ **8**   Use the Offset command to copy the building perimeter 6 inches inward.

> Command: **OFFSET**
> Offset distance or Through <Through>: **6**
> Select object to offset: *Pick any part of the Pline*
> Side to offset? *Move cursor inward*
> Select object to offset: ⏎ or button 2

✦ **9**   As the book progresses, you will continue to develop this plan by adding interior walls, doors, a window wall, and finally a furniture

layout. For now, end the drawing by pressing button 2, typing
END, and pressing ⏎. This saves the drawing and returns you to
the Main Menu, where you can select 0 to exit AutoCAD.

When you have finished your PLAN drawing at the end of the book, it will look
like this:

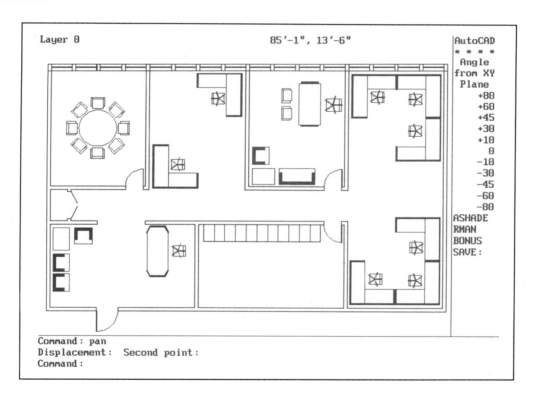

Here is a 3-D view of the final drawing, with hidden lines removed:

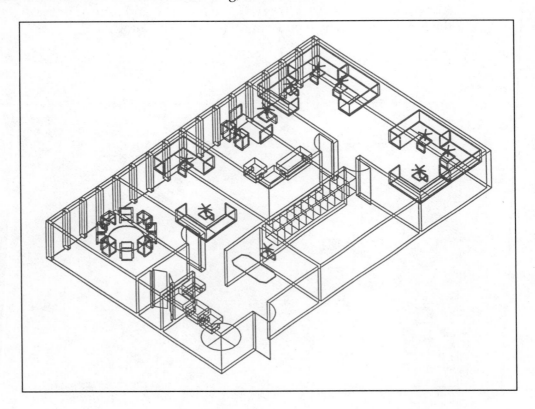

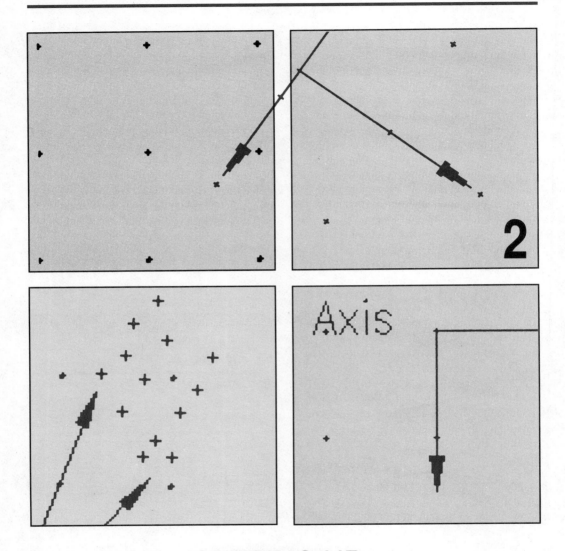

SETTING UP
THE DRAWING
ENVIRONMENT

When you set up your drawing space, you establish certain parameters, such as the units of measurement for your work (feet and inches, decimal, or metric), a grid for your drawing area, an increment for your cursor movement, and the size of the drawing space. AutoCAD calls this *model space* to distinguish it from *paper space,* which is the space you manipulate when plotting drawings.

In this chapter you'll learn about some basic setup commands. There are additional commands for controlling your drawing environment that will be useful as you get further into your drawing (see Chapter 14).

+ Units

+ Limits

+ Snap

+ Grid

+ Axis

+ Blipmode

+ Ortho

+ Function keys

+ Layer

✦ UNITS

Lets you select the system of measurement units and the degree of precision appropriate to the type of drawing you are working on.

Command Finder

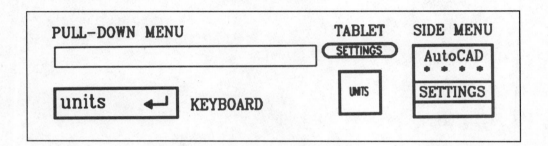

✦ Units Options

- System of units
- Denominator of smallest fraction to display
- System of angle measure
- Number of fractional places for display of angles

✦ Using the Units Command

In setting up your drawing space, you start by defining the type of units you will be working with. Your choices are

- Scientific
- Decimal

- Engineering
- Architectural
- Fractional

```
Report formats:       (Examples)

    1.   Scientific     1.55E+01
    2.   Decimal        15.50
    3.   Engineering    1'-3.50"
    4.   Architectural  1'-3 1/2"
    5.   Fractional     15 1/2

With the exception of Engineering and Architectural formats,
these formats can be used with any basic unit of measurement.
For example, Decimal mode is perfect for metric units as well
as decimal English units.

Enter choice, 1 to 5 <4>:
Denominator of smallest fraction to display
<1, 2, 4, 8, 16, 32, or 64> <1>:
```

The examples in this book use architectural units, which comprise feet and inches. Fractions of inches are displayed as fractions. However, this system allows both fractional and decimal input.

When you choose architectural or fractional units, you see the prompt "Denominator of smallest fraction to display." Use your judgment in setting this. For example, if you are drawing a floor plan, you certainly don't want units shown to 1/64 of an inch. On the other hand, if you are detailing something, you will want to work in smaller parts of inches. The number you select only controls the *display* of units; AutoCAD keeps track of your drawing with much greater accuracy than you specify.

The other Units options deal with angle measurements and are more appropriate to surveying than architecture.

✦ **Note**

Although AutoCAD displays dimensions in the Units menu with inch marks (such as *1'-3 1/2"*), you cannot enter the dimension this way. The valid entry would be *1'3-1/2* or *1'3.5*. The dash is required to separate inches from parts of inches; AutoCAD doesn't require you to indicate inches with the " symbol.

✦ LIMITS

Establishes the size of your drawing space.

Command Finder

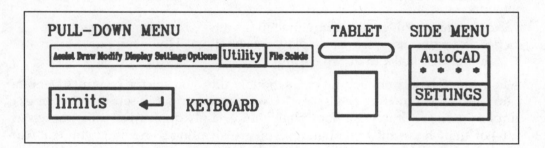

✦ Using the Limits Command

Unlike a manual drafting sheet, the AutoCAD drawing space can be sized to match the actual size of the object you are drawing. For example, if your building plan is 60' × 20', your computer drawing space can represent that size, plus an allowance for notes and dimensions. You would enter the coordinates for your limits as Lower-left 0,0 and Upper-right 70′,30′ to accommodate the 60′ × 20′ building plan.

The input format for specifying limits requires a comma and no spaces between the coordinates. Dashes are allowed only between the inch settings and fractions of inches (3-1/2). The format that AutoCAD shows you as the default, <1′-0,0′-9">, is written that way for clarity of display only. You will get an error message if you input your coordinates this way.

When you specify limits, you will be in text screen mode. To return to the drawing screen, press [F1]. This is unnecessary if you are working with dual monitors.

Always use the All option under the Zoom command after changing limits. (For details on use of the Zoom command, see Chapter 4.) AutoCAD doesn't resize the screen after you change limits; the All option will display the new limits.

When checking on the size of objects or text, remember that the denominator that you specified in the Units command controls the precision of the dimension you are given (see "Units" in this chapter). For example, if you have selected *1* as the smallest fraction to display, you will only get whole inches in response to any inquiry, even if the object's dimension is ½ inch.

✦   **Tip**

If you get the error message "Invalid 2D point," you are probably in the wrong system of units. Check to see that the coordinates you are specifying are in the same system of units that you selected with the Units command. For example, if you are in AutoCAD's default unit system, Decimal, you will get an error message if you specify 44 feet as *44′*. The Units screen shows the acceptable input format.

✦ SNAP

Sets the cursor movement to a fixed increment.

Command Finder

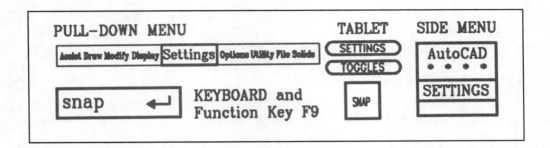

✦ Snap Options

- Snap spacing
- On
- Off
- Aspect
- Rotate (covered in Chapter 14)
- Style (covered in Chapter 14)

✦ Using the Snap Command

Set the snap spacing to the smallest usable increment. This increment will depend upon what you are drawing. For working on details, 1/8" works well, but if you are working on a site plan, 1' is more appropriate. The default is 1".

When you specify a snap increment, the Snap function is turned on automatically. If you don't want your cursor to move in specific increments, you can turn off Snap by selecting Off or pressing F9. Remember that a function key acts as a switch, turning a function on or off each time it is pressed. Function keys also work while you are in the middle of using another command. (See Chapter 1 for a discussion of transparent commands.)

Aspect is used when you want the x-axis snap movement to be different from the y-axis movement.

The Drawing Tools dialog box under Settings in the pull-down menus offers an easy way to set Snap, as well as other settings for your drawing environment.

Snap			
X Spacing	0'3"	Snap	✓
Y Spacing	0'3"	Grid	✓
		Axis	✓
Snap angle	0	Ortho	✓
X Base	0'0"	Blips	
Y Base	0'0"		

Isoplane

✓	Left
	Top
	Right

Grid		
X Spacing	0'0"	
Y Spacing	0'0"	

Isometric	

Axis		
X Spacing	1'0"	
Y Spacing	1'0"	

[OK]   [Cancel]

♦ GRID

Places a grid of dots on your computer drawing sheet.

Command Finder

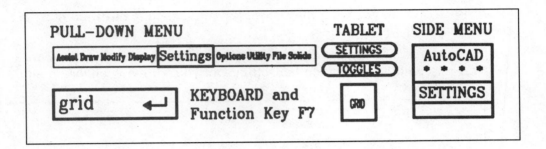

✦ Grid Options

- Grid spacing
- On
- Off
- Snap
- Aspect

✦ Using the Grid Command

To set the grid, specify a single number for both x- and y-axis spacing. If you enter an *X* after the number, your grid will be that multiple of the snap spacing. If you enter 0, the grid spacing will be the same as the snap spacing.

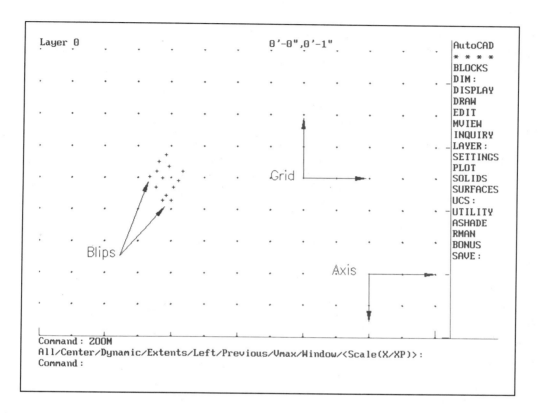

You can turn the grid on and off by selecting the appropriate option in the Grid command or by pressing the **F7** key. Remember that function keys will work while you are in the middle of using another command. The grid, like blips and the cursor, appears on the screen only and does not plot or print.

The Snap option sets the grid spacing to match the snap spacing, which is the same as the 0 setting for the Grid Spacing option.

You use the Aspect option when you want the x-axis grid spacing to be different from the y-axis spacing.

The Drawing Tools dialog box under Settings in the pull-down menus offers an easy way to set Grid and other settings for your drawing environment.

```
                        Snap

        ┌─────────────────────┐        ┌──────────┬───┐
        │ X Spacing │ 0'3"    │        │ Snap     │ ✓ │
        │ Y Spacing │ 0'3"    │        │ Grid     │ ✓ │
        └─────────────────────┘        │ Axis     │ ✓ │
                                       │ Ortho    │ ✓ │
        ┌─────────────────────┐        │ Blips    │   │
        │ Snap angle │ 0      │        └──────────┴───┘
        │ X Base     │ 0'0"   │
        │ Y Base     │ 0'0"   │            Isoplane

                        Grid            ┌───┬───────┐
                                        │ ✓ │ Left  │
        ┌─────────────────────┐         │   │ Top   │
        │ X Spacing │ 0'0"    │         │   │ Right │
        │ Y Spacing │ 0'0"    │         └───┴───────┘
        └─────────────────────┘
                        Axis            │ Isometric │   │

        ┌─────────────────────┐
        │ X Spacing │ 1'0"    │
        │ Y Spacing │ 1'0"    │
        └─────────────────────┘
              ┌────────┐          ┌──────────┐
              │   OK   │          │  Cancel  │
              └────────┘          └──────────┘
```

✦ Grid Notes

If you get the message "Grid too dense to display," either zoom in or increase your grid size. If the grid doesn't appear at all, you may have zoomed in too close. Using the Zoom command with the All option should fix this.

Sometimes the grid will not cover the entire area displayed on the monitor. This is because the area that has a grid is controlled by the limits of your drawing. If you want to extend the grid, increase your limits (see "Limits" in this chapter).

After drawing and editing, some of the grid dots will disappear. Use the Redraw command to restore your grid. (You can type *Redraw* or press **F7** twice.)

✦ AXIS

*Displays rulerlike divisions called **ticks** on the bottom and right sides of the screen drawing area. These ticks can be used as a drawing aid.*

Command Finder

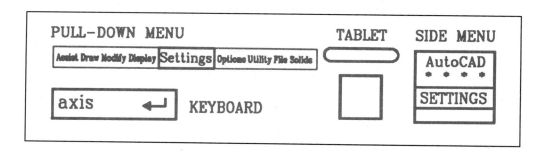

```
PULL-DOWN MENU                          TABLET    SIDE MENU
 Assist Draw Modify Display Settings Options Utility File Solids              AutoCAD
                                                         • • • •
 axis          ←       KEYBOARD                     SETTINGS
```

✦ Axis Options

- Tick spacing
- On
- Off
- Snap
- Aspect

✦ Using the Axis Command

To set the axis tick spacing, specify a single number for both X Spacing and Y Spacing. If you enter an X after the number, the tick spacing will be that multiple of the snap spacing. If you enter 0, the tick spacing will be the same as the snap spacing.

You can turn the display of ticks on the axes on and off by selecting the appropriate option in the Axis command.

The Snap option sets the tick spacing to match the snap spacing, which is the same as the 0 setting for the Axis Tick Spacing option.

You use the Aspect option when you want the x-axis tick spacing to be different from the y-axis tick spacing.

The Drawing Tools dialog box under Settings in the pull-down menus offers an easy way to set Axis and other settings for your drawing environment.

Snap

| X Spacing | 0'3" |
| Y Spacing | 0'3" |

Snap angle	0
X Base	0'0"
Y Base	0'0"

Grid

| X Spacing | 0'0" |
| Y Spacing | 0'0" |

Axis

| X Spacing | 1'0" |
| Y Spacing | 1'0" |

Snap	✓
Grid	✓
Axis	✓
Ortho	✓
Blips	

Isoplane

✓	Left
	Top
	Right

| Isometric | |

OK   Cancel

✦   **Note**

Ticks on axes are generally set to a larger increment than the grid; the snap increment is usually the smallest of all.

✦ BLIPMODE

Displays tiny crosses, called blips, that appear on your screen as you select a point. They remain on the screen after some editing commands are used.

Command Finder

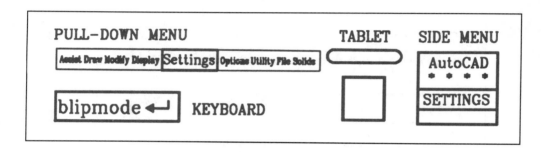

✦ Using the Blipmode Command

You control the display of blips by selecting the On or Off option.

The Drawing Tools dialog box under Settings in the pull-down menus offers an easy way to set Blips and other settings for your drawing environment.

✦ **Tip**

Use the Redraw command to clean up your screen; it removes blip marks. (You can type *Redraw* or press **F7** twice.)

✦ ORTHO

Not a command but a mode that constrains all lines and cursor movement to the horizontal and vertical directions only.

Command Finder

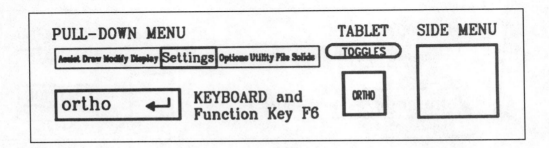

✦ Using the Ortho Mode

Ortho can be turned on and off by pressing [F8] or can be set in the Drawing Tools dialog box under Settings in the pull-down menus.

✦ FUNCTION KEYS

Some commands and features are used so frequently in AutoCAD that function keys have been assigned to them. These allow you to turn the commands on and off easily by pressing just one key. You cannot use function keys to assign values to these commands; to do that, you must go into the command menus themselves.

✦ Using the Function Keys

The drawings that follow illustrate the uses of the function keys:

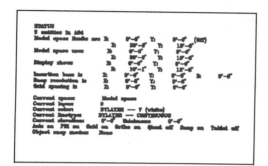 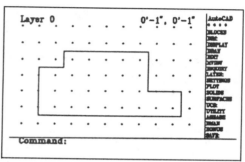

F1 switches from the text screen to the graphics screen.

F6 sets the upper-right coordinates to follow the cursor movement dynamically so that you get a readout of the x and y locations as you move the cursor. When set to Off, the coordinates will give a readout only after a command is activated. The drawings show how the readout changes as the location of the cursor changes.

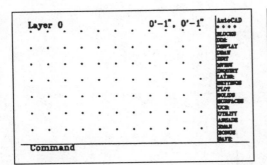 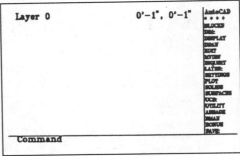

⌨**F7** turns the grid on or off.

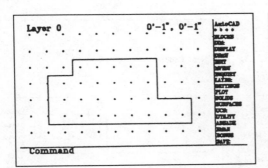 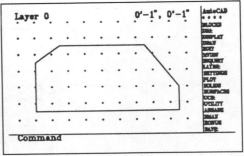

⌨**F8** turns Ortho on, which constrains lines and cursor placement to horizontal and vertical directions. Setting Ortho to Off enables you to draw diagonal lines.

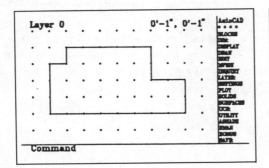 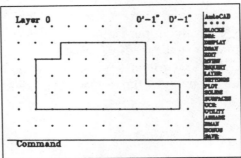

⌨**F9** turns Snap on, which constrains lines and cursor placement to the snap increments that have been previously set. If the grid spacing is the same as the snap increment, then you can only draw from point to point on the grid. Setting Snap to Off removes this constraint.

`F10` turns the tablet mode on to act as a digitizer, or off to act as a standard command template.

✦ LAYER

Using layers is similar to doing overlays in drafting. By placing different items on different layers, you can produce many different kinds of plans by selecting which layers you want to see.

Command Finder

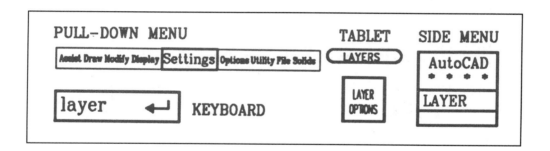

✦ Layer Options
- ?
- Make
- Set
- New
- On
- Off

- Color
- Ltype
- Freeze
- Thaw

◆ Using the Layer Command

When working with layers, it is easier to set options in the Layer Control dialog box: Select Layer Control on the Settings pull-down menu. The dialog box displays ten layers at a time. To see more than ten layers, use the arrow bars on the right side to scroll through the list.

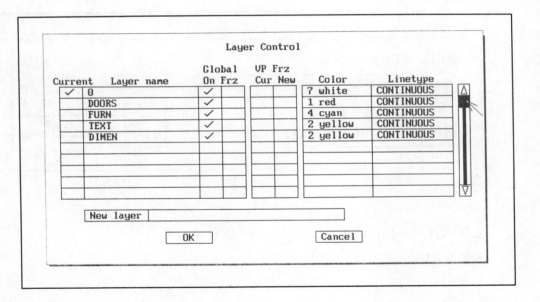

New Layers To add new layers, select the box to the right of *New layer* by pressing the pick button, type in the layer name, and press ⏎. If you want to create an additional layer, leave the box highlighted and type the next name.

Setting Current Layer   There can be only one current layer. To make a layer current, move the arrow into the Current column; when the highlight appears next to the layer you want, press the pick button on your puck or mouse. A check appears in the box indicating that it is the current layer.

On/Off   A layer is turned on if a check mark appears in the On box. To turn it off, move the arrow into the box and press the pick button.

Freeze/Thaw   A layer is frozen if a check mark appears next to its name in the Frz box; it is thawed if there is no check. Highlight the appropriate box and press the pick button to add or remove the check mark.

VP Frz   Refers to the Vplayer command; selectively turns layers on and off in different viewports. It is used to control paper-space views when preparing a drawing for plotting.

Color   Any layer color, other than white, is selected by picking the existing Color box. The Select Color dialog box opens, showing the colors available. Move the arrow to the box next to the color name, and press the pick button to select it. The new name appears in the box above *Color code*. Highlight OK to leave the dialog box.

Linetype   To change a linetype to something other than continuous, highlight the Linetype box that you want to change. A second dialog box opens, showing what linetypes are available. Use the arrow to highlight the box next to the linetype you want to set for that layer. Highlight OK to leave the dialog box. For a linetype to be available, you must first load it by using the Linetype command.

The Layer command functions differently when accessed from the side menu or entered from the keyboard. Here are the options you can use:

?	Lists the existing layers
Make	Makes a new layer and sets it up to be the currently active layer
Set	Sets the layer named to be the active drawing layer
New	Makes new layers; you separate multiple layer names with commas, as in *DOOR, FURN, TEXT*
Color	Assigns the color chosen to the layer specified

Ltype	Assigns a different linetype to a layer
Freeze	Turns off a layer so that AutoCAD does not reference or search it; helps to speed up the regeneration time of a drawing
Thaw	Turns on a layer that is frozen

♦ TUTORIAL: SETTING UP A DRAWING ENVIRONMENT

In this exercise you will set up the drawing environment for a furniture library. (The commands used that are not covered in this chapter are Zoom and Line.)

♦ **1**   Start AutoCAD by typing **ACAD** at the DOS prompt.

♦ **2**   From the Main Menu, select *1. Begin a NEW Drawing.*

        Enter selection: **1**
        Enter Name of drawing: **A24**

♦ **3**   Use the Units command to set the format to Architectural and the denominator to 1, since you will not be using fractions for this drawing setup.

        Command: **UNITS**
        Systems of units: (AutoCAD shows examples)
        Enter choice, 1 to 5 <2>: **4**
        Denominator of smallest fraction to display
        (1, 2, 4, 8, 16, 32, or 64) <16>: **1**

♦ **4**   Accept the default values for the next four prompts.

♦ **5**   Press [F1] to return to the graphics screen from the text screen.

♦ **6**   Use the Drawing Tools dialog box for additional settings. From the pull-down menu, select Settings and then Drawing Tools.

✦**7**   Set the snap spacing to 3": With the mouse or puck, place the arrow in the rectangle where the dimension is indicated for X Spacing, type **3**, and then press ⏎. The number 3 will appear automatically in the Y Spacing box.

✦**8**   Leave the grid spacing at 0 so that it will automatically be the same as the snap increment.

✦**9**   Set the axis spacing: Move the arrow into the rectangle where the X Spacing dimension is indicated, type **1'**, and press ⏎. The dimension 1'-0" appears automatically in the Y Spacing box.

✦**10**   Move the arrow to the box in the upper-right section of the dialog box. Use the pick button on your puck or mouse to place checks in the Snap, Grid, Axis, and Ortho boxes.

✦**11**   Move the arrow to the box next to Blips, and press the pick button to turn Blips off.

✦**12**   Move the arrow to the OK box and pick it to exit the Drawing Tools dialog box.

✦**13**   Press F6 to toggle Coordinates on.

✦**14**   The AutoCAD standard drawing space is 9 × 12 inches. Architectural drawings need much more room, so you need to reset the limits.

Command: **LIMITS**
Reset Model space limits:

ON/OFF/<Lower left corner> <0'-0",0'-0">: ⏎
Upper right corner <1'-0",0'-9">: **20',15'**

+ **15**   When changing limits, you must use Zoom, All for the screen to show the extent of the new setting.

Command: **ZOOM**
All/Center/Dynamic/Extents/Left/Previous/Vmax/Window/<Scale(X/XP)>: **A**
Regenerating drawing.

+ **16**   Make a border encompassing the limits by drawing a line around the grid.

Command: **LINE**
From point: **0,0**
To point: **20',0**
To point: **20',15'**
To point: **0,15'**
To point: **C**

+ **17**   Now you have a drawing setup from which you will begin drawing furniture for an office space. End this drawing and use what you have learned (as well as the following parameters) to do a setup for the drawing plan that you started in Chapter 1.

Command: **END**

+ **18**   Select *2. Edit an EXISTING drawing* on the Main Menu, and enter **PLAN** as the name.

+ **19**   Edit the drawing by setting the following values:

Denominator: **1**
Snap: **1'** and set to On
Grid: **2'** and set to On

Blips: On
Ortho: On
Axis: Off

✦ **20**   The PLAN drawing will have layers. Use the Layer Control option on the Settings pull-down menu to make new layers, and assign the indicated colors to them. Keep layer 0 as the current layer and leave it white.

DOORS: red
FURN: cyan
TEXT: yellow
DIMEN: yellow

You have now established a drawing environment for the PLAN drawing, which you will find useful as you continue working on it. Use the End command to save your drawing; you return to the Main Menu.

USING THE UTILITY COMMANDS
TO MANAGE YOUR FILES

The commands in this chapter enable you to manage your files. (You may think of your drawings as drawings; AutoCAD thinks of them as files.) With these commands, you can access and manipulate files, save your work, and exit a file or AutoCAD. Because this chapter does not cover any commands related to drawing, there is no tutorial.

+ End

+ Save

+ Quit

+ Files

+ Rename

+ Purge

♦ END

Saves the work you have done in your drawing and returns you to the Main Menu.

Command Finder

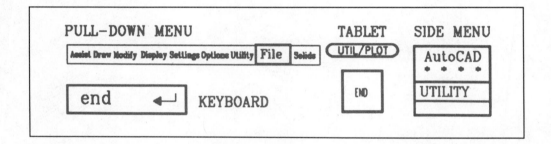

♦ Using the End Command

The End command saves your work and returns you to the Main Menu. To exit AutoCAD, you select *Exit AutoCAD*. You can also choose other options, such as beginning or editing another drawing.

Here's how End compares with other AutoCAD saving and exiting commands:

- *End* saves your work and exits the drawing editor.
- *Save* saves your work without leaving the file or exiting the program.
- *Quit* returns you to the Main Menu without saving your work.

♦ SAVE

Saves your drawing to disk without leaving the file or exiting AutoCAD.

Command Finder

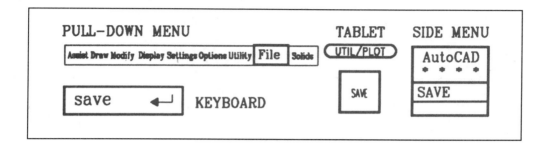

♦ Using the Save Command

The Save command brings up a dialog box that shows all the drawing files in your current directory. The name of your current drawing file appears next to the box named File. The first time you save a drawing, you simply select the OK box. If you want to, you can press ⏎ instead.

Saving your work as you continue with your drawing is called *updating* your drawing. To update the current file, select the OK box. You get the message "The specified file already exists. Do you want to replace it?" Select the OK box.

If you want to save the drawing with another name or to a floppy disk, select *Type it* or type in the new name or drive letter and file name.

Do not type a space between the drive specification and the drawing name. You do not have to specify the file extension .DWG; AutoCAD adds it automatically.

♦ **Tip**

It is a good practice to save your drawing often during a work session and before you plot the drawing. When you have completed part of a drawing and find yourself sitting back to take a breath, that is a good time to save the drawing.

✦ QUIT

Returns you to the Main Menu without saving your work.

Command Finder

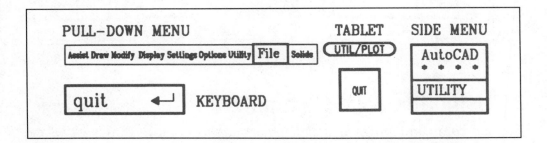

✦ Using the Quit Command

The Quit command returns you to the Main Menu and discards all changes made to your drawing during that work session. AutoCAD prompts you to make sure that this is your intention:

Really want to discard all changes to drawings?

Press Y for Yes or N for No.

✦ FILES

Accesses and manipulates files. The command can be accessed from the Main Menu or from within the drawing editor.

Command Finder

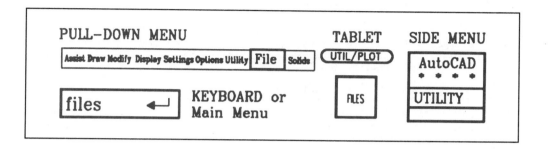

✦ Files Options

- Exit File Utility Menu
- List Drawing files
- List user specified files
- Delete files
- Rename files
- Copy file

✦ Using the Files Command

The Files command works the same way whether you access it from the Main Menu or from within the drawing editor.

To select files from the Main Menu, choose the File Utilities option to see the menu that shows the file options.

```
               A U T O C A D  (R)
        Copyright (c) 1982-90  Autodesk, Inc.  All Rights Reserved.
        Release 11 (10/17/90) 386 DOS Extender
        Serial Number:  100-10000000
        Licensed to:    Genevieve Katz, Metron Studios
        Obtained from:  Autodesk, Inc. - 332 2344 Fax 331 8093


        File Utility Menu

           0.  Exit File Utility Menu
           1.  List Drawing files
           2.  List user specified files
           3.  Delete files
           4.  Rename files
           5.  Copy file
           6.  Unlock file

        Enter selection (0 to 6) <0>:
```

You will see this prompt at the bottom of the screen:

   Enter selection (0 to 6) <0>:

The next prompt you see depends on which option you choose.

The *Exit File Utility Menu* option returns you to the drawing screen or to the Main Menu, depending on where you were before you used the command.

If you choose *List Drawing Files*, you'll see this prompt:

   Enter drive or directory:

Press ⏎ to list all the drawings in your current directory. To see the drawings on your floppy disk in drive A, you would type **A:** and press ⏎.

The *List User Specified Files* option displays this prompt:

   Enter file search specification:

To specify the files you want, you can use the wildcard convention, the asterisk (*), to represent any character or any number of characters in a file name. The wildcard can be typed either before or after the period that separates the file name from its extension. (A file extension is made up of the three letters after the period in a file name. It generally indicates the type of file—for example, the extension .DWG denotes a drawing file, .BAK denotes a backup file, and .SLD denotes a slide file.) Because you can specify a file with an extension other than .DWG, you must include the extension in your file specification (see "Files Notes").

Use the wildcard to list all the backup files in your current directory by typing ***.BAK**. To list all the slide files in your current directory, type ***.SLD**. To list all the drawing files that begin with the letter *p,* type **P*.DWG**.

When starting a work session, you can also use the List Drawing Files option to help you remember the name of your drawing.

When you choose the *Delete Files* option, you see this prompt:

Enter file deletion specification:

Remember to include the file extension in your specification. When you use a wildcard, AutoCAD lists all the files included in the selection and specifically asks you whether you want the file deleted. To erase all the backup files in your current directory, type ***.BAK**. To erase a specific drawing file in your current directory—for example, one named *HOUSE*—you would type **HOUSE.DWG**.

When you choose the *Rename Files* option, you see two prompts:

Enter current filename:

then

Enter new filename:

You can only rename one file at a time, and you must specify the extension. You can rename both the file name and the extension. You cannot have two files with the same name. To rename a backup file so that you can use it, first type the current file name, such as **HOUSE.BAK**. Then, in response to the prompt for a new file name, you would type **HOUSE1.DWG**.

The *Copy File* option also displays two prompts:

> Enter name of source file:

then

> Enter name of destination file:

To copy the file HOUSE.DWG from your hard disk to a floppy disk in drive A, you would type **HOUSE.DWG** when prompted for the source file. Then, in response to the prompt for the destination file, you would type **A:HOUSE.DWG**. You must specify both the drive and the file name, including the extension.

✦ Files Notes

File names can only be eight characters long. No two files in the same directory can have the same name, because the last one written will overwrite the new one.

It is easy to make a copy of a file on a floppy disk while still in a drawing: You use the Save command and precede the file name with the drive letter (see "Save" in this chapter).

AutoCAD makes a backup copy of your drawing file each time you edit a drawing. This file has the same name, but the extension is .BAK instead of .DWG. If something happens to the drawing, you can use the backup file, but you first have to rename it.

✦ RENAME

Changes the names of various items used in your drawings.

Command Finder

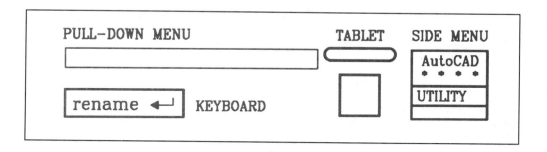

✦ Rename Options

- Block
- LAyer
- LType
- Style
- Ucs
- VIew
- VPort

✦ Using the Rename Command

When you specify the type of item you want to rename, AutoCAD prompts you for the old name and then the new name.

As you do more complex drawings, you will find this command quite useful. For example, you can use the option for renaming layers when, as the drawing progresses, you find that some of the layer names you originally chose need more descriptive names or that you have made a spelling mistake.

✦ **Note**

You cannot rename files with the Rename command; you must use the Rename Files option in the Files command (see "Files" in this chapter).

✦ PURGE

Removes certain unused items from a drawing. This reduces the size of the drawing, which enables AutoCAD to load it faster.

Command Finder

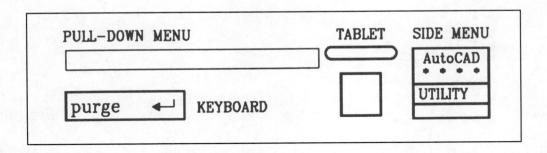

✦ Purge Options
- Blocks
- SHapes
- STyles
- All
- LAyers
- LTypes

◆ Using the Purge Command

The Purge command only works at the beginning of a drawing session, before you have made any changes to the entities. You can use commands that do not change the entities, such as inquiry commands, and display commands, such as List and Zoom.

After you have selected the option specifying the types of items to be purged, AutoCAD steps through a list of the selected items and asks you whether you want to purge each one. Press Y to purge the item. If you accept the default value (N) by pressing ⏎, the item will not be purged.

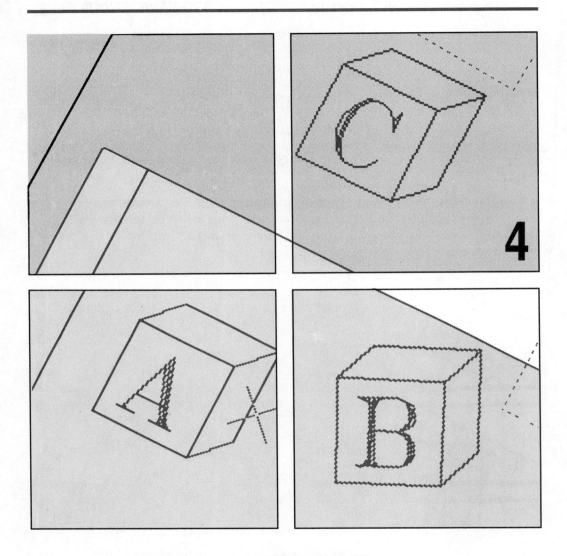

DISPLAY COMMANDS

4

Because you no longer have to work on drafting-table-size sheets of paper, you can use AutoCAD's many commands to get about your small-screen-size drawing area. These commands manipulate the screen images only—they do not change your drawing size. Beginners often work with too small an image. Save your eyes—work large enough for comfort!

- ✦ Zoom
- ✦ Pan
- ✦ Redraw and Redrawall
- ✦ Regen
- ✦ Regenauto
- ✦ View
- ✦ Viewres

✦ ZOOM

Manipulates the screen display of your image; you can zoom in to show more detail and zoom out for a "bird's-eye view." Zoom only changes the screen view; it does not change the scale or size of your drawing.

Command Finder

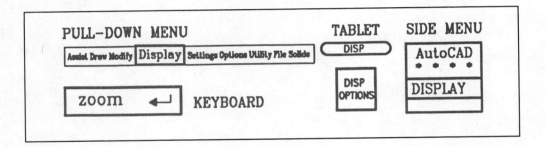

✦ Zoom Options

- All
- Extents
- Window
- Scale (X/XP)
- Center
- Left
- Previous
- Dynamic
- Vmax

✦ Using the Zoom Command

When entering the options for the Zoom command from the keyboard, you only have to specify the first letter.

Most zooms can be done transparently, which means that you can call them up while in another command. The All and Extents options cannot be used transparently because they require a *regen*. (When the screen is regenerated, AutoCAD recalculates the coordinates for all the entities in the drawing. This takes time—more or less, depending upon the speed of your computer.) Other zooms will also sometimes require a regen. This depends on the extents of your virtual screen, which are set automatically by your last regen. Zooms entered from the keyboard are not transparent unless preceded by an apostrophe (').

The following pictures illustrate the uses of the Zoom options:

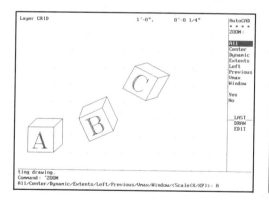 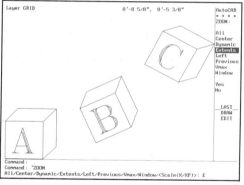

The All (A) option displays your drawing up to the drawing limits specified in the Limits command or up to the border placed during the Setup procedure. If you have drawn objects outside of the limits, they will also be included in the screen view. The Extents option (see the drawing to the right) fills your screen with all the entities in your drawing and disregards limits unless they are defined with a border.

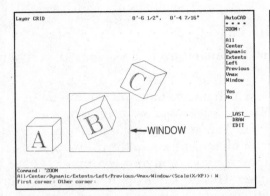
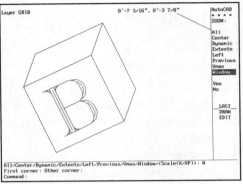

The Window (W) option fills the screen with the area you have specified within your window box.

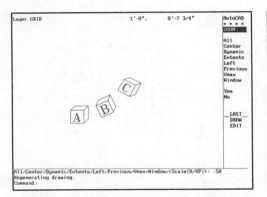
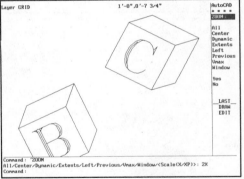

There are two options when specifying Scale in model space. Placing an X after the value indicates that the scale will operate on the existing screen display. Specifying a value without the X uses the limits of the drawing as the base for change. Scale changes are indicated numerically; .5 reduces the view by half and 2 enlarges it two times. To use the Scale option, do not enter S—just type in the numerical value you want. The XP option is used when working in paper space to scale the image inside the viewports to a specific scale for plotting (you will use this option in Chapter 17).

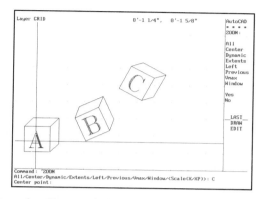 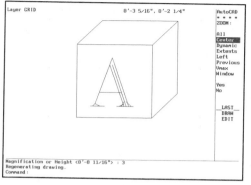

Using the Center (C) option is a little like combining a pan (moving a camera to get a different view) with a zoom. You specify the point on your drawing to become the new center and a height based upon screen height or scale (X). The current height is given as the default, making it easier for you to determine the new height.

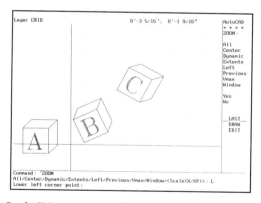 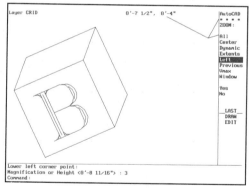

The Left (L) option is similar to the Center option, only you specify the point on your drawing to be the lower-left corner. Again, the new height is determined from the current height—for example, if the current screen height is 7", specifying 3.5" enlarges the image by a factor of 2.

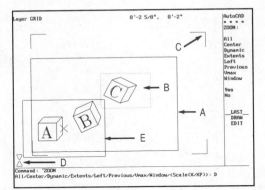
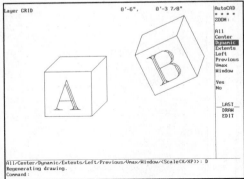

The Dynamic (D) option is useful for avoiding time-consuming regens when zooming in large drawings. After you select the option, you see a special screen showing the following:

A View of drawing at last regen enclosed in a white border

B Last zoomed view enclosed in a dotted green border

C Corner angle in red defining the area you can zoom to without causing a regen; this defines the limits of your virtual screen

D Hourglass icon in lower-left corner indicating that the limits of the virtual screen have been exceeded; a regen is required

E View box that moves and changes size as you move your mouse or puck. The pick button alternately activates the sizing and panning operations. When the arrow icon is visible, the box can be resized by moving your mouse or puck. When the X appears in the middle of the box, the box can be moved about the screen. The new view is activated when button 2 or ⏎ is pressed.

The Previous option restores the previous view and can stack up to ten views. In addition to the views available with the Zoom command, views available with the Pan, Plan, Vpoint, Dview, and View commands are also included in the stack.

Vmax is a new option in Release 11. It allows you to zoom out to the maximum extents allowed, without causing a regen.

✦ Zoom Notes

- Use the All option after you have changed your limits to display your new drawing limits.
- The Extents option is useful in locating objects that may have "disappeared" during the Move command when your base point was not placed on or near the object you were moving.
- It is easier to get enlarged views of your drawing than reduced views. One of the simplest ways to get a reduced view is to use the Scale option and specify a number smaller than 1.

✦ PAN

Moves the screen image from one place to another.

Command Finder

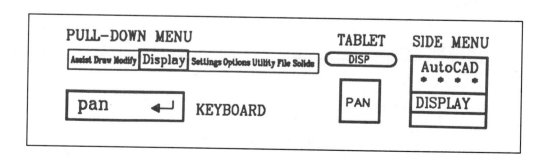

✦ Using the Pan Command

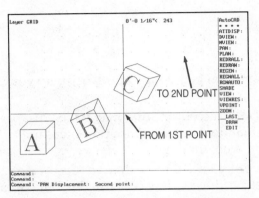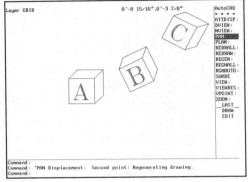

To pan your drawing, you first indicate the displacement by picking the *from point* and then the *to point.* You can give these points as coordinates, although the pointing method is generally used. Pan is one of the transparent commands, so it can be used while in another command.

✦ REDRAW AND REDRAWALL

These commands redraw entire entities that appear broken (but actually are not); they restore missing grid points and clear blip marks from the screen.

Command Finder

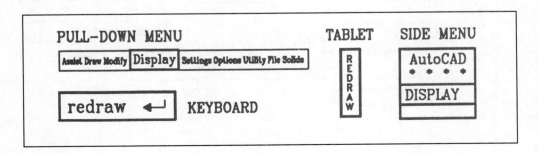

✦ Using the Redraw Command

Redraw cleans up your screen. Redrawall works the same way, except that it acts on all viewports simultaneously. Both commands are transparent, so they can be used while in another command.

✦ **Note**

Turning off Grid or Layer causes an automatic redraw.

✦ REGEN AND REGENALL

These commands recalculate the drawing display and redraw the screen based upon this information.

Command Finder

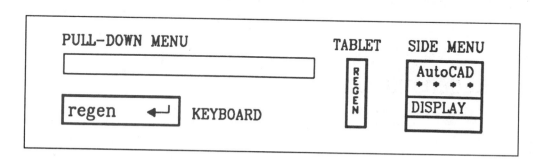

PULL-DOWN MENU	TABLET	SIDE MENU
	R E G E N	AutoCAD ✦ ✦ ✦ ✦
regen ↵ KEYBOARD		DISPLAY

✦ Using the Regen Command

The Regen command is necessary to show the changes made to drawings when you use certain command options, such as turning Fill on or off, changing linetypes, and redefining Style or Blocks. Generally, the regen is done automatically, unless you have set Regenauto to Off (see "Regenauto").

✦ REGENAUTO

Certain options available with some commands regenerate the screen automatically, such as Fill, Layer; making changes in linetypes, style, and linetype scale; and updating or redefining blocks. Regenauto allows you to control whether the regeneration is automatic.

Command Finder

```
┌─────────────────────────────────────────────────────────────────────┐
│  PULL-DOWN MENU                          TABLET    SIDE MENU          │
│  ┌──────────────────────────────────┐   ⬭         ┌──────────┐      │
│  └──────────────────────────────────┘             │ AutoCAD  │      │
│                                          ┌───┐     │ • • • •  │      │
│  ┌──────────────────────┐               │   │     ├──────────┤      │
│  │ regenauto ⏎          │ KEYBOARD      └───┘     │ DISPLAY  │      │
│  └──────────────────────┘                         ├──────────┤      │
│                                                    │          │      │
│                                                    └──────────┘      │
└─────────────────────────────────────────────────────────────────────┘
```

✦ Regenauto Options
- On
- Off

✦ Using the Regenauto Command

The On option (the default setting) updates your screen automatically to reflect the changes you have made to your drawing. If you select Off, AutoCAD asks your permission before it regenerates the drawing.

✦ **Tip**

If you are a beginner, you should keep Regenauto turned on; otherwise, you may be confused by the effect of some commands if the screen is not regenerated to show the result of a change you have made.

✦ VIEW

Saves screen views that you have defined so that you can recall them by using the View command instead of the Zoom command. Both plan and 3-D views can be accessed this way.

Command Finder

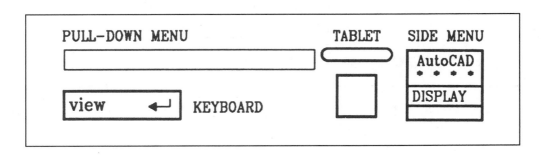

✦ View Options

- ?—shows you a list of views saved
- Delete (D)—removes the views you no longer want
- Restore (R)—recalls the view you request
- Save (S)—saves the current screen view with the name you supply (can be up to 30 characters long)
- Window (W)—allows you to define only part of the screen to be saved as a view

✦ Using the View Command

By saving views of different parts of your screen, you can avoid going back and forth between Zoom, Previous and Zoom, Window.

It is useful to save a screen view that is slightly larger than the screen that you get when you use Zoom, All. This allows you to select parts of the drawing that are at the very edge of the screen. You can also use this view instead of Zoom, All to avoid a regen.

The View command is one of the transparent commands, which means that it can be accessed while in another command; however, the view requested must be the same size or smaller than the screen displayed at the last regen. (The screen display resulting from the last regen is known as the *virtual screen*.)

✦ VIEWRES

Controls whether your zooms are done at redraw or regen speed and how many sections will be drawn to display arcs, circles, or linetypes.

Command Finder

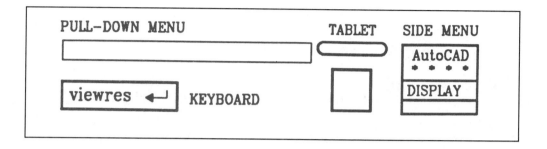

◆ Viewres Options

- Yes
- No
- Enter circle zoom percent

◆ Using the Viewres Command

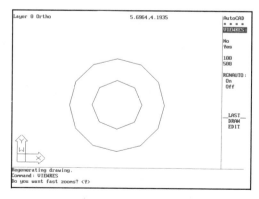 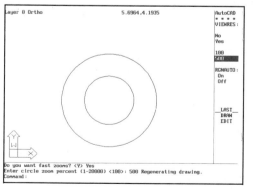

The Yes option gives you zooms done at redraw speed. The No option gives you zooms done at regen speed. The default value for circle zoom percent is 100. The larger the number is, the more segments are used to draw curves and the longer it takes to redraw the image.

✦ Viewres Notes

If you don't want your circles to look like polygons, you can increase the number for circle zoom percent to 500, without slowing down the display time.

Sometimes your linetypes, such as dashed and hidden, will look like solid lines. If this is not caused by an incorrectly set Ltscale (which sets the scale of the linetype), increasing the circle zoom percent will produce a more accurate screen view of the linetype. Regardless of how polygon-like your circles and arcs appear on the screen, they will plot perfectly rounded.

Why wouldn't you always want fast zooms? The trade-off is how your drawing looks on the screen. Without fast zooms, you can get better display resolution, but it takes longer to update your screen.

✦ TUTORIAL: USING VIEWS IN A PLAN

In this lesson, you will use the View command to save screen displays of areas that you anticipate working on. By saving views in the upper-right and lower-left portions of the drawing, you can avoid the intermediate step of zooming to full size to pick the other end of the plan. You will also save a view of the entire plan.

Absolute coordinates are given for the screen windows to ensure that you are at the right locations for the exercise. In real life, you simply window the area you desire with your pointing device.

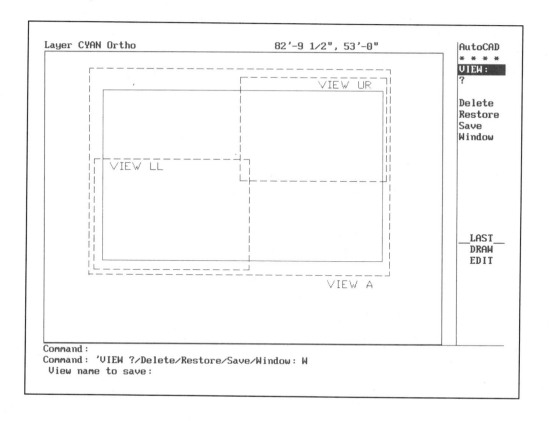

Use the PLAN drawing that you started in Chapter 1. If you haven't done that drawing, refer to chapters 1 and 2 for setup and drawing instructions.

♦1   From the Main Menu, select 2 to edit the existing PLAN drawing.

♦2   Save a view of the entire plan by zooming in to get the view you want to save.

    Command: **ZOOM**
    All/Center/Dynamic/Extents/Left/Previous/Window/<Scale (X)>: **W**
    First corner: **10',14'**
    Other corner: **70',55'**

    Command: **VIEW**
    ?/Delete/Restore/Save/Window: **S**
    View name to save: **A**

♦3   Use the Window option of the View command to save two more views, lower-left and upper-right.

    Command: **VIEW**
    ?/Delete/Restore/Save/Window: **W**
    View name to save: **LL**
    First corner: **10',15'**
    Other corner: **41',38'**

    Command: **VIEW**
    ?/Delete/Restore/Save/Window: **W**
    View name to save: **UR**
    First corner: **39',33'**
    Other corner: **69',54'**

✦ **4**   To see how the View command restores your view, reenter the command.

       Command: **VIEW**
       ?/Delete/Restore/Save/Window: **R**
       View name to restore: **LL**

✦ **5**   End the drawing.

       Command: **END**

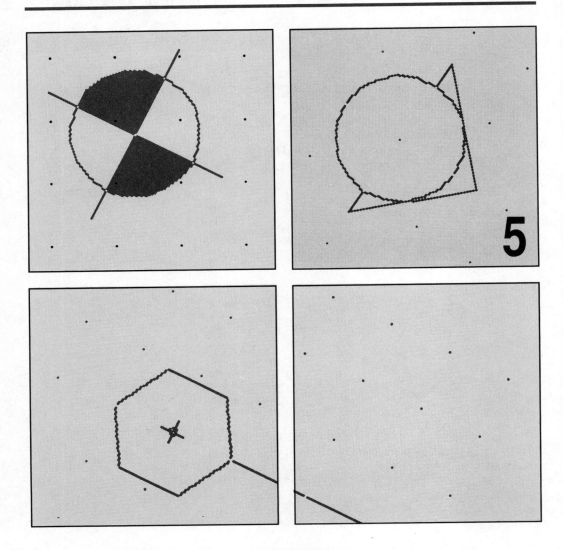

DRAWING COMMANDS

The graphic primitives available in AutoCAD to "lay down line" are not very different from the ones you have been accustomed to using in manual drafting. You will find, however that drawing lines, circles, and polygons with various line weights is much easier with a CADD system. Not only are the "templates" for all these objects available to you, but you also can get information on the entities you use in your drawing by using the inquiry command List.

In spite of the help CADD systems give you for drafting, you will find that laying down line still takes time. The real speed of these systems lies in their powerful editing commands. The goal to aim for is to draw as little as possible, to edit as much as possible, and to not throw away any lines that you can use somewhere else.

- Line

- Circle

- Ellipse

- Arc

- Donut

- Polygon

- Point

✦ LINE

Draws straight lines between two or more points. The Line command can also be used to undo a line segment you have drawn, to continue a line from where you left off, or to close a polygon automatically.

Command Finder

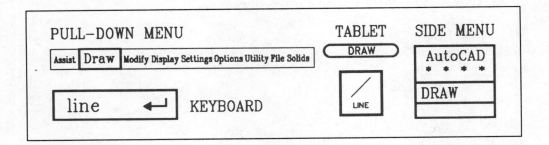

✦ Line Options

- Continue
- Close (C)
- Undo (U)

✦ Using the Line Command

To start a line, move the cursor to the point where you want the line to begin and press the pick button. Then move the cursor to the next point desired and press the pick button again.

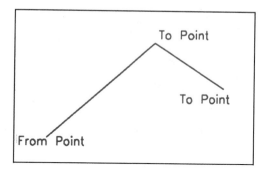
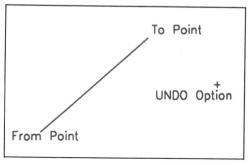

As you move the cursor from the first point to the endpoint, a rubber-banding line tracks your movement. To disengage the line from the cursor, press the second mouse button or press ⏎. Additional line segments are drawn by moving the cursor and pressing the pick button. While using the Line command, the Undo option will erase the previous line segment. You can undo all the lines you have drawn with the current Line command.

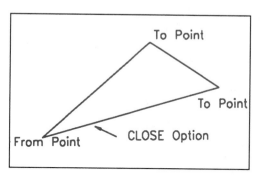
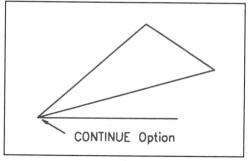

The Close option automatically closes a polygon by drawing a line from the last point to the beginning point. The Continue option restarts the line where you left off.

✦ Line Notes

- Other line types, such as hidden and dashed, are also drawn with the Line command, except that the lines are drawn on a layer to which that special linetype has been assigned (see the Linetype command in Chapter 14).

- The Ortho setting constrains the line to orthogonal directions, and Snap allows the line to begin and end only at snap locations.
- The Continue option allows you to come back after you have finished using the Line command and continue the line from where you left off. With this handy option, you can interrupt your drawing with other commands (except Pline and Arc).

✦ CIRCLE

Draws a circle after you specify its radius or diameter. AutoCAD provides five ways to draw a circle.

Command Finder

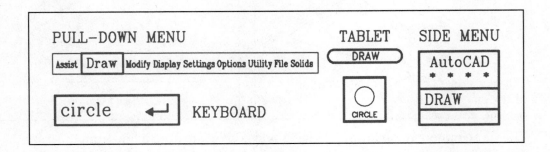

✦ Circle Options

These are the most commonly used circle drawing options:

- Center Point (Radius)
- 2P (2 Point)

You may also want to investigate these options:

- *3P* (3 Point) prompts you for three points on a circle.
- *TTR* draws a circle based on two tangent points and a radius.
- *Cen,Dia* is like the Center Point option except that you specify a diameter instead of a radius.

• Using the Circle Command

In this section we'll look at two methods for drawing circles: Center Point and 2 Point.

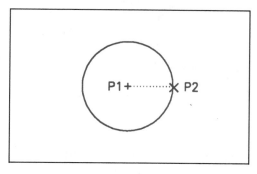
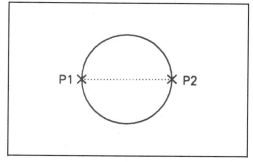

With Center Point—the default option—you pick the first point (P1) as the center of the circle; the second point (P2) indicates the radius length. With the 2 Point option, you specify the two points at the ends of the diameter.

• Tip

If your circles seem to be drawn with straight sides, it's because AutoCAD is trying to save you time in regenerating the screen. If you would rather trade time for rounder circles, set Viewres to a larger number, such as 200.

✦ ELLIPSE

Draws ellipses from major and minor axes. You specify the axes by indicating their endpoints.

Command Finder

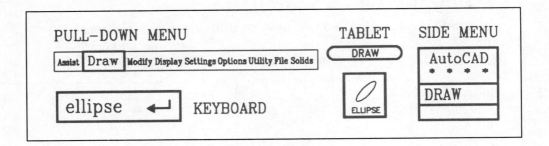

✦ Ellipse Options

AutoCAD provides several ways to draw ellipses; two of them are explained in this section:

- Pick the endpoints of one axis and specify the mid-distance for the second axis (the default option).
- Specify the center of the ellipse to pick the endpoints of the two axes.

✦ Using the Ellipse Command

You can draw an ellipse using two different methods.

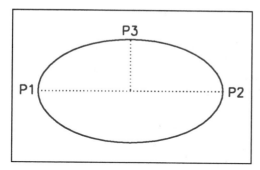 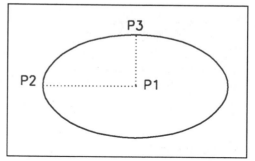

With the first method, after specifying the endpoints of the first axis, a rubber-banding line from the axis's center appears. You use the cursor to indicate the distance between that center point and one endpoint on the second axis. With the second method, you first specify the ellipse's center point. You then indicate the first axis's endpoint with a rubber-banding line from the center point. Finally, you indicate the distance for the other axis with another rubber-banding line from the center point.

◆ ARC

Draws a segment of a circle. You specify three items: a starting point, an ending or a center point, and one other option, which can be an angle, a radius chord, a direction, or a second point.

Command Finder

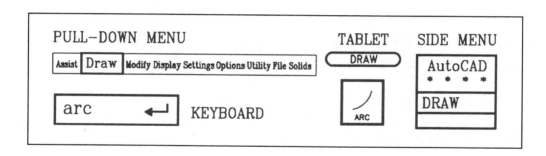

✦ Arc Options

The Arc menu has 11 options for drawing arcs. Most of them are represented by letters that are abbreviations of the points you must specify to draw an arc. The order in which the letters are shown is the order in which you pick the points.

Here are five frequently used Arc options:

- 3 Point (the default option)
- S,C,E (**S**tarting point, **C**enter, **E**nding point)
- S,E,A (**S**tarting point, **E**nding point, included **A**ngle)
- S,E,D (**S**tarting point, **E**nding point, **D**irection from starting point)
- Contin (for continuing an arc or a line from the last point drawn)

Other Arc options use radius (R) and the length of a chord (L).

✦ Using the Arc Command

An arc requires a starting point, an ending or center point, and an angle, a radius, a chord, a direction, or a second point. An arc is not drawn on the screen until after you place the second point. As you place the third point, the image is dragged along with the cursor, showing the arc as it is being formed. In this section you'll learn about five frequently used methods of drawing arcs.

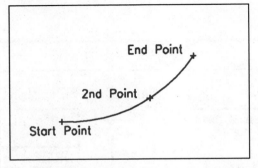
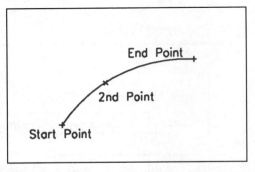

The 3-point arc is the default arc. This arc can be drawn in any direction, depending on the points chosen.

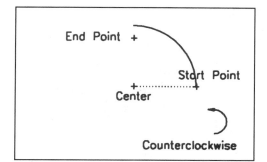

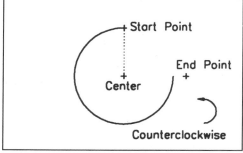

With the S,C,E (start, center, end) method, the arc is always drawn counterclock-wise around the center from the start point toward the endpoint. Because the radius for the arc is determined by the distance from the starting point to the center, it may not always pass through the endpoint specified.

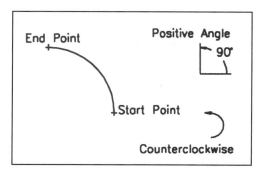

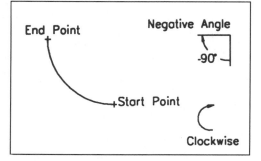

The S,E,A (start, end, angle) method is also direction-sensitive. Specifying a positive angle draws the arc in a counterclockwise direction; specifying a negative angle draws the arc in a clockwise direction.

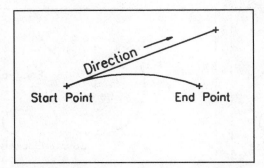 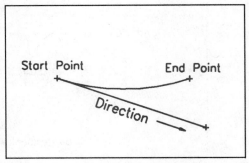

The S,E,D (start, end, direction) method draws an arc in any direction. The direction is determined by the location of the cursor and is tangent to the rubber-banding line from the starting point of the arc to the cursor.

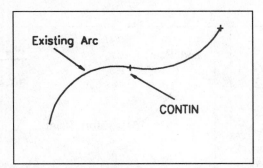 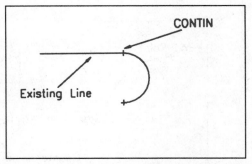

The Contin option will start drawing an arc from the endpoint of a previously drawn line or arc. (Similarly, the Contin option in the Line command will draw a line from the endpoint of a previously drawn line or arc. Both are very handy options.)

✦ Arc Notes

Make sure that Ortho mode is turned off when drawing arcs.

You need to pay attention to clockwise and counterclockwise directions when specifying points in an arc or you will get surprising results. The only three Arc options that draw arcs in any direction are 3 Point (the default), S,E,D, and Contin. All other options draw arcs in a counterclockwise direction unless you specify a negative value.

A good way to decide which arc drawing option to use is to ask yourself what information you have to draw the arc and whether you want to use the center or start point as your first specification point. After you have answered these questions, go to the Arc menu and pick the most appropriate option.

The best option for drawing an arc depends on the drawing problem to be solved. The 3-point option is often used when drawing land contours because you don't have information that would be required to use any of the other options. The S,E,R option is used when laying out roads and driveways, where a specific turning radius is required. For drawing "flattish" types of arcs, the S,E,D and 3-point options work well because they allow the center of the arc to be off the screen.

◆ DONUT

Draws solid circles and donut shapes.

Command Finder

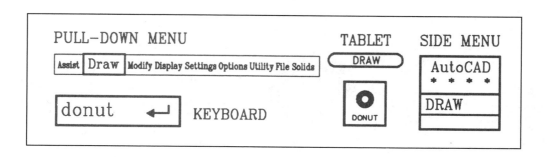

✦ Using the Donut Command

Donuts are drawn by specifying the inside diameter, the outside diameter, and the center of the donut. If you use the keyboard, you can type in *donut* or *dough-nut*—AutoCAD recognizes either spelling. Once you have drawn a donut, you can place multiple copies of it. To cancel the command, press ⏎ or button 2 at the second *Center of doughnut:* prompt.

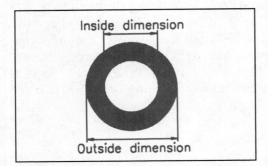
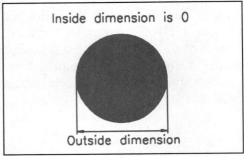

When drawing a donut, the inside dimension is the diameter of the hole and the outside dimension is the size of the donut. To draw a solid circle, specify 0 for the inside diameter, then enter the outside diameter. When Fill (covered in Chapter 7) is on, the donuts and circles are drawn solid. When Fill is off, AutoCAD draws lines instead of solid filled areas. Any changes to Fill require a regeneration of the drawing before you can see the changes on-screen.

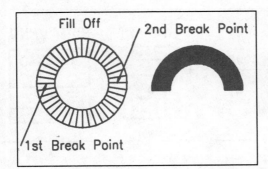
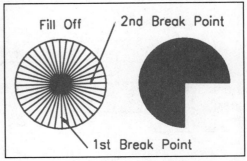

If you want only a segment of a circle or donut, turn Fill off and break the drawing at the segment lines.

✦ POLYGON

Constructs an equal-sided polygon, given the number of sides and the radius or the specification of a single side.

Command Finder

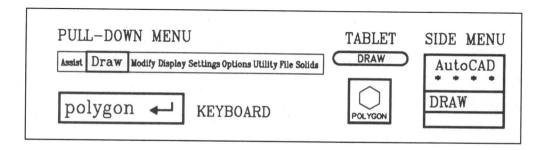

✦ Polygon Options

- Edge
- I-scribe (inscribed in a circle)
- C-scribe (circumscribed about a circle)

✦ Using the Polygon Command

You can draw a polygon in three ways. With all three, you first specify the number of sides. In the Edge method, you specify the endpoints of a side of the polygon. With the other two methods, AutoCAD draws the polygon inside or outside a circle (you provide the radius).

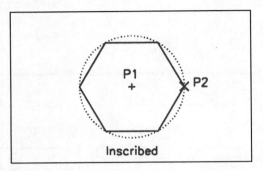
Inscribed

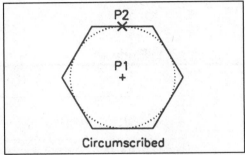
Circumscribed

The I-scribe option inscribes the polygon in a circle. The C-scribe option circumscribes the polygon about a circle.

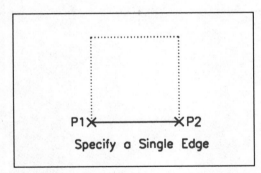
Specify a Single Edge

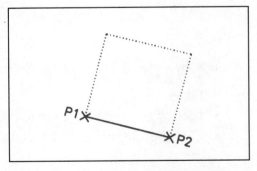

The Edge option draws equal sides of a length you specify. The placement of the second point determines the orientation of the polygon.

✦ Polygon Notes

Polygon orientation is determined by how you select the diameter. When drawing a polygon inscribed in a circle, the point picked positions the endpoint of one of the sides. When drawing a polygon circumscribed about a circle, the point picked will be the midpoint of one of the sides. If you enter the diameter as a value, the side of the polygon is drawn parallel to the x-axis.

✦ POINT

Draws a pixel-sized point. Points are used to mark locations that you want to reference. The drawing tool Osnap can be set to locate points automatically (see Chapter 6).

Command Finder

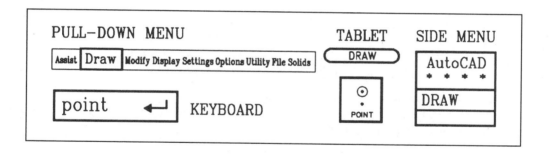

✦ Using the Point Command

Because the small size of the default point makes it difficult to see, AutoCAD provides many sizes and styles. Pdmode offers 20 variations from which to select a point style most appropriate for your application. With Pdsize you indicate the actual size for the point style selected. Only one style or size can be used at a time. Changes in Pdmode or Pdsize take effect only after you regenerate a drawing.

Here are some point examples:

```
┌──────────────────────────────────────────────────────────────┬──────────┐
│ Layer 0                        2.6128,0.0108                   │AutoCAD   │
│                                                                │* * * *   │
│                                                                │POINT:    │
│                               +     ×     |                    │.x        │
│                                                                │.y        │
│            O      1      2     3     4                         │.z        │
│                                                                │.xy       │
│                                                                │.xz       │
│                                                                │.yz       │
│                                                                │          │
│           ⬡      ⬡     ⬕     ⊠     ◔                          │Complex   │
│                                                                │Points    │
│           32     33     34    35    36                         │example:  │
│                                                                │remove    │
│                                                                │example:  │
│           □      □      ⊞     ⊠     ◳                          │Pdmode:   │
│                                                                │Pdsize:   │
│           64     65     66    67    68                         │__LAST__  │
│                                                                │  DRAW    │
│                                                                │  EDIT    │
│           ⊡      ⊡      ⊞     ⊠     ◳                          │          │
│                                                                │          │
│           96     97     98    99   100                         │          │
├────────────────────────────────────────────────────────────────┴────────┤
│ Command: VSLIDE                                                           │
│ Slide file <POINT>: acad(points)                                          │
│ Command:                                                                  │
└───────────────────────────────────────────────────────────────────────────┘
```

◆   **Tip**

To see the different styles available in Pdmode, select *Complex Points example:* under the Point command. To remove the slide, pick *remove example:* from the menu or enter **redraw**.

✦ TUTORIAL: DRAWING A FURNITURE LIBRARY

With this lesson, you will start building a furniture library. You'll draw a desk, a workstation, and chairs, which you will use in planning an office you design in later chapters. Do not copy the dimensions or text shown on the illustration into your drawing.

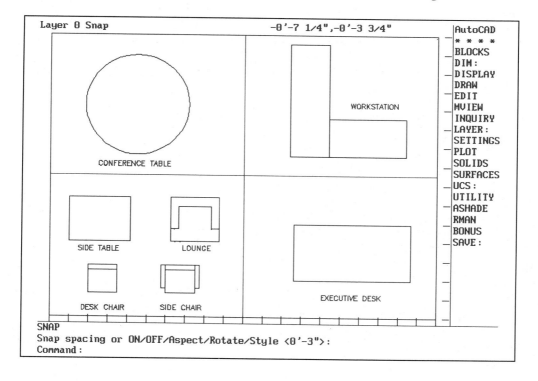

You already set the limits, units, and settings for snap, grid, and axis in the prototype drawing you did in Chapter 2. If you have not done the prototype drawing, refer to Chapter 2 for the settings. (The new commands used in this lesson that are not covered in this chapter are Ucsicon, Erase, and Osnap overrides.)

✦**1**   Begin a new drawing by selecting 1 on the Main Menu. To use a prototype drawing as the base for a new drawing, type an equal sign and the name of the prototype after the new drawing's name.

Enter NAME of drawing: **LIB-F=A24**

✦**2**   Divide the screen into four quadrants, as shown in the drawing. Use the Osnap override Mid to pick the midpoints of the boundary lines (Osnap is covered in the next chapter). You use Osnap overrides to snap to special points on your entities. In this case, AutoCAD finds the midpoints of the lines without your having to measure them.

Command: **LINE**
From point: **MID** of   *Pick the bottom line of the border*
To point: **MID** of   *Pick the top line of the border*
To point: ⏎ or button 2

Command: **LINE**
From point: **MID** of   *Pick the left line of the border*
To point: **MID** of   *Pick the right line of the border*
To point: ⏎ or button 2

✦**3**   Turn off the arrow icon at the bottom of the screen—right now it is in the way. (It is useful when you work in 3-D space.)

Command: **UCSICON**
ON/OFF/All/Noorigin/ORigin <ON>: **OFF**

◆**4**   Zoom to the lower-left quadrant to start drawing the chairs.

> Command: **ZOOM**
> All/Center/Dynamic/Extents/Left/Previous/Window/<Scale(X)>: **W**
> First corner: Other corner: *Window the lower-left quadrant*

◆**5**   Draw the desk chair, using the dimensions, grid, and axis ticks shown in the following drawing for reference:

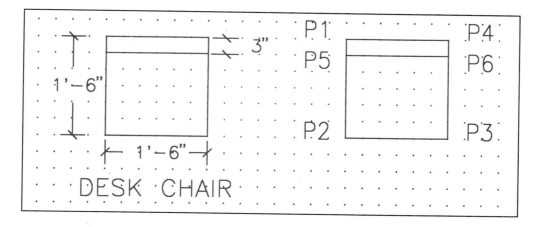

Make sure that the coordinate readout in the upper-right portion of your screen follows your cursor movement. Use the readout to give you playback on the length of line you are drawing. The [F6] key toggles this function on and off.

Command: **LINE**
From point: *Pick point 1*
To point: *Pick point 2*
To point: *Pick point 3*
To point: *Pick point 4*
To point: **C** (to close the figure)

Command: **LINE**
From point: *Pick point 5*
To point: *Pick point 6*
To point: ↵ or button 2

✦**6** Draw the side chair next to the desk chair, using the same dimensions as those for the desk chair. Add the side arms, using the
dimensions shown in the following drawing:

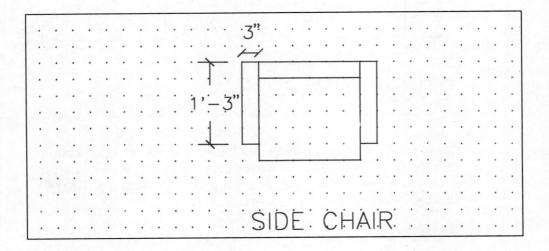

Check the coordinate readout to make sure that the lines you draw are the same length as those shown in the drawing.

♦ **7** Move your cursor to the upper-left portion of your screen, and use the same technique to draw the side table. Use the dimensions shown in the illustration, and check the coordinate readout for the line lengths. Select Drawing Tools on the Settings pull-down menu, and change your snap spacing to 1 inch (leave the grid spacing at 3 inches).

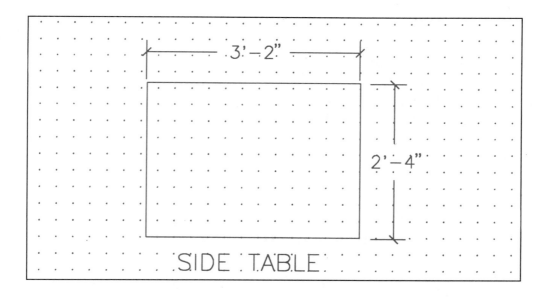

♦ **8** Move your cursor to the upper-right portion of your screen, and draw the lounge chair. Follow the points and use the dimensions shown in the illustration.

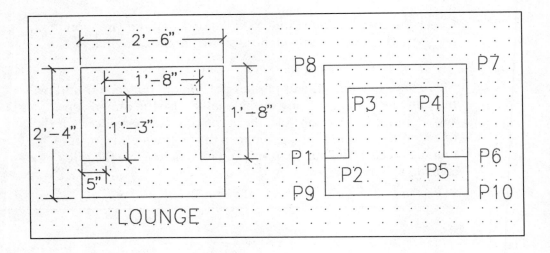

Command: **LINE**
From point: *Pick point 1*
To point: *Pick points 2 to 10 in sequence*
To point: *Return to point 6*
To point: ⏎ or button 2

✦**9**   Zoom back to the full-screen view.

> Command: **ZOOM**
> All/Center/Dynamic/Extents/Left/Previous/Window/<Scale(X)>: **P**

✦**10**   Zoom to the lower-right quadrant to start drawing the executive desk.

> Command: **ZOOM**
> All/Center/Dynamic/Extents/Left/Previous/Window/<Scale(X)>: **W**
> First corner: Other corner: *Window lower-right quadrant*

◆ **11** Draw the executive desk, using the dimensions shown in the following illustration:

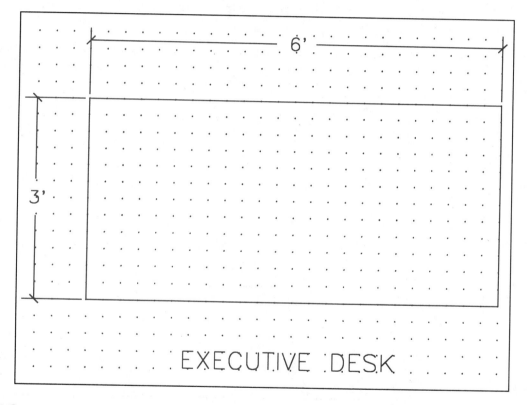

EXECUTIVE DESK

◆ **12** Zoom back to the full-screen view.

Command: **ZOOM**
All/Center/Dynamic/Extents/Left/Previous/Window/<Scale(X)>: **P**

◆ **13** Zoom to the upper-right quadrant to draw the workstation.

Command: **ZOOM**

All/Center/Dynamic/Extents/Left/Previous/Window/<Scale(X)>: **W**
First corner: Other corner: *Window the upper-right quadrant*

♦ **14**   Draw the workstation, using the dimensions shown in the following illustration:

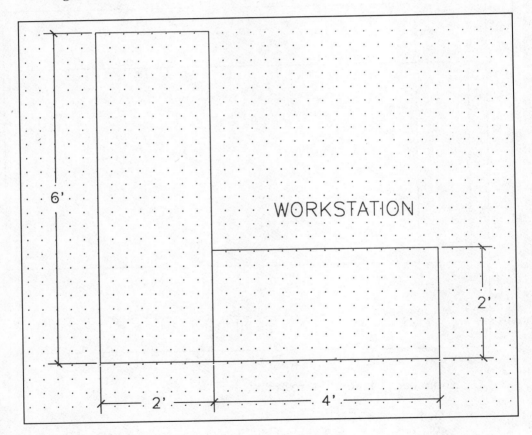

♦ **15**   Zoom back to the full-screen view.

Command: **ZOOM**
All/Center/Dynamic/Extents/Left/Previous/Window/<Scale(X)>: **P**

♦16   Zoom to the upper-left quadrant to draw the conference table.

Command: **ZOOM**
All/Center/Dynamic/Extents/Left/Previous/Window/<Scale(X)>: **W**
First corner: Other corner: *Window the upper-left quadrant*

♦17   Draw the conference table using the diameter option of the Circle command.

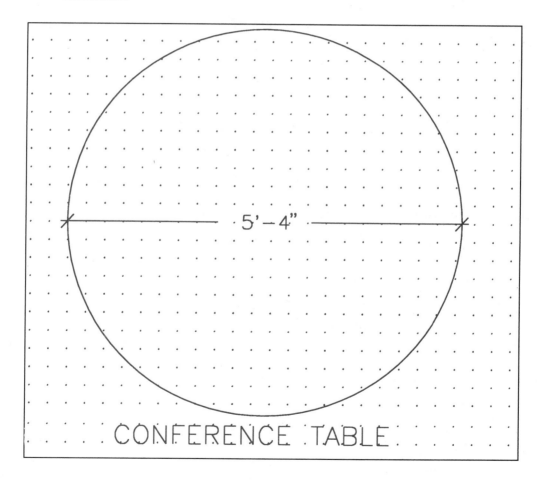

Command: **CIRCLE**
3P/2P/TTR/<Center point>: *Pick a point in the center of the screen*
Diameter/<Radius>: **D**
Diameter: **5′4**

✦**18**   End the drawing session.

Command: **END**

From the Main Menu, select 0 to exit AutoCAD. You have completed the basic
furniture you need to lay out the office you will design later in the book.

✦ TUTORIAL: DRAWING ARCHITECTURAL SYMBOLS

In this lesson, you will use the Polygon, Point, and Donut commands to create three architectural symbols: a column-line symbol, a section symbol, and a work point symbol. The size for all the symbols is ½ inch. Although the snap setting makes it easy to locate points, this lesson also makes use of filters and Osnap overrides to demonstrate their use. (You may want to take a look at the next chapter's material on Osnap before proceeding.)

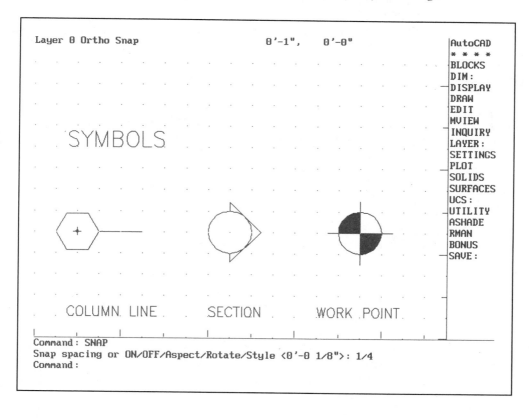

✦**1**   Start a new drawing called **LIB-S**.

✦**2**   Establish the following settings:

> Units: **4** (Architectural)
> Denominator: **4**
> Limits: Lower left **0,0**; Upper right **6,3**
> Snap: **1/4** and set to On
> Grid: **1/4** and set to On
> Axis: **1/2** and set to On
> Blipmode (Blips): Off
> F6 Function Key: <Coords On>
> F8 Function Key: <Ortho On>
> Ucsicon: Off
> Zoom: All

✦**3**   Start the column-line symbol by drawing a hexagon in the left third of your screen.

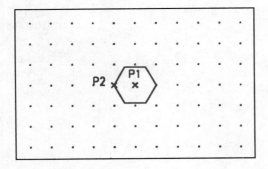

Command: **POLYGON**
Number of sides: **6**
Edge/<Center of polygon>: *Pick point 1*

Inscribed in circle/Circumscribed about circle (I/C): **I**
Radius of circle: *Pick point 2*

◆**4** Draw a line from the right point of the hexagon to indicate
column direction.

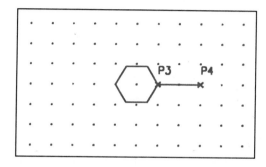

Command: **LINE**
From point: *Pick point 3*
To point: *Pick point 4*
To point: ⏎ or button 2

◆**5** Mark the center of the hexagon with a point for future insertion of
a letter. Select a complex point so that the point will be visible. By
using the side menu to choose Complex Points, you can select
both the mode and size for the point; otherwise, you have to type
pdmode and **pdsize** to change these settings. Toggle Snap off
(press F9).

Command: **POINT**
(Select *example* to bring up the slide; select Pdmode to pick the point style)
PDMODE: New value for PDMODE <0>: **2**
(Select Pdsize to pick the point size)
PDSIZE: New value for PDSIZE <0>: **1/8**
(Select *remove example* to remove the slide)

✦**6**   Use the filters listed under the Point command to place the point in the center of the hexagon.

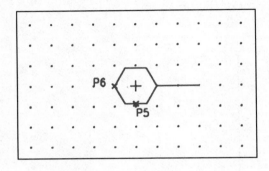

Command: **POINT**
(Select .x, type **mid**, press ⏎, and pick point 5. Then type **end**, press ⏎, and pick point 6)

✦**7**   Start the section identification symbol by drawing a circle. Toggle Snap on (press F9).

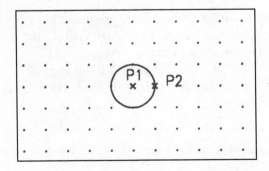

Command: **CIRCLE**
3P/2P/TTR/<Center point>: *Pick point 1*
Diameter/<Radius>: *Pick point 2*

⋆**8**   Draw a square around the circle.

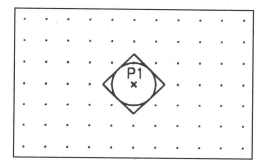

Command: **POLYGON**
Number of sides: **4**
Edge/<Center of polygon>: *Pick point 1*
Inscribed in circle/Circumscribed about circle (I/C): **C**
Radius of circle: **@1/4<45** (or pick it from the numerical pad on a tablet)

⋆**9**   Draw a line bisecting the symbol using the end Osnap override.
Toggle Snap off (press F9).

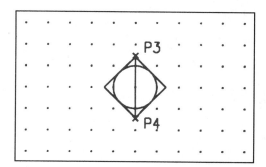

Command: **LINE**
From point: end (Select Osnap override from the four stars on the side menu) of   *Pick point 3*
To point: end (Select Osnap override) of   *Pick point 4*
To point: ⏎ or button 2

✦**10**   Zoom in to see more detail.

Command: **ZOOM**
All/Center/Dynamic/Extents/Left/Previous/Window/<Scale(X)>: **W**
First corner: Other corner: *Window the section symbol*

✦**11**   Use the Trim command to erase half of the polygon. (A full explanation of the Trim command is given in Chapter 8.)

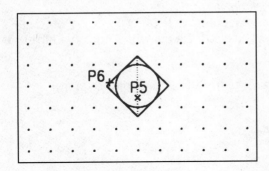

Command: **TRIM**
Select cutting edge(s)...   *Pick point 5*
Select objects: 1 selected, 1 found

Select objects: ↵ or button 2
Select object to trim: *Pick point 6*
Select object to trim: ↵ or button 2

♦ **12**   Use the Trim command to erase the line through the circle.

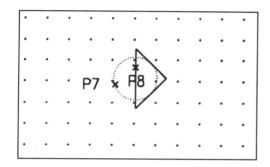

Command: **TRIM**
Select cutting edge(s)…   *Pick point 7* (the circle is the cutting edge)
Select objects: 1 selected, 1 found
Select objects: ↵ or button 2
Select object to trim: *Pick point 8*
Select object to trim: ↵ or button 2

♦ **13**   Zoom back to the previous view.

Command: **ZOOM**
All/Center/Dynamic/Extents/Left/Previous/Window/<Scale(X)>: **P**

✦ **14**   The next symbol you will draw is referred to as a *work point* or a
datum point. Start by drawing a circle. Toggle Snap on (press ⌷F9⌷).

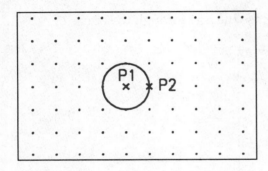

Command: **CIRCLE**
3P/2P/TTR/<Center point>: *Pick point 1*
Diameter/<Radius>: *Pick point 2*

✦ **15**   Zoom in to work on the symbol.

Command: **ZOOM**
All/Center/Dynamic/Extents/Left/Previous/Window/<Scale(X)>: **W**
First corner: Other corner: *Window the section symbol*

✦ **16**   Use the Donut command to draw the filled sections.

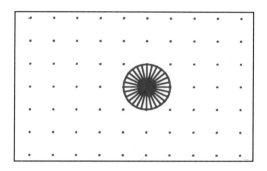

Command: **DONUT**
Inside diameter <0'-0">: **0**
Outside diameter <0'-0">: **1/2**
Center of doughnut: *Pick the same center as that for the circle, then press*
⏎ *or button 2 to finish Donut command*

✦**17**   Turn Fill off to make it easier to work with the donut.

Command: **FILL**
ON/OFF <On>: **OFF**

To see the effect, you have to regenerate the drawing.

Command: **REGEN**
Regenerating drawing.

✦**18.** Change the snap spacing before drawing the crossing lines that extend 1/8" on either side of the circle.

> Command: **SNAP**
> Snap spacing or ON/OFF/Aspect/Rotate/Style <0'-0 1/4">: **1/8**

✦**19** Draw the first and second crossing lines.

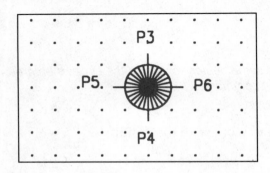

> Command: **LINE**
> From point: *Pick point 3*
> To point: *Pick point 4*
> To point: ⏎ or button 2
>
> Command: **LINE**
> From point: *Pick point 5*
> To point: *Pick point 6*
> To point: ⏎ or button 2

♦ **20**   Use the Trim command to erase parts of the donut.

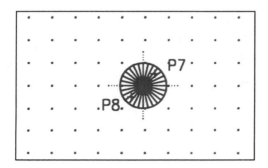

Command: **TRIM**
Select cutting edge(s)...   *Pick one of the crossing lines*
Select objects: 1 selected, 1 found
Select objects: 1 selected, 1 found   *Pick the other crossing line*
Select objects: ⏎ or button 2
Select object to trim: *Pick point 7*
Select object to trim: *Pick point 8*
Select object to trim: ⏎ or button 2

Sections of the donut are trimmed:

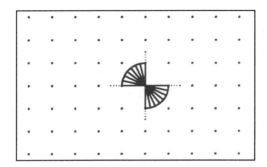

✦ **21**   Use Redraw to restore the missing pieces of the symbol.

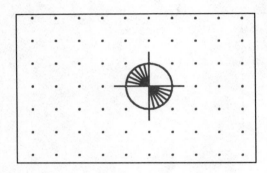

Command: **REDRAW**

✦ **22**   Zoom back to the full view and turn on Fill.

Command: **ZOOM**
All/Center/Dynamic/Extents/Left/Previous/Window/<Scale(X)>: **P**

Command: **FILL**
ON/OFF <Off>: **ON**

✦ **23**   Regenerate the screen to see the effect of Fill turned on. Your work
point drawing should now look like the full-screen image at the
beginning of the tutorial.

Command: **REGEN**

✦ **24**   End the drawing.

Command: **END**

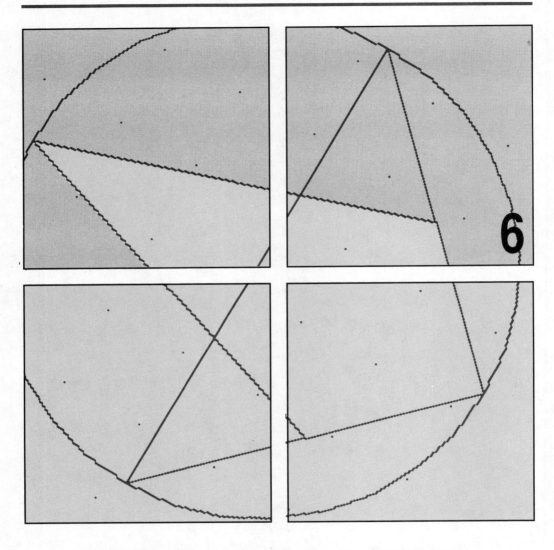

6

DRAWING TOOLS AND AIDS

The drawing assistance commands are found on the Assist and Utility pull-down menus and under the four stars (****) on the root menu. To the beginner, learning Osnaps and Filters often seems like an additional complication, but to the pro, learning them makes drawing easier and increases speed and accuracy.

- Help

- Undo/U

- Redo

- Cancel

- Osnap

- Filters

✦ HELP

*Provides on-screen information about AutoCAD commands. In Release 11 the help is **contextual**, which means that you can access it while in a command. It gives you information specific not only to the command but also to the option you are working with.*

Command Finder

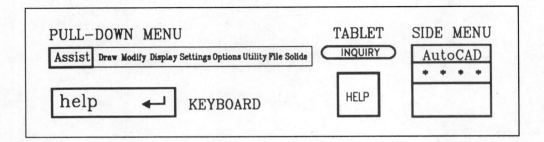

✦ Using the Help Command

The Help command provides information on a specific command or provides a list of commands from which you can make a choice. If you select Help from the tablet or screen while in another command, you see information specific to that command. Help is one of the transparent commands, which means that you can use it while inside another command.

✦ Help Notes

- You can get "trapped" in the Help command—if you do, you will keep seeing lists of commands. Use the Cancel command or press CTRL C to cancel Help.

- You can type ? instead of typing *Help* to access the command from the keyboard.
- If you use the apostrophe (') before typing *Help* or ?, the command can be used while inside another command.

✦ UNDO AND U

These commands allow you to step back sequentially and undo previous commands.

Command Finder

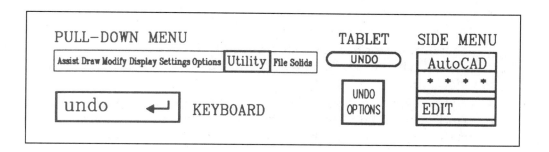

✦ Undo Options
- Number
- Mark
- Back

✦ Using the Undo Command

When you select the Undo command, the default choice is Number. If you press ⏎, AutoCAD assumes that you mean the number **1** and will undo the last command. If you type a number, AutoCAD undoes that number of previous commands.

When trying out a new design, it is sometimes useful to be able to mark a point in the process so that you can return to that point should you decide not to go with the changes. To do this, use the Mark option of the Undo command to mark the stage in your drawing that you may want to return to. Continue drawing; if you want to restore your drawing to that stage, select Undo and then Back.

U will undo only a single command. Because it has no options, it works as soon as you use it.

◆ Undo Notes

- If you use Undo too many times, you can use Redo to undo the effects of the last Undo. Redo will redo only one Undo.
- Other options for this command, such as Auto, Control, Group, and End, are used when working with menu macros and large drawings; they are outside the scope of this book.
- The U option used inside of a command is different from U used as a command. When used inside a command, it undoes the last step taken while inside that command. When used as a separate command, it undoes all the steps taken in the last command.

◆ REDO

Reverses the effect of the last undone command. Redo will redo only one Undo.

Command Finder

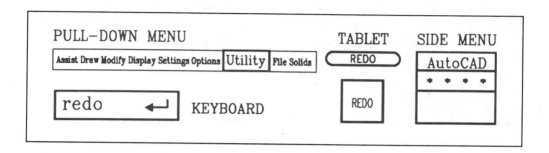

◆ CANCEL

Terminates the existing command and returns you to the Command prompt.

Command Finder

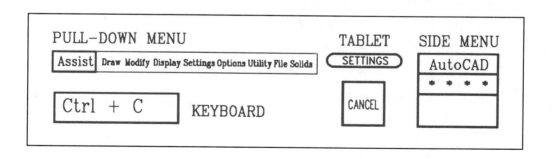

✦ Using the Cancel Function

Cancel is not really a command but a function that allows you to terminate a command. You can select it from the screen or the tablet menu. If you want to access Cancel from the keyboard, hold down [CTRL] while pressing [C].

✦ OSNAP

*The Osnap command (short for **object snap**) makes it easier to pick specific points on entities, such as endpoints and midpoints of lines and centers of circles and arcs. It does this by allowing you to prespecify the kind of point you want to pick and giving you a large enough target box to make picking easier.*

✦ Osnap Options

- ENDpoint
- INTersection
- MIDpoint
- CENter
- QUAdrant
- PERpendicular

- TANgent
- NODe
- INSert
- NEArest
- QUIck
- NONe

Command Finder

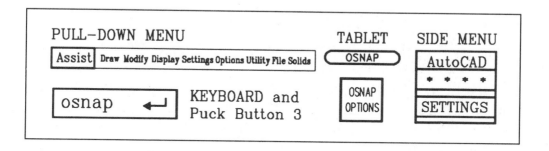

✦ Using the Osnap Command

There are two forms of the Osnap command. The standard form activates the mode you specify and keeps it active until you specify None. The other form works for one instance only and is referred to as an *Osnap override,* because it will override a standard Osnap. Because Osnaps are so useful, there are many ways to access them.

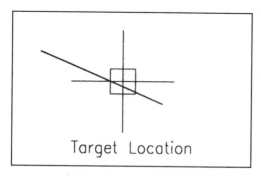

Target Location

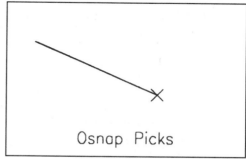

Osnap Picks

In selecting the ENDpoint Osnap, the target can be placed anywhere between the middle of a line and the desired endpoint.

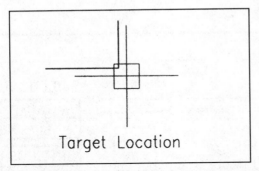

Target Location

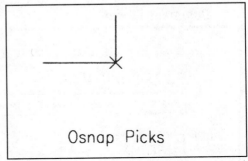

Osnap Picks

In selecting the INTersection Osnap, both lines comprising the intersection must be within the target.

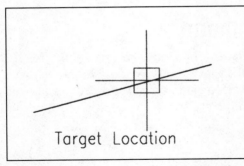

Target Location

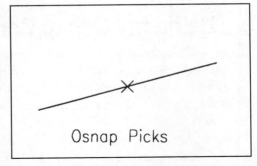

Osnap Picks

The MIDpoint Osnap finds the midpoint of a line; it can also find the midpoint of an arc. The target can be placed anywhere on the entity.

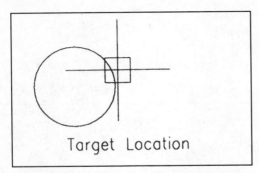

Target Location

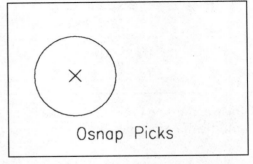

Osnap Picks

The CENter Osnap can find the center of a circle. The target can be placed anywhere on the circle's perimeter. The CENter Osnap can also be used to pick the center of an arc.

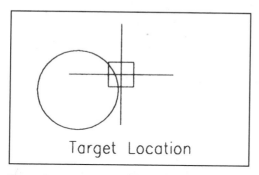

Target Location

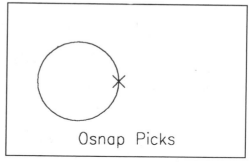

Osnap Picks

The QUAdrant Osnap can find the points on a circle or an arc that indicate their cardinal quadrants—0, 90, 180, and 270 degrees. The target should be placed on the perimeter of the circle, nearest to the quadrant point desired.

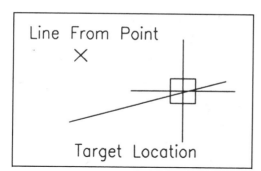

Line From Point

Target Location

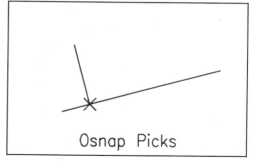

Osnap Picks

The PERpendicular Osnap is usually used to draw a line perpendicular to the start point. It can also be used to start a line perpendicular *from* the start point. The target can be placed anywhere on the entity that the line is being drawn to.

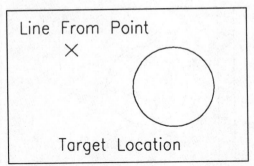

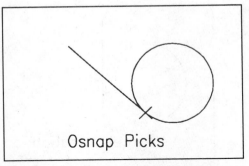

The TANgent Osnap snaps to a point that is tangent to a circle. There are two tangents possible from a point to a circle. Either side of the circle can be specified.

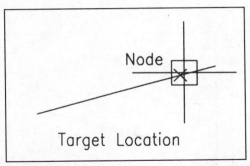

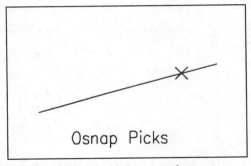

The NODe Osnap snaps to a point. The point must be inside the target box.

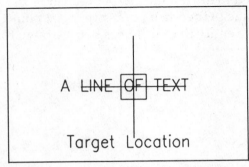

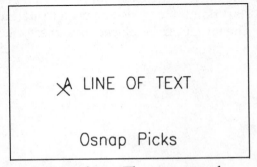

The INSert Osnap snaps to the insertion point of a line of text. The target can be placed anywhere on the line of text. This mode also snaps to the insertion point of a block.

The NEArest Osnap snaps to a point on an entity that is nearest to the cross hairs.

The QUIck option modifies any of the other Osnap modes except INTersection. When your drawings are large, this option speeds up selection.

✦ Osnap Notes

- Use the Status command to find out what Osnap modes are active.
- You can tell that you have Osnap turned on when a target box appears around the cross hairs and the pick box.
- You can change the size of the target box. Size is controlled by the variable Aperture. Type **Aperture** and enter a number for the target box size.
- When using the standard Osnap, you can specify more than one mode by separating them with a comma, such as *MID,END*.
- If you are using a four-button puck, Osnaps can be accessed by pressing button 4.

✦ FILTERS

Not a command but a way of constructing a point by giving x, y, and z coordinates separately instead of all at once. You can enter the coordinates in any order that is convenient to the construction of the point. You can use filters to construct points in either 2-D or 3-D space.

✦ Filter Options

- .X
- .Y
- .Z

- .XY
- .XZ
- .YZ

Command Finder

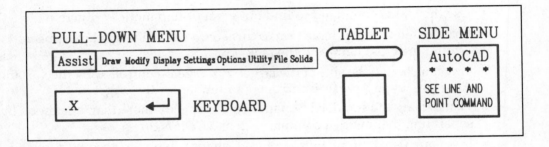

✦ Using Filters

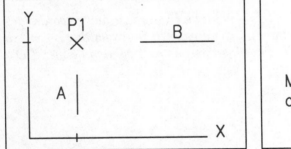 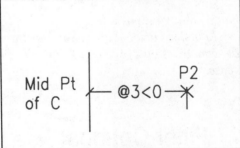

With filters you can derive the coordinates of point P1 from the x-coordinate of the vertical line A and the y-coordinate of the horizontal line B. By using Osnaps in combination with relative coordinates, you can use filters to place a point P2 a specific distance from the midpoint of line C.

✦ Filter Notes

- Filters can be used to start lines a specific distance from an existing object without drawing construction lines.
- When using filters in 3-D space, use the .XY filter to pick a point in the x-y plane and then specify the z-coordinate.

✦ TUTORIAL:
DRAWING A NORTH ARROW

This lesson shows how to use Osnaps and demonstrates how useful they can be in drawing. Osnaps are used all the time in production drawings and throughout this book.

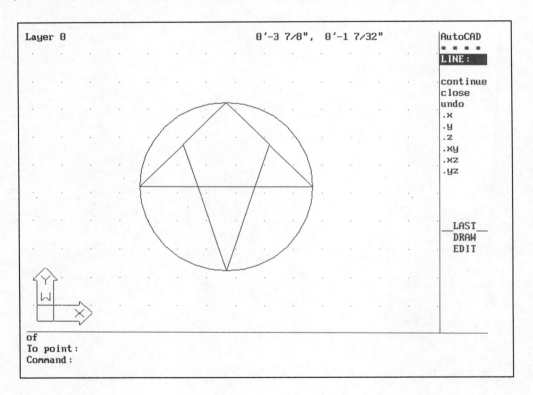

✦**1**   Start a new drawing called NORTH.

✦**2**   Establish these settings:

> Units: **4** (Architectural))
> Denominator: **32**
> Limits: Lower left **0,0**; Upper right **2,1-1/2**
> Snap: **1/16** and set to On
> Grid: **1/8** and set to On
> Blipmode: Off
> Zoom: All

✦**3**   Draw a circle with a radius 3/8".

> Command: **CIRCLE**
> 3P/2P/TTR/<Center point>: *Select a point in the middle of the screen*
> Diameter/<Radius>: **3/8**

✦**4**   We will use the standard Osnap for the QUAdrant mode because we will be drawing to the quadrant of the circle a number of times, but we will use the Osnap overrides for those modes that are needed only once.

> Command: **OSNAP**
> Object snap modes: **QUA**

✦**5**   Draw the top part of the arrow using the Osnap target to pick the points (shown in the illustration at the beginning of the tutorial). The QUAdrant Osnap remains active until it is canceled. The CENter override overrides the QUAdrant Osnap for a single pick. Remember, it is not necessary to pick the points exactly when using Osnaps.

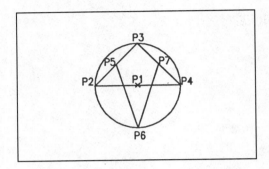

Command: **LINE**
From point: CEN of   *Pick a point on the perimeter of the circle* (the line starts at P1)
To point: *Pick a point near P2*
To point: *Pick a point near P3*
To point: *Pick a point near P4*
To point: CEN of   *Pick a point on the perimeter of the circle*
To point: ⏎ or button 2

✦6   Begin another line for the bottom of the arrow. For these points we will use the MIDpoint Osnap override.

Command: **LINE**
From point: MID of   *Pick a point near P5*
To point: *Pick a point near P6*
To point: MID of   *Pick a point near P7*
To point: ⏎ or button 2

✦7   You are now finished with the outline of the north arrow symbol. In the next chapter, you will add a hatch pattern and a solid fill to complete the design.

Command: **END**

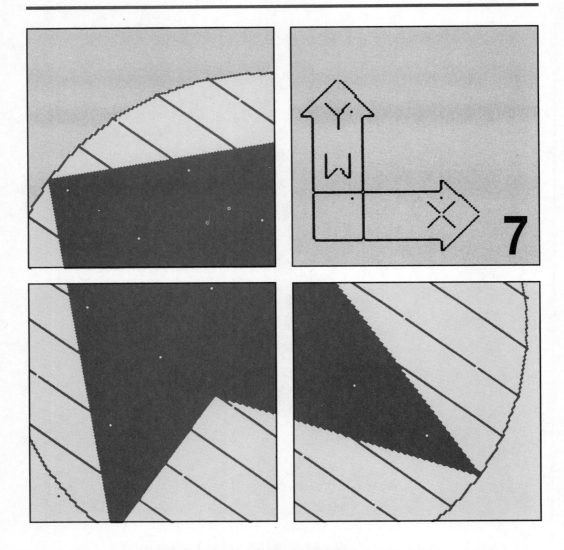

AREA FILL COMMANDS

The area-fill commands cover a defined area with a solid fill or one of the many textures available in AutoCAD's hatch patterns.

- ✦ Hatch

- ✦ Solid

- ✦ Fill

♦ HATCH

Fills a specified area with a pattern. Aside from the 65 hatch patterns that AutoCAD provides, you can define your own simple line pattern. The Normal option is the default and is chosen automatically when you select a hatch. The other options are specified by placing a comma and the option letter after the pattern name.

Command Finder

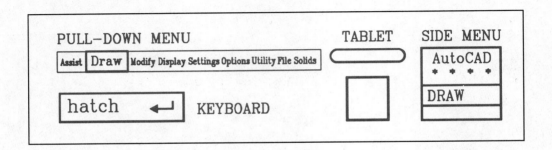

♦ Hatch Options

- Outermost (O)
- Ignore (I)
- User Defined (U)

◆ Using the Hatch Command

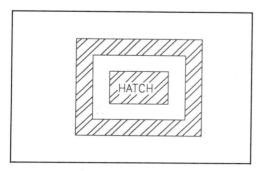
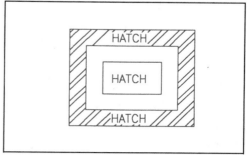

The default (or Normal) option starts hatching at the outermost area and alternately hatches and ignores successive areas; text is not hatched over. The Outermost (O) option fills only the outermost area; text is not hatched over.

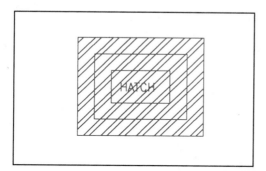
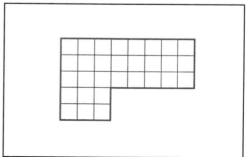

The Ignore (I) option hatches over all the areas, including text. For the User Defined (U) option, you specify the angle for the crosshatch lines, the spacing between the lines, and whether or not you want double hatching. Double hatching will crisscross a second set of lines 90 degrees over the first set. This option is particularly useful for drawing tiles on floor plans.

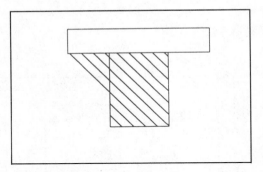
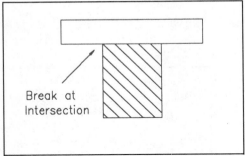

Break at
Intersection

Sometimes when the boundaries of an area are ambiguous, hatching produces unexpected and undesirable results. The simple solution is to do a *pixel break* at the problem intersections, which is to cut the line in two so that it no longer is a continuous line.

✦ Hatch Notes

Typing a question mark after a Hatch command lists names of hatch patterns. The ANSI (American National Standards Institute) hatches are used more often in mechanical design. (For a list of hatch names, see Appendix C.)

Selecting Hatch Options on the Options pull-down menu displays illustrations of the available hatch patterns. Picking a hatch here preselects the pattern when using Hatch on the pull-down menu. In Release 11, AutoCAD added some hatches specific to architecture. Some of the more useful ones are shown in the illustration.

The hatch patterns are reproduced at the angle illustrated. If you want to change this, enter your choice when prompted for an angle.

One common error is to specify too small a scale for the hatch pattern. Many of the patterns are symbols for materials, such as brass (ANSI34) and steel (ANSI32). The size of these patterns has been designed for 1"=1" scale for use in mechanical drafting. If you are designing in 1/4"=1' scale (or 1"=48") and want to use these hatches, you must multiply the hatch scale factor by 48 to compensate for the reduction that will be made when you plot the drawing. The newly added architectural hatches (they have an AR prefix) are actual textures or surfaces drawn at full scale, and as such, can be entered at the full-scale value of 1.

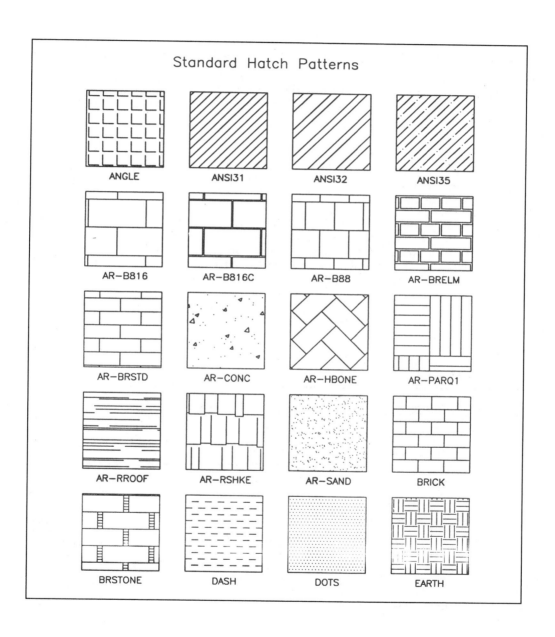

Standard Hatch Patterns

Hatch acts as a block. To erase it, select any line. Hatch can be exploded into its component parts for editing; however, it will revert to layer 0 regardless of the layer it was on originally and can substantially increase the size of your drawing.

✦ **Tip**

Because hatches slow down the time it takes to display your drawing after regeneration, a good drawing procedure is to put them on a separate layer so that layer can be frozen.

If you still have trouble with hatch boundaries after you have tried the pixel break, here is a "last resort" procedure: Go to a separate layer, outline the area with a pline (polylines, or *plines*, are discussed in Chapter 9), turn off all the layers except the layer with the pline, and then window the area you want to hatch. Although this is tedious, it almost always works.

✦ SOLID

Produces a solid-filled area that is bounded by straight line segments.

Command Finder

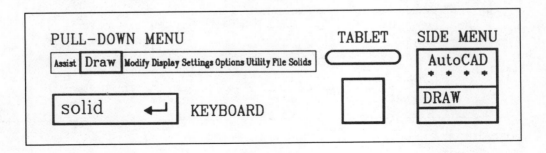

✦ Using the Solid Command

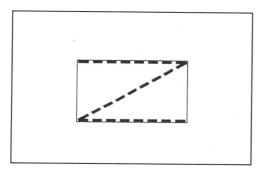 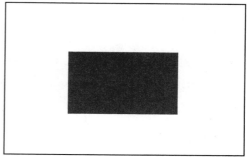

The area to be filled is specified by picking points in the shape of the letter Z. AutoCAD fills the areas in triangular sections.

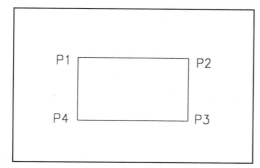 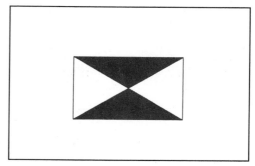

If you get a "bow tie," you incorrectly selected the points by picking them around the perimeter.

✦ Solid Notes

For a drawing to be solid, the auxiliary command Fill must be turned on; however, drawings with Fill on take longer to display after regeneration, so it is a good practice to keep Fill off while you are drawing.

To erase a solid area, use Undo immediately after you have created it; otherwise, use Erase with a crossing window (the solid will become lined), and then use R to remove any lines that you do not want erased. Redraw will bring back the border lines.

AutoCAD prompts "Third point, Fourth point" to allow you to continue to fill in more complex areas. If you get unexpected results this way, start the command again and work on the sections separately.

To fill curved sections, use wide plines (discussed in Chapter 9).

✦ FILL

Fills in wide plines, donuts, solids, and arrows.

Command Finder

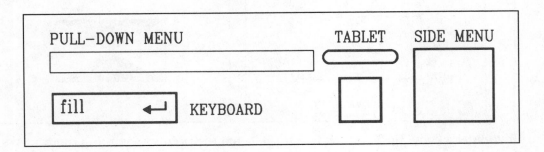

✦ Fill Options

- On
- Off

✦ Using the Fill Command

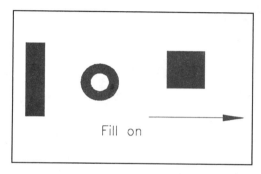

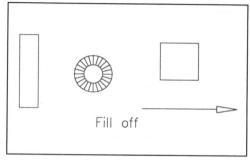

If you turn Fill on, objects will appear solid. If you turn Fill off, only the outline of the entity will be drawn.

Changes in Fill options are only visible after you regenerate your drawing. Fill can be either on or off, but it will affect all the items in a drawing.

✦ Fill Notes

Drawings with Fill turned on take longer to regenerate, so Fill is generally left off until plotting. Objects with Fill turned on appear solid only in plan views.

The Solid command on the side menu provides access to the Fill command. It is a convenient way to use Fill while working with the Solid command; otherwise, it is simpler to just type in *Fill*.

◆ TUTORIAL: USING HATCH AND SOLID IN THE NORTH ARROW

In this lesson you will use a hatch pattern and a solid fill to finish the north arrow that you worked on in Chapter 6.

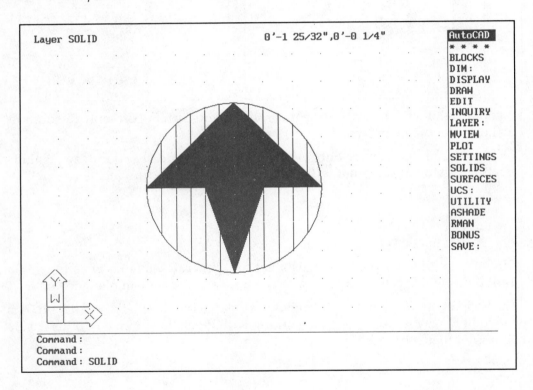

◆1   Select the existing drawing called NORTH for editing.

◆2   Using the Hatch command, select the User Defined option. The default option will hatch only the area outside of the arrow.

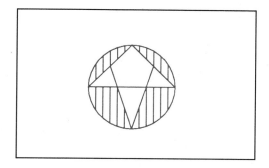

Command: **HATCH**
Pattern (? or name/U,style): **U**
Angle for crosshatch lines <0>: **90**
Spacing between lines <1.0000>: **1/16**
Double hatch area? <N>: ⏎
Select objects: **W** (Window the whole object)
First corner: Other corner: 7 found
Select objects: ⏎

◆**3**   Fill the arrow using the Solid command, utilizing Osnaps to pick
the exact points. Remember that the QUAdrant Osnap was activated in the previous drawing session. Set Fill to On if it is not already turned on.

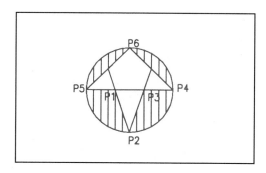

Command: **SOLID**
First point: INT of   *Pick point 1*
Second point: INT of   *Pick point 2*
Third point: INT of   *Pick point 3*
Fourth point: ⏎

✦**4**   Use the Solid command again and fill in the other section of the arrow.

Command: **SOLID**
First point: *Pick point 4*
Second point: *Pick point 5*
Third point: *Pick point 6*
Fourth point: ⏎

✦**5**   End the drawing. You now have a symbol that can be rotated to indicate the north direction in a plan.

Command: **END**

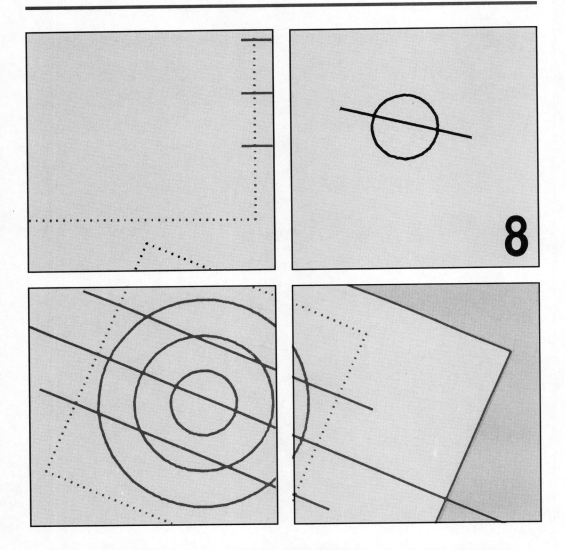

8

ERASING AND MOVING OBJECTS

Probably as soon as you have drawn some objects, you will want to move, erase, or copy some of them. In this chapter you will learn about these basic editing commands, plus some more. Some of the more powerful editing commands are covered in Chapter 11.

- Erase
- Oops
- Break
- Trim
- Move
- Copy
- Offset
- Mirror
- Rotate

◆ ERASE

Erases whatever object or group of objects is selected, such as lines, circles, and polylines. It will not erase parts of these entities. To erase parts of entities, use the Break command. The effectiveness of this command is enhanced by using the selection sets in specifying what objects are to be erased.

Command Finder

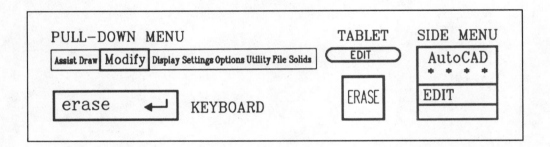

◆ Using the Erase Command

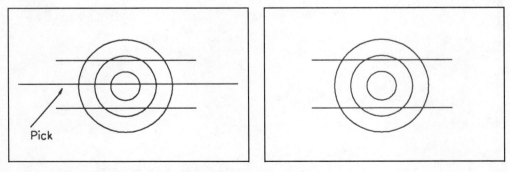

Objects can be erased simply by picking them.

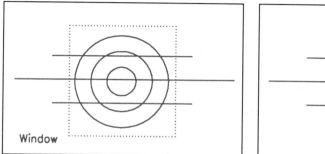

Specific groups of objects can be erased by selecting them with the Window option. Only objects completely within the window area are erased.

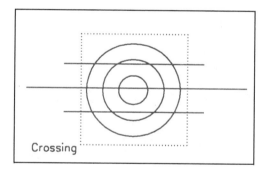

You can also select objects by using the Crossing option. All objects inside of this box and any object crossed by the box are erased.

◆ Erase Notes

The Oops command (see the next section) brings back all objects erased with the last command until you either plot or exit the drawing. The U or Undo command undoes the last command and can step backward to the beginning of your drawing (or to your last Mark command).

Sometimes when erasing, the remaining lines will look as though they were broken or partly erased—this is normal. Use the Redraw command to restore the complete appearance of these lines.

Erase, when selected from the pull-down menu, will stay active in the Auto mode until you cancel the command or select another.

◆ OOPS

Restores the entity or entities that were erased with the last use of the Erase command.

Command Finder

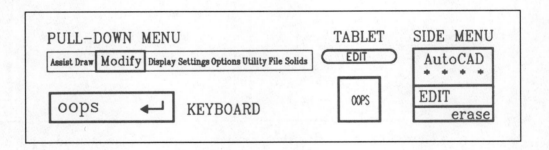

◆ Using the Oops Command

Oops is useful in restoring drawings that disappear when you are making blocks (discussed in Chapter 10). It brings back the original drawing should you wish to make additional blocks from that image. If you use Undo in this situation, it brings back the image but undoes the block just made.

✦ BREAK

You can use the Break command to erase part of a line, a pline, a circle, or an arc. You can also use it to cut these objects without erasing any part of them.

Command Finder

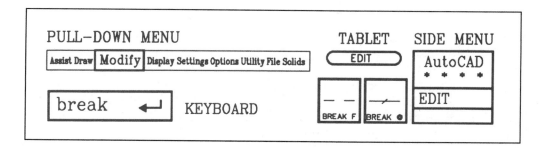

✦ Break Options

- 2-point break
- F break
- @ (at) break

◆ Using the Break Command

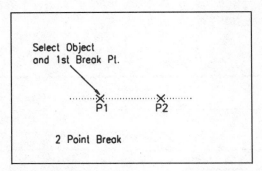
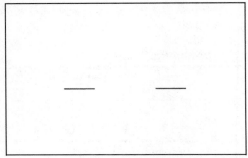

In the 2-point break (the default), the point you use to select the object becomes the first point of the break; you then select the endpoint of the break. This option requires you to pick only two points: The first point indicates the beginning of the break and the second point the end of the break. The section between is erased after you press button 2.

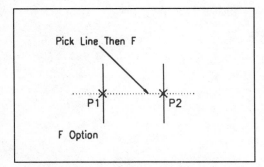
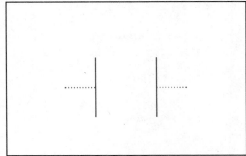

The F break allows you to indicate the object to be broken before you give the first and second points. You use this option when the points where you want to break are too close to other lines. First, pick the object that you want to break, then enter **F** to indicate that you are initiating the break sequence and pick the two points for the break.

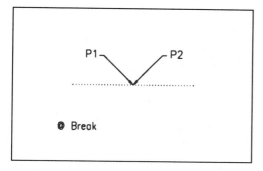

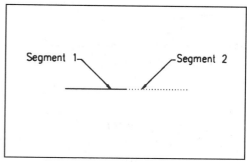

The @ break cuts the line without erasing it, because the first and second points are the same.

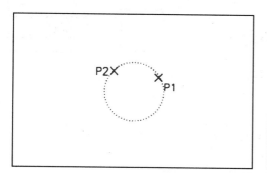

To break a circle, you select the break points in the counterclockwise direction.

✦ Break Notes

The @ sign is a shorthand message to AutoCAD to use the last specified location. In the pixel break, AutoCAD uses the first point you specified as the second point, and in effect, makes the break at the same place. The @ sign is also used when specifying a relative distance from another point.

If you use the tablet menu, you can choose the F option or the @ option. If you choose the F option, you don't have to enter the F. If you choose the @ option, the @ point is automatically entered as soon as you pick the first point.

✦ TRIM

Erases those parts of objects that intersect the cutting plane on the side of the cutting line you specify.

Command Finder

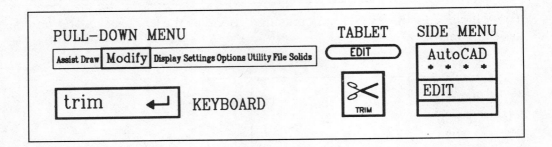

✦ Using the Trim Command

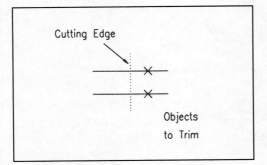

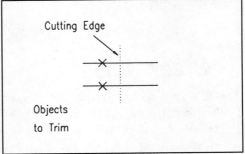

You are asked to select a cutting edge; after you press ⏎, you are prompted to select objects to trim. You can select objects on either side of the cutting edge.

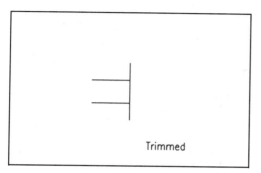

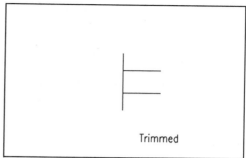

The point you specify determines what sections are erased.

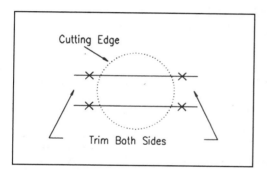

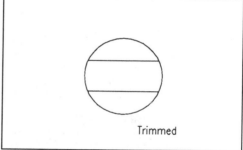

A cutting edge can be something other than a straight line; circles, arcs, and even polygons work fine.

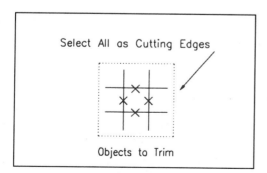

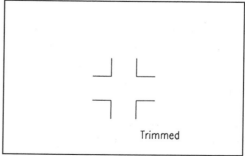

You can have more than one cutting edge. An object that you select as a cutting edge can itself be an object to be trimmed.

✦ **Tip**

A common error is to forget to press ⏎ after selecting the cutting edge. After you make your selection, you must press ⏎ or button two on your mouse or puck to complete the selection before you select the objects to be trimmed. Also, you cannot use a block as a cutting edge or an object to be trimmed.

✦ MOVE

Moves objects from one location on the drawing to another. You can indicate the distance on the screen by moving your cursor or by typing in the x and y displacements.

Command Finder

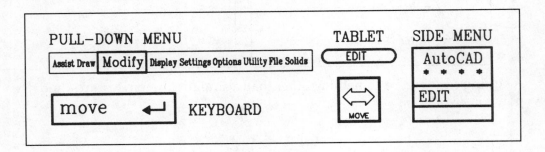

✦ Using the Move Command

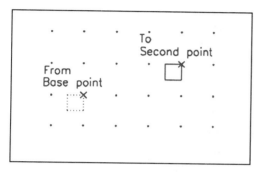
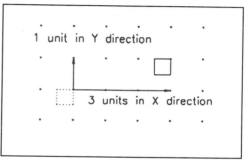

After you select the objects to be moved and they are highlighted, AutoCAD prompts with *Base point or displacement:*. The base point is the point *from* which you want to move the object and can be visualized as the handle on the object you want to move. After you have indicated the point, the next prompt is *Second point of displacement:*. This is the point *to* which you want to move the object. You can simply think of this as the From/To method. The second method (see the second drawing) involves typing the displacement vector. When prompted for *Base point or displacement:*, type in the distance you want to move the object in the x and y directions. When prompted for *Second point of displacement:*, simply press ⏎ or button 2 on your mouse or puck.

✦ Move Notes

- When groups of objects are moved, they keep the same relationship to one another that they had before being moved.
- You can move objects in 3-D space by indicating a z value for elevation.

✦   **Tip**

If you move something and it disappears, type **U** for Undo and try again. What you probably did was incorrectly enter the point where you wanted the object moved as the *from* point. If you want to find the object, you can use Zoom, All; it should be there in outer space.

✦ COPY

Structured very much like the Move command, except that it gives you the option of making more than one copy of an object.

Command Finder

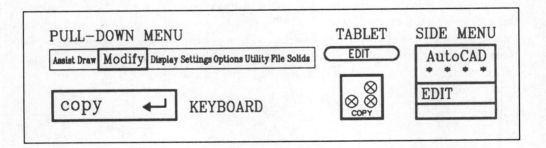

✦ Copy Options

- Multiple

✦ Using the Copy Command

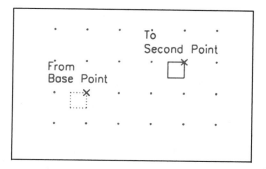
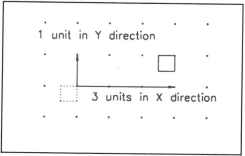

The procedure for copying single objects is the same as for moving them. The From/To method makes a copy from one place to another. The base point is the point on the object you are copying, and the second point is the point where you want the copied object to appear. The other method for copying objects is to type in the displacement vector (see the second drawing), as you do in the Move command. To the first prompt for *Base point or displacement:*, type in the x,y vector value, remembering to use the minus sign if the values go in a negative direction. Respond to the prompt *Second point of displacement:* by pressing ⏎ or button two on your mouse or puck.

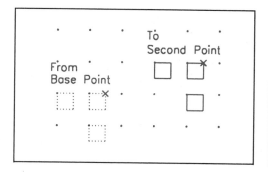
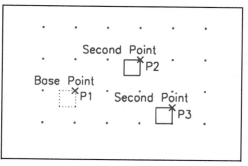

When groups of objects are copied, they keep the same relationship to one another that they had before being moved.

When you select the Multiple option, pick the first point on the object and continue picking multiple second-point locations on the screen.

✦ Copy Notes

- The response to the *Select object:* prompt can be Previous, in which case the original object is copied, or Last, in which case the last object placed is copied.
- As in the Move command, U undoes the last operation.
- Specifying x, y, and z coordinates copies an object in 3-D space.

✦ OFFSET

Copies lines and arcs parallel to the existing entity. Closed polylines, arcs, and circles are offset in a "nesting fashion." The distance to be offset can be indicated by screen pointing or by specifying a distance and direction.

Command Finder

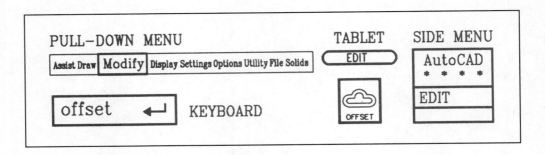

✦ Offset Options

- Through
- Offset distance

✦ Using the Offset Command

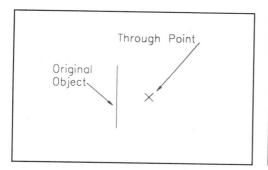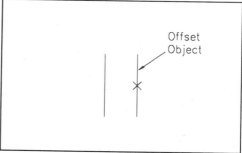

The Through option (the default) asks you to select an object and a point through which you want the duplicated object to pass. The point selected must be parallel to the existing object. The prompt repeats, so you can continue selecting objects and various points to copy through. You can terminate the command by pressing ⏎ or button 2 on your mouse or puck or by selecting *done* on the side menu.

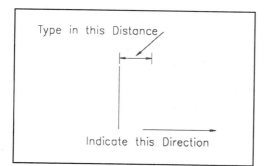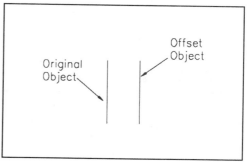

The Distance option asks you to select the offset distance, the object, and the side to be offset. When asked for the side to offset, you indicate the direction; the actual distance has already been specified. This distance remains in effect until you reenter the command and specify another distance or the Through option.

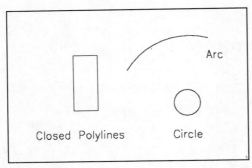 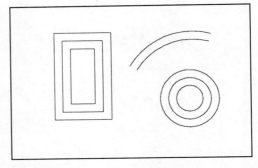

Closed polylines, polygons, circles, and arcs are offset in a "nesting fashion."

✦ Offset Notes

- Choosing the Distance option is the easiest method for making double lines for walls, because once the wall thickness is specified, you only have to indicate which side to offset the original single lines.
- You must explicitly select the object to be offset; you cannot use *P* for Previous or *L* for Last.
- Using Offset is the only way you can make concentric circles and arcs.

✦ Mirror

Makes a mirror image of an object. The location of the new image is controlled by the mirror line.

Command Finder

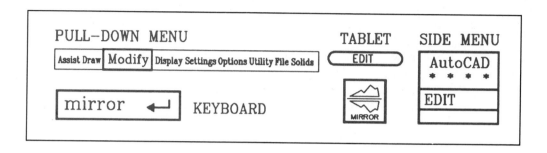

◆ Mirror Options

- Delete old objects (N)
- Delete old objects (Y)

◆ Using the Mirror Command

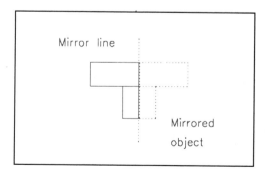

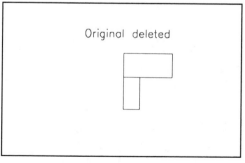

To specify a mirror line, select two points to indicate the reflection plane. If you want your mirror line to be perfectly orthogonal, press F8 to toggle the Ortho mode on. If you press Y after the prompt *Delete old objects*, the original object will be erased, leaving only the mirrored one. The default option leaves the old object.

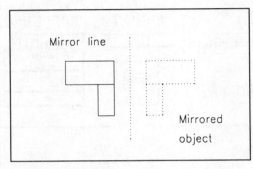
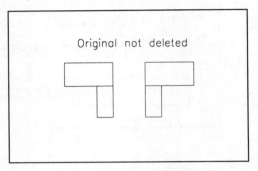

It may help to think of the mirror line as a reflecting mirror. Aside from reflecting the actual object, it also reflects the space between that object and the mirror.

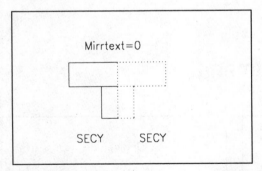
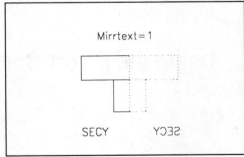

Text will be mirrored unless you set the variable Mirrtext to 0 (Mirrtext is covered in Chapter 14).

✦ Mirror Notes

- Text inside of blocks and dimensions is always mirrored, along with the object mirrored.

- Mirrored blocks cannot be exploded. (Exploded blocks revert to the original drawing and are no longer "glued together" as a single entity.)

✦ ROTATE

Rotates an object to a new orientation about a selected base point.

Command Finder

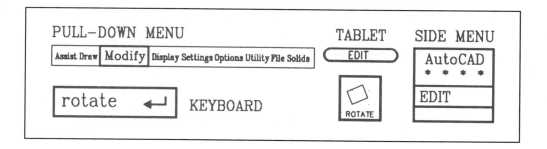

✦ Rotate Options
- Rotation Angle
- Reference

✦ Using the Rotate Command

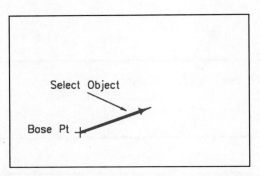

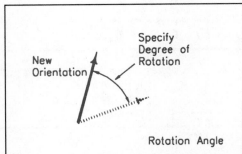

With the Rotation Angle option (the default), after you have selected the object to be rotated and have specified the base point, enter the number of degrees you want to rotate the object; remember that + is counterclockwise and – is clockwise. You can also use your cursor to drag the object into position.

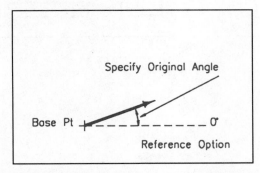

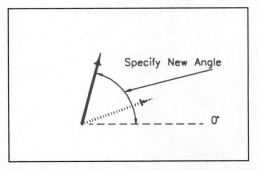

The Reference option allows you to type in the original angle (the angle you are moving *from*) and then the new angle (the angle you are moving *to*). You must first indicate the base point.

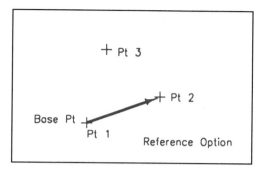
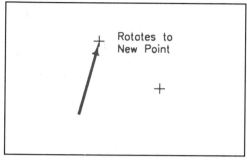

You can also indicate the rotation on the screen with the Reference option. After picking the base point and selecting Reference, pick two points on the object you want to rotate, in response to the *Reference angle* prompt. Respond to the *New angle* prompt by picking a point through which the rotation will pass.

✦ Rotate Notes

- When you drag an object into position, you can get a readout of the angle if you have your coordinates toggled on (press F6). Dragging is particularly useful if you don't know the angle of the original object.
- To find the angle of an object, use the List command. It gives you all the vital statistics on an object.

◆
TUTORIAL: DRAWING
WALLS AND MAKING A CLOSET

In this lesson you will add walls and a closet to your plan outline. You will use all the editing commands you have learned in this chapter, plus a few that are covered later in the book: a variable called Pickbox that controls the size of the box used to pick items; Fillet, which you will use to join corners at right angles; and Explode, which is used to unjoin plines.

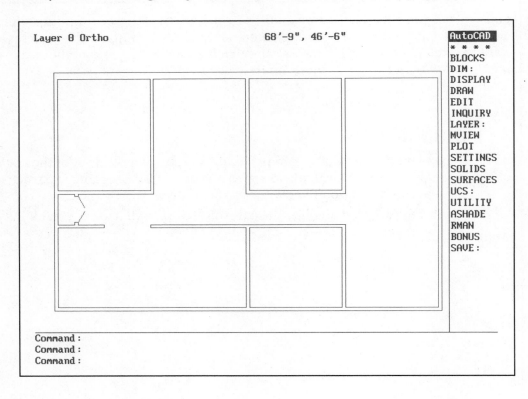

```
Layer 0 Ortho                          68'-9", 46'-6"              AutoCAD
                                                                  * * * *
                                                                  BLOCKS
                                                                  DIM:
                                                                  DISPLAY
                                                                  DRAW
                                                                  EDIT
                                                                  INQUIRY
                                                                  LAYER:
                                                                  MVIEW
                                                                  PLOT
                                                                  SETTINGS
                                                                  SOLIDS
                                                                  SURFACES
                                                                  UCS:
                                                                  UTILITY
                                                                  ASHADE
                                                                  RMAN
                                                                  BONUS
                                                                  SAVE:


Command:
Command:
Command:
```

◆**1**   Continue working on the PLAN drawing. To make the interior
         walls, you will use parts of the building perimeter that you have
         already drawn. To do this, you will have to first explode the pline
         into individual line segments. Turn Snap on so that you can pick
         the line.

Command: **EXPLODE**
Select block reference, polyline, dimension, or mesh: *Pick both rectangles*

◆**2**   Use the Copy command to make the walls that define the interior
         walls, which extend from the top to the bottom of the plan.

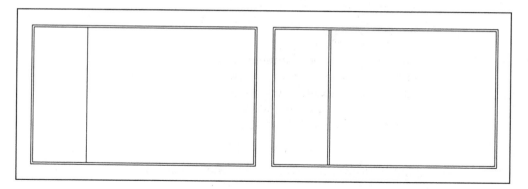

Command: **COPY**
Select objects: *Select the left interior wall line*
<Base point or displacement>/Multiple: **13'6,0**
Second point of displacement: ↵

Command: **COPY**
Select objects: **L** (Specifies last object selected)
<Base point or displacement>/Multiple: **6,0**
Second point of displacement: ↵

✦**3**　Select both lines and copy them 14 feet and 28 feet to the left.

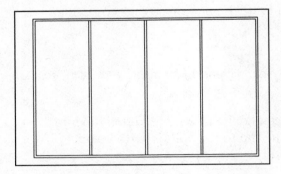

Command: **COPY**
Select objects: *Pick both lines*
<Base point or displacement>/Multiple: **M**
Base point: **0,0** (Another way of specifying displacement)
Second point of displacement: **14',0**
Second point of displacement: **28',0**
Second point of displacement: ⏎

✦**4**　Copy the bottom inner-wall line to make the corridor walls. Use
the same technique as you did for the previous walls.

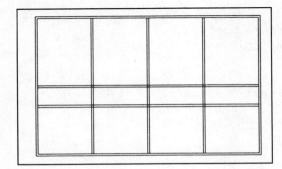

Command: **COPY**
Select objects: *Pick the interior bottom line*
<Base point or displacement>/Multiple: **0,12'**
Second point of displacement: ⏎

✦ **5** To make a wall that is 6 inches thick, copy this line 6 inches upward.

Command: **COPY**
Select objects: **L**
<Base point or displacement>/Multiple: **0,6**
Second point of displacement: ⏎

✦ **6** To make the other corridor wall, copy both lines upward 5 feet.

Command: **COPY**
Select objects: *Pick both lines*
<Base point or displacement>/Multiple: **0,5'**
Second point of displacement: ⏎

✦ **7** Use the Trim command to take out the lines in the corridor and to remove some of the walls as shown. If you have accidentally trimmed a line that you didn't want to trim, use the U option to bring it back. (If your pickbox is too small, type **PICKBOX** and follow the prompts to make it larger.)

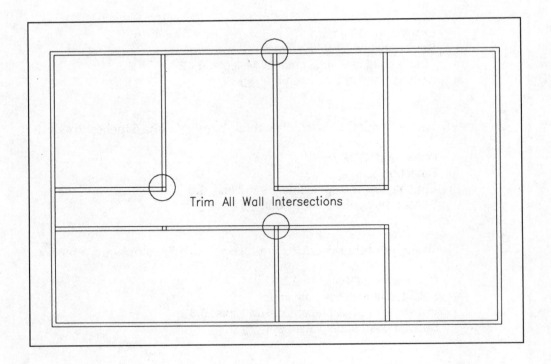

Trim All Wall Intersections

Command: **TRIM**
Select cutting edge(s)…   *Window the entire drawing*
Select objects: ⏎
<Select object to trim>Undo: *Pick the lines to be trimmed*

✦**8**   Continue to use Trim to clean up all the wall intersections. Zoom in or use the View command to enlarge the view so that it is easier to make your picks.

✦**9**   To take out part of the wall to make an entrance to the corridor,
use the Break command.

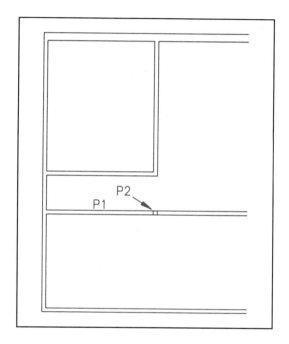

Command: **BREAK**
Select object: *Pick line P1*
Enter second point (or F for first point): **F**
Enter first point: INT of   *Pick P2*
Enter second point: **@–7′,0**

✦**10**   Repeat to break the other wall line.

✦**11**   Draw a line to finish off the end of the wall. Erase the remaining nib (the line left over from the wall intersection).

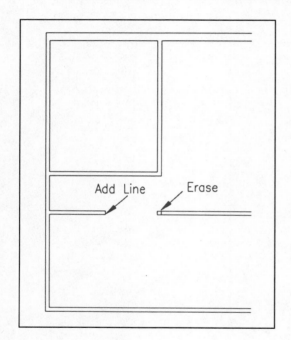

Add Line   Erase

✦**12**   To make a 12-inch-wide window wall, move the upper wall 6 inches up.

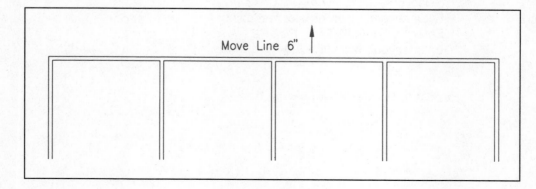

Move Line 6"

Command: **MOVE**
Select objects: *Pick upper line*
Base point or displacement: **0,6**
Second point of displacement: ⏎

✦ **13**   Use Fillet with a radius of 0 to connect the open edges of the wall
corners. Repeat for the other side.

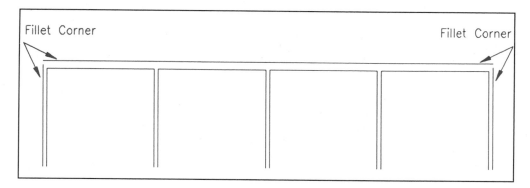

Command: **FILLET**
Polyline/Radius/<Select two objects>: **R**
Enter fillet radius <0'-0">: ⏎

Command: **FILLET**
Polyline/Radius/<Select first object>: *Pick one corner line*

Command: **FILLET**
Polyline/Radius/<Select second object>: *Pick the other corner line*

✦**14**   To make a closet at the left end of the corridor, copy the inside
wall line out into the corridor.

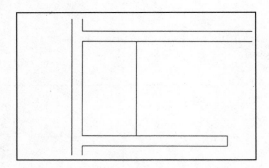

Command: **COPY**
Select objects: 1 selected
<Base point or displacement>/Multiple: **30,0**
Second point of displacement: ⏎

✦**15**   Copy this line 6 inches to the left to form the outer wall of the
closet.

Command: **COPY**
Select objects: **L**
<Base point or displacement>/Multiple: **6,0**
Second point of displacement: ⏎

✦**16**   Zoom in and trim the wall intersections.

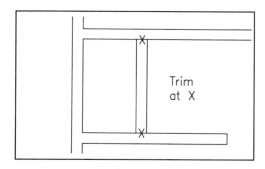

Command: **TRIM**
Select cutting edge(s)…   *Select the two walls you just made*
Select objects: ⏎
<Select object to trim:>/Undo: *Pick the wall intersections*

✦**17**   You will use relative coordinates to draw the jamb 4 inches from
the corner, but first you have to use the ID command to make the
corner the last point. The numerical values are irrelevant.

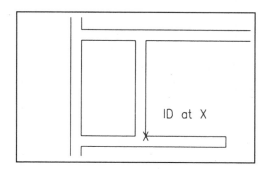

Command: **ID**
Point: INT of   *Select point X*   X=15′-0"   Y=30"-0"   Z=0′-0"

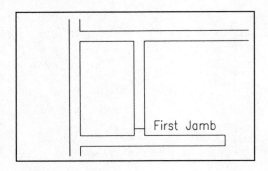

First Jamb

Command: **LINE**
From point: **@4<90**
To point: PER to   *Pick inside wall of closet*
To point: ⏎

✦**18**   Mirror the line to the other side using the midpoint of the wall line
in the back of the closet.

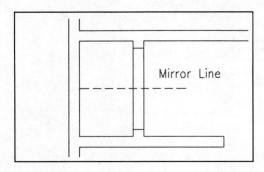

Mirror Line

Command: **MIRROR**
Select objects: 1 selected, 1 found
First point of mirror line: MID of   *Pick wall line in back of closet*
Second point: ⏎
Delete old objects? <N> ⏎

◆ **19**   Trim the double lines back to the jambs.

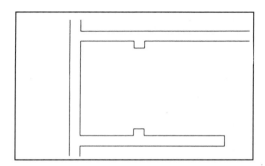

Command: **TRIM**
Select cutting edge(s)…   *Pick both jambs*
<Select object to trim:>/Undo: *Pick the lines between the jambs*

◆ **20**   Draw the first of the double doors by using filters.

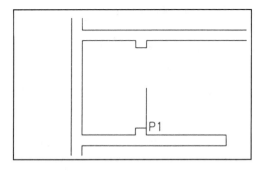

Command: **LINE**
From point: END of   *Pick P1*
To point: .x of @ (Specifies the x filter point)
(need YZ): MID of   *Pick back wall of closet as y filter point*
To point: ⏎

✦ **21**   Rotate the door 30 degrees and mirror it.

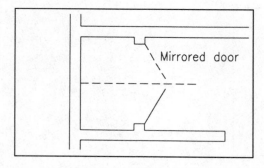

Command: **ROTATE**
Select objects: **L**
Base point: END of
<Rotation angle>/Reference: **–30**

Command: **MIRROR**
Select objects: *Pick door*
First point of mirror line: MID of   *Pick back wall of closet*
Second point: (see drawing)
Delete old objects? <N>: ⏎

Your drawing should look like the one at the beginning of the tutorial. End the drawing. You will continue in the following chapters to add the window wall and doors.

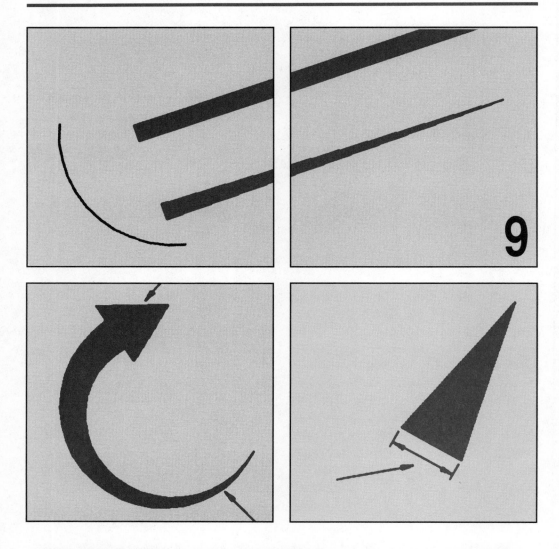

9

DRAWING AND EDITING POLYLINES

Polylines, or *plines,* are, as the term suggests, lines endowed with many properties. Editing plines is done with special commands used specifically for them. In this book we will deal with the simpler modifications to plines.

+ Pline

+ Pedit

✦ PLINE

A pline can be a line segment, an arc, or a combination of both. It can have uniform or varying width. When one is drawn as connected segments, it acts as a single object.

Command Finder

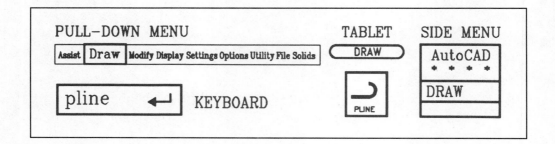

✦ Pline Options

- Width
- Halfwidth
- Arc
- Length
- Undo
- Close

✦ Using the Pline Command

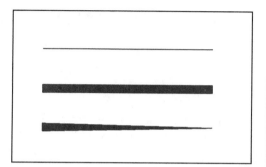
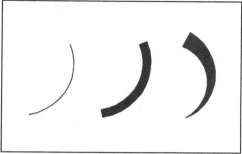

A line or arc drawn with the Pline command can have 0 width (in which case it looks like a regular line or arc), uniform width, or different beginning and ending widths.

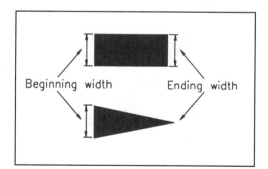
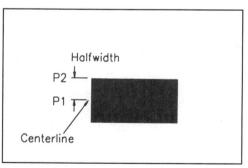

Pline width is specified by a beginning width and an ending width. Tapers are produced by specifying different beginning and ending widths. The Halfwidth option is useful when you are specifying a width using the screen cursor instead of typing in the value. For a pline having width, the cursor is attached to the pline's centerline. With the Halfwidth option, width is indicated by a rubber-banding line from the centerline of the pline to a point indicating its edge.

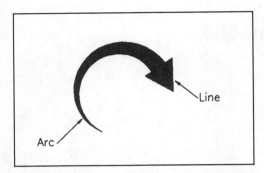

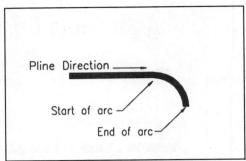

Pline arcs and lines can be combined; the widths of each can be varied to produce complex shapes. The default option for the pline arcs is S,E,D (start point, endpoint, and direction). Don't be surprised by the direction in which the arc is drawn—AutoCAD determines it from the last line or arc drawn. This option works best when you continue an arc from either a line or another arc.

As in the standard Arc command, there are many other options available for drawing pline arcs. See the discussion of the Arc command in Chapter 5 for other options.

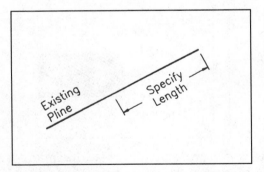

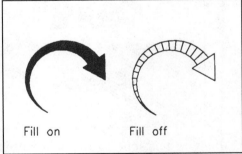

The Length option (L) draws a line segment of a specified length that continues in the same direction as the previous segment. (Do not confuse this with entering *L* for *Line* in the arc portion of the Line command; this changes you from arc drawing to line drawing.) When Fill is on, wide plines are drawn solid. When Fill is off, the individual segments are shown. Any change to Fill requires a regen before the change can appear on the screen.

Using Undo inside the Pline command is the same as using Undo in the Line command—it steps you back and erases one segment at a time. The Close option also works the same in the Pline command as it does in the Line command—it closes a polygon by drawing a pline from the last point to the starting point.

✦ Pline Notes

- As with the Line command, with Pline you must first specify the starting point before any other specification is accepted.
- Plines are very useful in area calculations since both the perimeter and enclosed area can be accessed through the List and Area commands. Plines are often used in mapping applications to draw contour lines and roads.
- The Break command works on plines as it does on other entities.
- To change regular lines and arcs into plines or to modify the widths of plines, use the Pedit command (see "Pedit" in this chapter).
- Plines can be disassembled into their component lines and arcs with the Explode command. When exploded, plines revert to 0 width.
- With a closed pline, the Fillet command works on all the vertices at one time.

✦ PEDIT

Has over 30 options and is used to edit 2-D plines, 3-D plines, and meshes. This book covers only the options that perform editing functions on the whole 2-D pline and does not deal with vertex editing. (Vertex editing involves modifying individual segments of polylines and is beyond the scope of this book.)

Command Finder

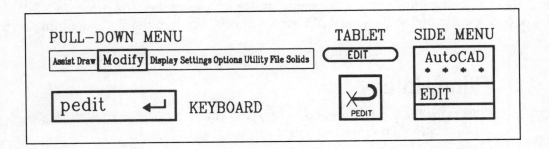

✦ Pedit Options

- Close
- Join
- Width
- Fit curve
- Spline curve
- Decurve
- Undo
- eXit

◆ Using the Pedit Command

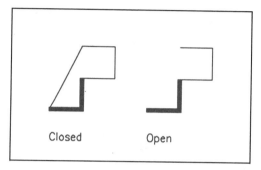

Closed   Open

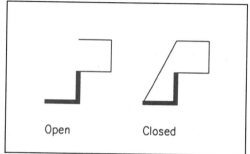

Open   Closed

Plines behave differently depending upon whether they are open or closed. Plines that have been used to make an enclosed form and whose last segment has been drawn with the Close (C) option are considered closed plines, and as such, act as single objects or entities. When you choose the Pedit command and select the pline to edit, AutoCAD already knows whether the pline selected is open or closed. If the pline is closed, you are offered the Open option; if it is open, you are offered the Close option.

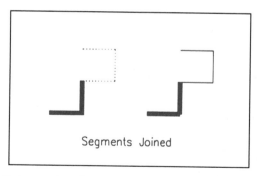

Segments Joined

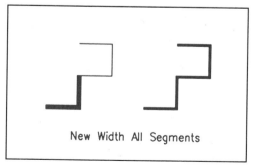

New Width All Segments

The Join option lets you join other plines to an existing one. If the lines you select are not plines, you are given the option of turning them into plines. For plines to be joined, they must meet at the *exact* same point. With the Width option, you can select a new width for the entire pline. This new width will affect *all* the segments of the pline.

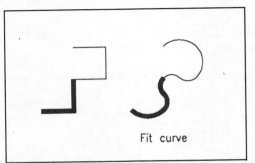

Fit curve

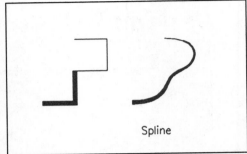

Spline

The Fit curve option replaces the straight lines between the vertices with arcs and results in a strongly curved line. The Spline curve option gives a smoother curve by "pulling" the line toward the vertices instead of requiring the line to pass through them.

- The Decurve option undoes the effect of both of the curve options and makes the lines straight again.
- The Undo option allows you to undo the last Pedit operation while remaining in the Pedit command.
- The Exit option exits you from the Pedit command.

✦   **Note**

Vertex editing is not covered in this book, because beginning users will find it easier to make new sections of plines than to edit them. For a more extensive exploration of editing plines, you can refer to *Mastering AutoCAD Release 11*, George Omura, SYBEX, 1991.

✦ TUTORIAL: DRAWING A DOOR AND WINDOW UNIT

In this lesson, you will use plines to make drawings of a door and a window unit to use in your PLAN drawing. In the next chapter, you will turn these drawings into blocks. Blocks are drawings that have been "glued" together to make a cohesive symbol, which is both easier to use and cuts down on the size of your drawing database.

You will be doing two different kinds of drawings that you will make into blocks: The first is a door designed to be a unit or 1-inch symbol; the second is a window unit designed to be used as a full-size block.

Because of your growing familiarity with AutoCAD, commands that have already been covered appear in a condensed form. New commands and commands that may be confusing appear in full. (This lesson uses Chprop, which is covered in Chapter 11; it is used to change the properties of an entity.) Use your own judgment about when to zoom, and remember to use Osnaps to help you place points.

*Doors have varying sizes and instead of making a drawing for each door size, you will make a unit door of 1 inch. When you use the block in a drawing, you will obtain the actual height and width by specifying multiples of 1 inch, such as **30 inches wide** and **96 inches high**.*

✦ **1** Start a new drawing called DOORWIN, with the following settings:

> Units: **4** (Architectural)
> Denominator: **32**
> Limits: (Accept default: **0,0** and **1',9"**)
> Snap: **1"** and set to On
> Grid: **0** and set to On
> Ortho: On
> Coordinates F6: On
> Blips: Off
> Ucsicon: Off

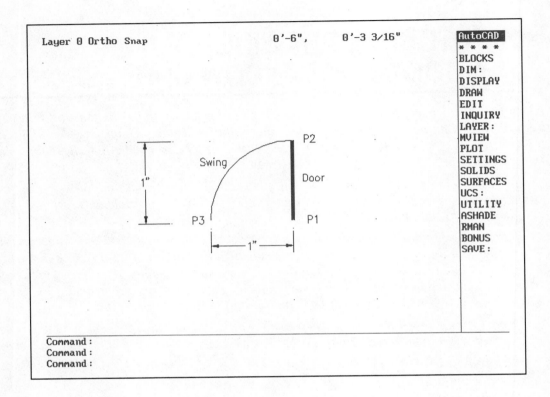

✦ **2**   Use Pline to draw a door that will have some thickness.

> Command: **PLINE**
> From point: *Start on a grid point*
> Current line-width is 0'-0"
> Arc/Close/Halfwidth/Length/Undo/Width/<Endpoint of line>: **W**
> Starting width <0'-0">: **1/32**
> Ending width <0'-0 1/32">: ⏎
> Arc/Close/Halfwidth/Length/Undo/Width/<Endpoint of line>: **Pt 1**
> Arc/Close/Halfwidth/Length/Undo/Width/<Endpoint of line>: **Pt 2**

✦ **3**   Draw an S,C,A (start, center, angle) arc for the door swing.

```
Command: ARC
Center/<Start point>: Pt 3
Center/End/<Second point>: C Center: Pt 1
Angle/Length of chord/<End point>: A
Included angle: -90
```

✦ **4**   The height of the door must be 1 inch so that you can multiply it later to get the actual door height. To do this, use the Chprop command to change its height. AutoCAD considers height to be thickness (a holdover from its beginnings as a mechanical design program). This command is not available in the pull-down menus.

```
Command: CHPROP
Select objects: Pick the door
Select objects: 1 selected, 1 found
Select objects: ⏎
Change what property (Color/LAyer/LType/Thickness)?  T
New thickness <0'-0">: 1
Change what property (Color/LAyer/LType/Thickness)?  ⏎
```

You have finished the door drawing. Use the same drawing to make the window unit for the building. Since this drawing will be at full size, you will have to increase the limits of the drawing.

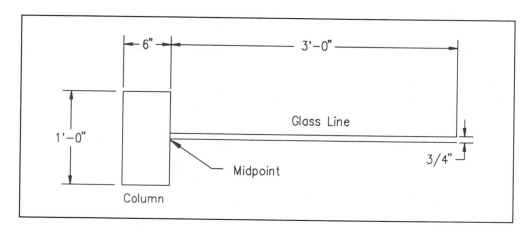

♦ **5**   Establish the following settings:

       Limits: **0,0** and **5′,3′**
       Snap: **6"**

♦ **6**   Use Zoom, All to reset the limits of the screen.

♦ **7**   Start the drawing for the window unit, following the dimensions in the illustration. Use Pline to draw the column, but first change the pline width from 1/32 back to 0.

       Command: **PLINE**
       From point: *Start the column*
       Current line-width is 0′-0 1/32"
       Arc/Close/Halfwidth/Length/Undo/Width/<Endpoint of line>: **W**

   Change the width:

       Starting width <0′-0 1/32">: **0**
       Ending width <0′-0">: ⏎
       Arc/Close/Halfwidth/Length/Undo/Width/<Endpoint of line>: *Continue drawing the three other points of the column and finish with C*

♦ **8**   Use the Line command to draw the glass line from the midpoint of the side of the column. Use Osnap to get the midpoint.

♦ **9**   Offset the glass line 3/4" upward.

♦ **10**   You want these two glass lines to appear at the top of the window frame, as they are shown in the 3-D drawing of the office at the end of Chapter 1. To get this effect, you must copy both lines upward 8′ in the z direction.

> Command: **COPY**
> Select objects: *Select both lines*
> \<Base point or displacement>/Multiple: **0,0,8'**
> Second point of displacement: ⏎

◆ **11**   To give the column height, you have to change its property of thickness, just as you did for the door.

> Command: **CHPROP**
> Select objects: *Select the column*
> Change what property (Color/LAyer/LType/Thickness)?   **T**
> New thickness \<0'-0">: **8'**

End this drawing and continue to the next chapter to find out how to make blocks out of the door and window drawings.

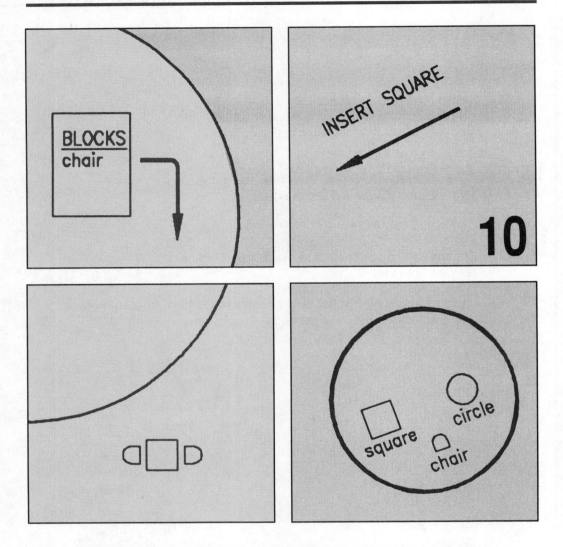

MAKING AND USING BLOCKS

The commands described in this chapter are used to create what you have been accustomed to thinking of as symbols—items you made by using templates. If you are going to use an object more than three or four times in your drawing, it is a good practice to make a block out of it, because blocks take up much less space in your drawing file. A particularly useful trait of blocks is their ability to be updated; all occurrences of a block in a drawing can be replaced (updated) by another one.

The commands in this chapter are more complicated than the simple drawing and editing commands because they are processes that affect the entire drawing. This chapter covers both the simple uses of the commands and the techniques for using and updating blocks in drawings.

- Block

- Wblock

- Insert

- Xref

- Xbind

- Explode

- Base

✦ BLOCK

"Cements" together diverse entities into a single symbol after you have responded to three prompts. At that point the drawing disappears. If you want to reuse the original drawing, you can bring it back with the Oops command. This command makes blocks that can only be used inside of the current drawing. You must use the Wblock command to make a block that can be used in other drawings.

Command Finder

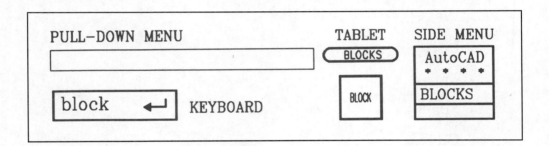

✦ Block Options

- Block name (or ?)
- Insertion base point
- Select object

Here is a summary of the Block options:

Block Name   Type in the name you want to give the symbol. Although you can make it as long as 31 characters, it is a good idea to keep it short. Typing ? lists all the blocks already in your drawing when you respond to the asterisk default by pressing ⏎. Remember that the asterisk stands for everything.

Insertion Base Point   The point on the block that is attached to your cursor when you insert the block back into your drawing.

Select Object When you select the object, make sure you get the entire object.

✦ Using the Block Command

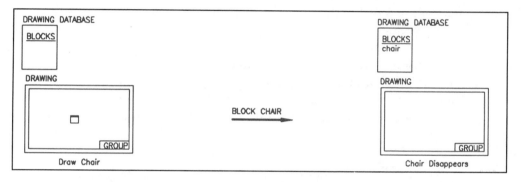

Making the chair inside the drawing called Group into a block causes the chair to disappear, as it should, and to be stored in that drawing's database as a block called *Chair*. This block can be used only in this drawing.

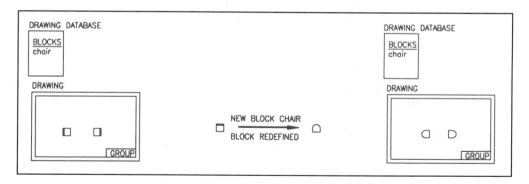

A block chair can be redefined inside a drawing by drawing another chair and blocking it with the same name, *Chair*. AutoCAD warns you that a block with that name already exists. When you specify Y to redefine it, all occurrences of that block are changed (updated) to the new block. The original drawing of the chair no longer exists, having been replaced by the new one.

✦ Block Notes

- Insertion points are standardly placed in the lower-left corner of the block, except when block usage would indicate otherwise. For example, circular objects, such as tables and trees, are easier to place if the insertion point is at the center.

- If you want to use the old chair block as a base for the new chair drawing, it must be exploded first. Make sure that the insertion base point is the same for both blocks; otherwise, the new one will be inserted with a different orientation. The old version of the chair symbol will no longer exist.

- Blocks made on layer 0 carry a special adaptive quality. They take on the color and linetype of whatever layer they are inserted into. Blocks made on other layers retain the properties of the layer on which they were made.

✦ WBLOCK

Writes the block definition onto your disk, allowing you to insert that block into any other drawing. You can Wblock an entirely new part of the drawing as a block or Wblock a block that already exists inside a drawing.

✦ Note

Although you may distinguish blocks as symbols or parts of drawings to be used in other drawings, AutoCAD sees them all as drawings and assigns to them the file extension .DWG.

Command Finder

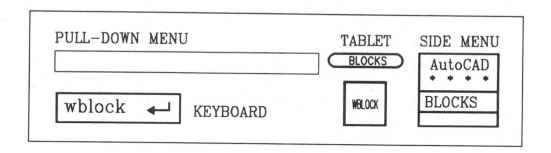

✦ **Wblock Options**

- File name
- Block name

Here is a summary of the Wblock options:

File Name Type in the name you want to give the block, either by first selecting the *Type it* box or simply by highlighting the rectangle next to the File box, typing the name in, and pressing ⏎ twice. Because it will be written to the disk, it can be no longer than 8 characters.

There is no ? option in the Wblock command; however, a dialog box appears that lists all the drawings in the current directory. If you want to look at other directories, highlight the rectangle next to the directory box and specify the path to the directory.

Block Name There are several possible responses to this prompt:

=   Indicates that the Wblock name is the same as an existing block already in the drawing. There will be no more prompts, and the block will be written to the disk.

⊖ Equivalent to a blank response; the process that follows is similar to that for making a block. You must specify the insertion point and indicate what part of the drawing is to be Wblocked. As in the Block command, the part being Wblocked will disappear. Using the Oops command will bring it back.

* A special response that causes the entire drawing to be written to the disk. There are no further prompts, and the drawing does not disappear. This is a quick way of purging unused items, such as blocks, layers, linetypes, and text styles. If you want to purge selectively, use the Purge command.

♦ Using the Wblock Command

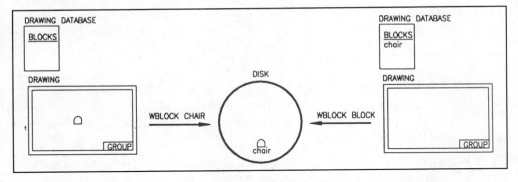

The Wblock command writes the block definition to your disk, which means that it is now available to be inserted in any other drawing. You can Wblock a block that already exists inside the drawing or Wblock an object that has not been blocked previously.

✦ **Tip**

Because drawings and blocks written to the disk are indistinguishable from one another, it is helpful to name drawings made expressly for use as blocks with some distinguishing character, such as a leading underbar. In this book, *b-* is used as a prefix for blocks, as in *b-desk*.

✦ INSERT

This is the command you use to bring blocks into drawings. You can insert blocks that are already in your current drawing or blocks that have been previously written to the disk. There are options that allow you to change the scale of the block at the time of insertion.

Command Finder

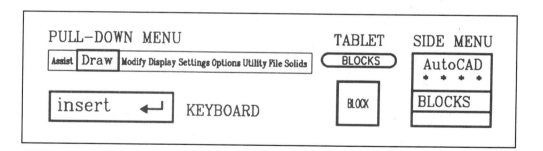

✦ Insert Options
- Block name (or ?)
- Insertion point
- X scale factor
- XYZ

- Corner
- Rotation

Here is a summary of the Insert options:

Block Name Give the name of the block you want to insert into the drawing. Typing the question mark produces a list of the blocks that are already in your drawing. The ~ (tilde) followed by ⏎ calls up a dialog box with a list of drawings (and blocks) in your current directory. The ~ response is also available in the side menu. You can select from this list either by highlighting the name or typing it in.

Insertion Point The point at which you want the block placed in your drawing.

X Scale Factor The scale in the x direction of the block as it was originally created. You will then be prompted for the Y scale factor, which defaults to the same value as the X scale factor unless you specify otherwise (the default is 1).

XYZ Select this option by typing in **XYZ** if you want to specify a Z (height) scale for the block. Prompts for specific X, Y, and Z scale factors will follow.

✦ Using the Insert Command

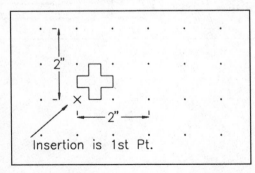

Insertion is 1st Pt.

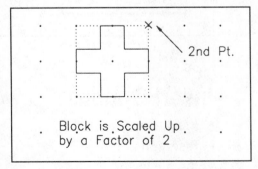

2nd Pt.

Block is Scaled Up by a Factor of 2

The Corner option (see the left-hand drawing) is a visual option for specifying both the X and Y scale factors. The insertion point is taken as the first corner, and the second corner dynamically follows your cursor location, as though you were making a window. The distance from the insertion point is both the X and Y scale factor and can be positive or negative (but not 0).

With the Rotation option (see the right-hand drawing), you can specify the degree of rotation or use your cursor to indicate the rotation on the screen. If you have the dynamic coordinate readout turned on (press `F6`), you can see the value of the angle (the default is 0).

Sometimes, you will want to insert a drawing just to bring in the blocks, or layers or settings, that are inside that drawing (the drawing *database*). In such a case, you don't want the actual drawing to appear in your current drawing. To insert only the database, respond to the *Insertion point* prompt by pressing `CTRL` `C`.

When inserting blocks into drawings, occasionally a large ghost image of the block will appear. Ignore it and continue to specify the scale for the block. (AutoCAD is dynamically scaling the block to your cursor movement—a confusing effect).

If you place a block on the wrong layer, use the Change or Chprop command to switch it to the correct layer.

✦   **Warning**

A common beginner's error is to use the Block command when you mean to use the Insert command. This can result in the original block being redefined as a blank block.

✦ Insert Notes

In Release 11, you can preset the name, scale factors, and rotation of a block by selecting Insert Options on the Options pull-down menu. You must then use the Insert command on the Draw pull-down menu for the presets to function. Typing in the Insert command or selecting it from the side menu gives you the standard (not preset) prompts.

If you precede a block name with an * (asterisk)—for example, ***chair**— the block will be inserted as its original (exploded) pieces. Do this if you want to modify the block you are inserting. This feature is not used very much now, because the Explode command is available. Explode will return a block to its original entities at any time.

✦ MORE ON USING BLOCKS

This section incorporates some additional information on using blocks in your drawings.

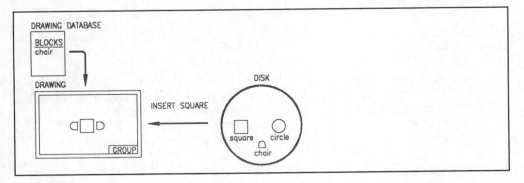

Blocks are inserted in a drawing from the current drawing database (when the block already exists there) or from the disk. The procedure that AutoCAD follows is to first look for the block inside of the current drawing, and if it cannot find it there, to look for it on the disk.

In the drawing called Group, the Insert command will insert the Chair block from within the drawing's database. The Square block, one of the blocks already on the disk, will come from the disk.

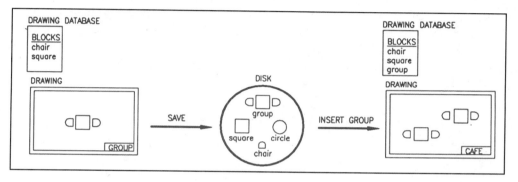

Blocks inserted from the disk can be simple blocks or *nested* blocks. Nested blocks are blocks contained within other blocks or drawings. An example of nested blocks is contained in the block drawing called Group. When Group is inserted in the drawing called Cafe, the blocks Chair and Square, which are nested inside of Group, are also brought into Cafe.

One of the advantages of using blocks is that you can automatically change all occurrences of a block in the drawing. *Redefining* is changing the block; *updating* is effecting the change in the drawing that contains the block.

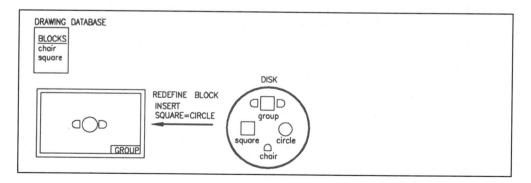

To exchange an old block with a new one without destroying the old one, you have to use blocks that are taken from the disk. Because AutoCAD first looks for

the block inside the current drawing when inserting blocks, you have to signal it to go to the disk to get the new block.

Placing an = (equal sign) after the block name when inserting it instructs AutoCAD to go directly to the disk to get the block for insertion. In the Group drawing, the square can be changed into a circle by accessing the Circle block, which had been previously stored on disk. You do this by specifying *Square= Circle* when asked for the block name in the Insert command. It is important to note that the table now resembles a circle but is still called Square in the drawing Cafe, and that the blocks/drawings Group, Circle, and Square residing on the disk have not changed their identities.

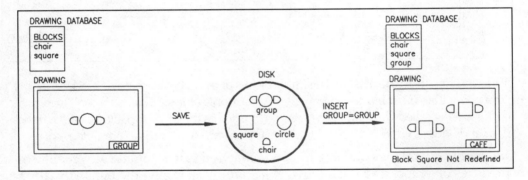

At this point, to bring the changes made in the Group drawing back into the Cafe drawing, you would normally use the Insert command with Group=Group. A problem arises, however, because the Cafe drawing already has the Square block in its database. The nested block is not redefined, because AutoCAD uses it from inside the existing Cafe drawing.

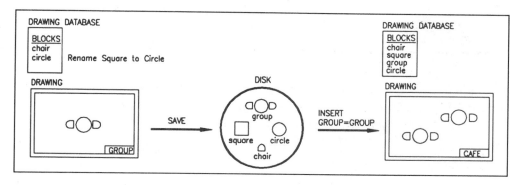

One solution to this predicament is to rename the block from *Square* to *Circle* in the Group drawing. When inserted in Cafe, AutoCAD will be unable to find a block named *Square* in the Cafe drawing and will then look on the disk and insert the Circle block from the disk.

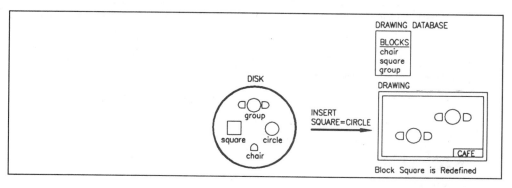

The other solution is to redefine the Square block to Circle within the Cafe drawing. This is sloppy block management, however, because blocks that look different wind up having identical names.

✦ **Tip**

In the Insert command, *Block=Block* can be abbreviated to *Block=* if the block name is the same.

✦ XREF

*In Release 11, AutoCAD has added a long-awaited function to its collection of block-type commands. Xref, which stands for **external reference,** allows you to bring a block (drawing) into another drawing on "temporary loan." Because the block is loaned temporarily, or externally referenced, your drawing size does not increase and the block is updated automatically in the drawing into which it is inserted. This last property is of great help when updating blocks, a process that can confound even experienced users.*

Command Finder

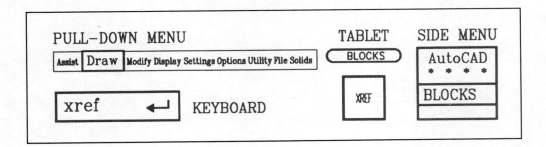

✦ Xref Options

- Attach
- Bind
- Detach
- Path
- Reload
- ?

◆ Using the Xref Command

The Attach option temporarily attaches the Xref to your current drawing. If you respond with a ~ (tilde), a dialog box appears from which you can make your choice. AutoCAD will then prompt you for the insertion point, scale, and rotation, just as in the Insert command. Nested blocks and layers that are attached along with the Xref carry the Xref's name as a prefix separated by ¦ (vertical bar). The blocks that come with the Xref are not available to be used independently. Externally referenced layers can be turned on and off but cannot be made the current layer.

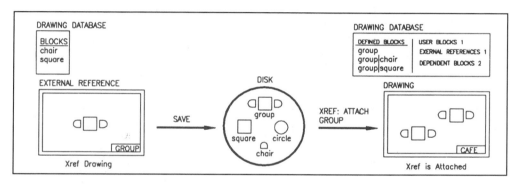

When you Xref the Group block into the Cafe drawing, it is only on loan. If you use the ? option of the Xref command, it will tell you that you have an externally referenced block named Group, with two Group-dependent (nested) blocks called *Group ¦ Chair* and *Group ¦ Square*.

The Detach option removes Xrefs from your drawing.

When you edit your drawing, the latest version of the Xref drawing is loaded automatically into your drawing. The Reload option is used when you want to update the Xref while in your current drawing. This is not a single-user function; it is used in a network environment, where someone else may be working on the Xref'ed drawing.

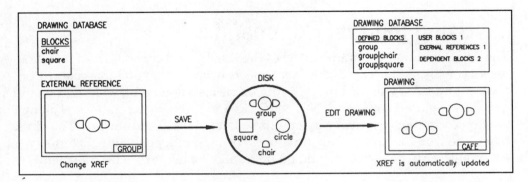

When you make your changes to Group and then go back to work on Cafe, the changes made to Group are carried automatically into the Cafe drawing.

The Bind option attaches the Xref to your current drawing (this is much like inserting a block).

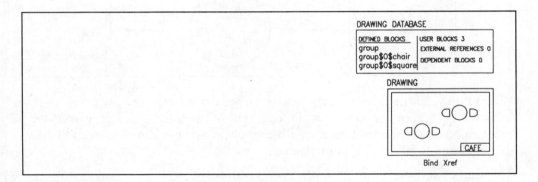

If you decide to keep these blocks permanently in the Cafe drawing, use the Bind option of the Xref command. The information in the drawing database will be changed to reflect this binding and will show that there are no longer any external references and that the nested blocks have been renamed *Group0Chair* and *Group0Square*. In the interest of block management, Group0Square should probably be renamed *Group0Circle*.

The Path option shows the path that AutoCAD uses to find the Xref. If you change the location of the Xref'ed drawing, you can edit this file to show the new path.

The ? option lists the Xrefs in your drawing.

✦ XBIND

*Used when you do not want to bind the entire Xref, but only parts of it, such as its layer setup or blocks. These parts are referred to as **independent symbols**.*

Command Finder

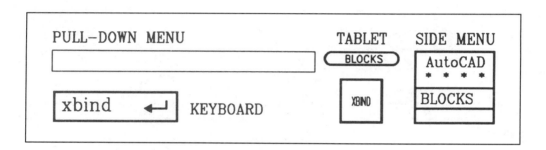

PULL-DOWN MENU		TABLET	SIDE MENU
		BLOCKS	AutoCAD
xbind ⏎ KEYBOARD		XBIND	BLOCKS

✦ Xbind Options

- Block
- Dimstyle
- LAyer
- LType
- Style

✦ EXPLODE

Breaks apart blocks, plines, hatches, dimensions, and meshes into their original component parts. You can explode only one entity at a time.

Command Finder

✦ Using the Explode Command

Explode has these effects on the following entities:

Blocks   Blocks return to the original, simple entities that made up the block. With nested blocks, Explode works on only one level at a time.

Plines   Plines change into simple lines and arcs without width.

Hatches   Hatches can be exploded into their component parts for editing, but doing so will greatly increase the size of your drawing database. The resulting hatch is placed on layer 0.

Dimensions   The lines, text, and arrows that make up the dimensioning annotations are inserted as a single block. Exploding a dimension causes it to revert to single entities. The dimensions are placed on layer 0; various dimensioning options, such as updating and the associative dimensioning function, will no longer work on these dimensions. (Refer to Chapter 15 for an explanation of dimension options.)

Meshes   Meshes are replaced with 3-D faces. (Meshes are not covered in this book. If you want information on them, refer to *Mastering AutoCAD Release 11*, George Omura, SYBEX, 1991.)

✦ Explode Notes

- Blocks inserted with different X, Y, and Z scale factors, and Xrefs and their dependent blocks, cannot be exploded. A block inserted with scale factors of X=1 and Y=−1 cannot be exploded because the scale values are not the same. This is why blocks that have been mirrored cannot be exploded.

- If you explode something by accident, use the Undo command to restore it.

✦ BASE

Relocates the insertion point in a drawing.

Command Finder

PULL–DOWN MENU   TABLET   SIDE MENU

AutoCAD

BLOCKS

base ↵ KEYBOARD

✦ Using the Base Command

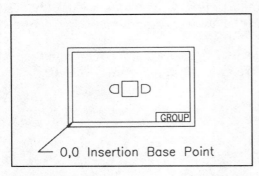
0,0 Insertion Base Point

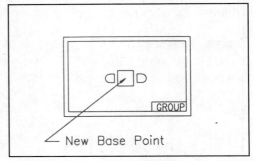
New Base Point

The standard insertion point for drawings is 0,0. Sometimes, depending on how you plan to insert a drawing, a different insertion base point is more useful. Relocating the base point does not change the location of 0,0.

♦ TUTORIAL:
MAKING AND INSERTING BLOCKS

In this lesson you will convert drawings you have already made into blocks and insert them in the PLAN drawing. The door and window drawings will be Wblocked; the furniture drawings will be simply blocked; and the entire furniture library drawing, LIB-F, will be brought into the PLAN drawing. All blocks in this book are made on layer 0, so they will take on the characteristics of whatever layer on which they are inserted.

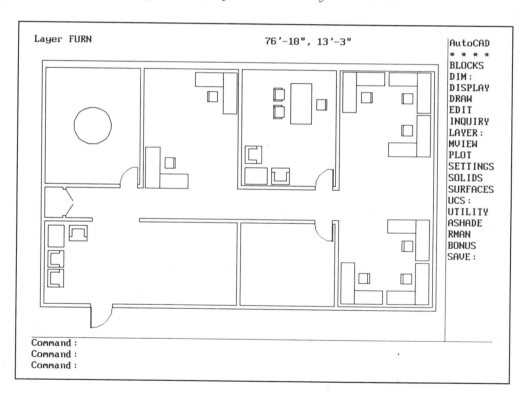

♦**1**   Start by editing the existing DOORWIN drawing. You will Wblock the drawings directly to the hard disk. Wblock the door drawing first. When the dialog box appears, highlight the file rectangle in the dialog box and type in the name, then press ⏎ and ⏎ again to leave the box (alternatively, you can select OK twice).

> Command: **WBLOCK**
> Filename: **B-DOOR**
> Block name: ⏎
> Insertion base point: *Pick the hinge point*
> Select objects: **W** (Window the door and the swing)
> First corner: Other corner: 2 found
> Select objects: ⏎ (Object should disappear)

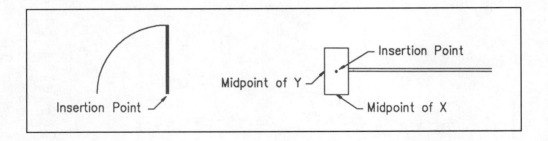

♦**2**   Wblock the window unit. Use XY filters to place the insertion point of the block at the center of the column.

> Command: **WBLOCK**
> File name: **B-WINDOW**
> Block name: ⏎
> Insertion base point: .X of MID
> of   *Pick midpoint of X*
> of (need YZ): MID
> of   *Pick midpoint of Y*
> Select objects: **W**
> First corner: Other corner: 5 found
> Object disappears.

You would use the Oops command to bring the drawing back if you planned to use it to make other window units.

✦ **3**   End the DOORWIN drawing.

✦ **4**   Edit the existing LIB-F drawing, and block the executive desk.

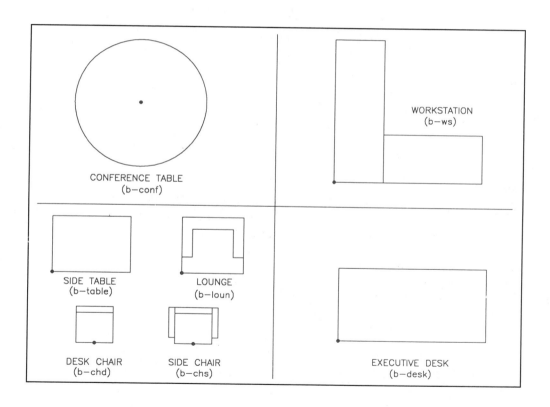

Command: **BLOCK**
Block name (or ?): **B-DESK**
Insertion base point: *Pick the point indicated by the dot*
Select object: **W** (Window the desk; the desk disappears)

Bring the drawing back by using the Oops command. Do not use Undo, because that will undo the block.

✦ **5**   Continue to make blocks out of the other furniture. The dots indicate the recommended insertion points. To simplify updating the 2-D blocks to 3-D blocks in later chapters, give the blocks the names in the parentheses. When you finish making the blocks, end the drawing.

✦ **6**   You are now ready to insert blocks in the PLAN drawing. Edit the existing PLAN drawing.

✦ **7**   Make the DOORS layer current before inserting the doors.

✦ **8**   Insert the b-door symbol 4 inches from the corner of the room by using relative coordinates. First, use the ID command to set the corner of the room as the "last point" from which to specify relative distances.

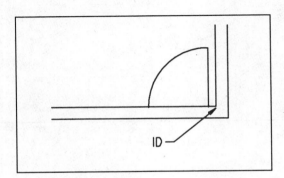

Command: **ID**
Point: END of *Pick the corner of the room*

✦ **9**   Insert the door, using relative coordinates. To specify both height and width, enter **XYZ** at the prompt for the X scale factor.

Command: **INSERT**
Block name (or ?): **B-DOOR**
Insertion point: @–4,0
X scale factor <1>/Corner/XYZ: **XYZ**
X scale factor <1>/Corner: **30** (Door width)
Y scale factor (default=X): [↵]
Z scale factor (default=X): **96** (Door height)
Rotation angle <0>: [↵]

✦ **10**   After inserting the door, draw the doorjambs, using the Osnap overrides to draw a line from the end of the door perpendicular to the wall and another from the end of the door swing perpendicular to the wall.

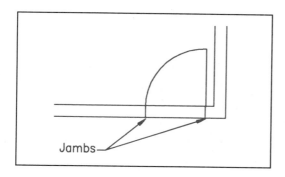

✦ **11**   At this point you could insert the other door blocks, but since you have already drawn doorjambs, it is more efficient to copy and mirror both the door and the jambs: Copy door A and the jambs to

230 TEACH YOURSELF AUTOCAD ✦ CH 10

the location for door B. Mirror door B to door C, using the mid-point of the back of the closet wall as the start of the mirror line.

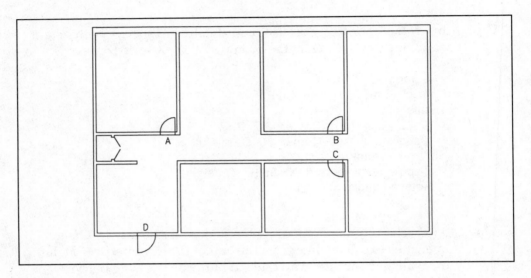

✦ **12**   Insert the door for the entrance. It will be 36 inches wide and rotated 180 degrees.

> Command: **INSERT**
> Block name (B-DOOR): [↵]
> Insertion point: *Line up door with left-hand side of corridor opening*
> X scale factor <30>/Corner/XYZ: **XYZ**
> X scale factor <30>/Corner: **36**
> Y scale factor (default=X): [↵]
> Z scale factor (default=X): **96**
> Rotation angle <0>: **180**

✦ **13**   Trim out the wall between the jambs.

✦ **14**   Before inserting furniture in the plan, make FURN the current layer.

✦ **15**   To insert the furniture blocks, insert the LIB-F drawing in the PLAN drawing. This will bring in all the associated furniture blocks. Because you don't actually want to place the LIB-F drawing in the PLAN drawing, but just want to·insert it so you can bring in the blocks, respond to the prompt for "Insertion point" by selecting Cancel, or press [CTRL][C] . This is a standard way of inserting a whole library of blocks into a drawing.

> Command: **INSERT**
> Block name (B-DOOR): **LIB-F**
> Insertion point: **CANCEL**

✦ **16**   Place the furniture as shown in the drawing at the beginning of the tutorial. It is more efficient to place a workstation, along with its associated chair, and then to copy, mirror, and rotate them into place, than it is to place these blocks individually.

In the next chapter, you will complete the office layout with the help of other editing commands.

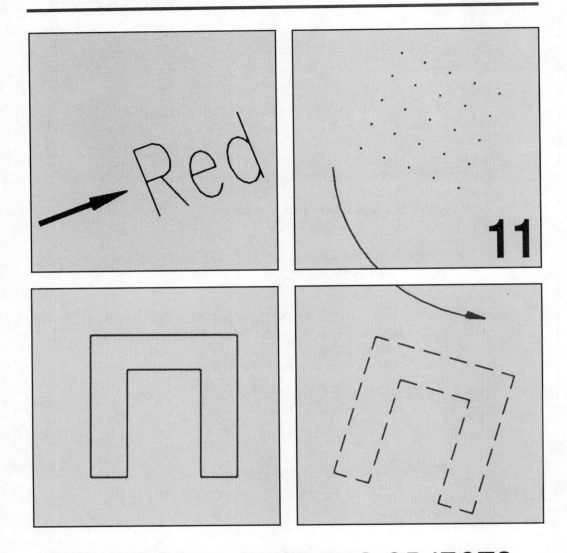

USING AND MODIFYING OBJECTS

This chapter introduces you to AutoCAD's power editing commands—those that modify and add to the line work you have already done. In using them, you will experience the advantage that the computer gives you over manual drafting. You will be able to do things easily that were either difficult or nearly impossible to do by hand. This is truly "new drafting."

+ Change

+ Chprop

+ Array

+ Extend

+ Stretch

+ Scale

+ Measure

+ Divide

+ Fillet

+ Chamfer

✦ CHANGE

Produces three different types of effects: changes in size and/or location of some types of objects, changes in all the options relating to text, and changes in the properties of objects. (The last kind of change is covered in "Chprop.")

Command Finder

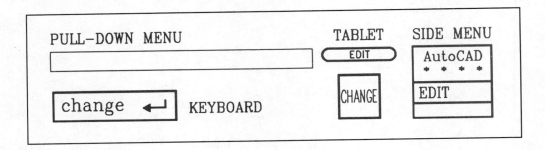

✦ Change Options

- Change Point
- Properties

✦ Using the Change Command

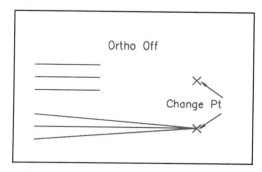
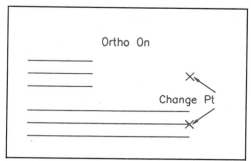

With the Change Point option (the default), lines are extended to the new point specified. If the Ortho mode is on, lines that are parallel are extended to line up to the new point but remain parallel.

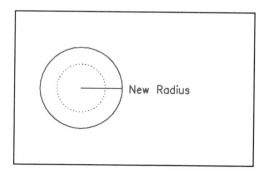
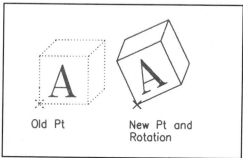

Circles are changed by varying the length of the radius. Blocks can be given a new rotation or their insertion location can be changed. The "insertion point" of the block does not change. To do this, you have to redefine the block.

```
┌─────────────────────────────┐  ┌─────────────────────────────┐
│                             │  │  Height                     │
│  Height                     │  │               Location      │
│  Location                   │  │  Style                      │
│  Style                      │  │  New Text String            │
│  Text String                │  │  Rotation                   │
│  Rotation                   │  │                             │
└─────────────────────────────┘  └─────────────────────────────┘
```

All the options for text can be changed: height, location, style, text string, and rotation. Style can be changed only if another existing style has been created.

The Change command also redefines the properties of objects. The Chprop command, introduced in Release 10, also works on properties. This represents AutoCAD's attempt to divide the Change functions into two separate commands, one dealing with text and location and one dealing with properties.

At this time, the Change command still works on the properties listed below. For descriptions of these options, refer to "Chprop."

- Layer
- Linetype
- Thickness
- Color

◆ Tips

You can straighten lines that have "jogs" in them or are not quite straight by using Change with Ortho mode turned on and picking one end of the line as the "Change point."

If the text you are changing has been inserted with a fixed height, the option to change height is not available. The way to get around this is to define a style with the new height, and change the height by changing the style. Global changes to text are possible using some LISP programs.

✦ CHPROP

Changes some properties of an object. To change text or the length and size of lines and circles or to move and rotate blocks, use the Change command.

Command Finder

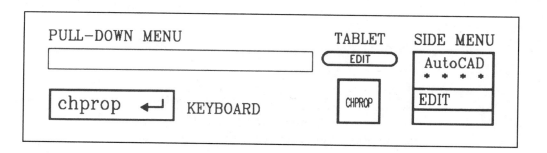

✦ Chprop Options

- Layer
- Linetype
- Thickness
- Color

✦ Using the Chprop Command

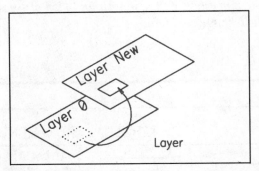

Layer

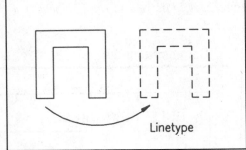

Linetype

The Layer option moves an object from one layer to another. This does not change the active layer. To do this, use the Layer command. The Ltype option changes the linetype of an object. If you are going to have more than a few special lines, it is better to assign a linetype to a layer and move those lines to that layer.

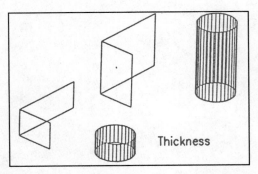

Thickness

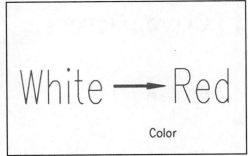

Color

Thickness is AutoCAD's term for what architects call height. You can use the Thickness option to give extruded height to lines, circles, arcs, plines, donuts, polygons, hatches, and even text. Chprop does not change the height of blocks, solids, or 3-D faces. The Color option changes the color of an object, independent of what layer it is on.

Don't use the Color option if you expect to use color as a guide to layer identification. Set your colors by layer, and let the object take on the color of the layer. This way the color of an item will be an indication of the layer it is on.

✦ ARRAY

Repeats an object in a rectangular or circular pattern.

Command Finder

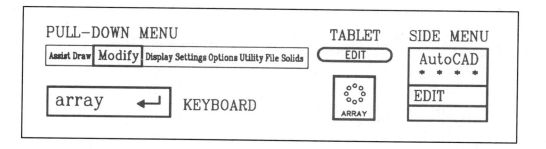

✦ ARRAY OPTIONS

- Rectangular (R)
- Polar (P)

✦ # Using the Array Command

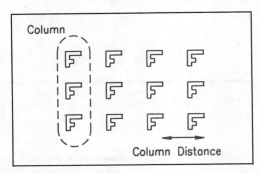
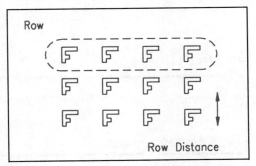

Rectangular arrays are made up of columns and rows and the spaces between each unit.

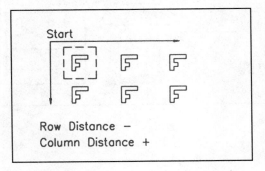
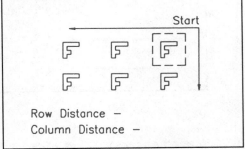
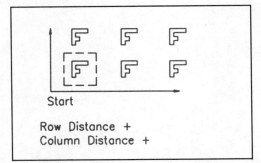
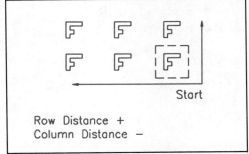

The direction for the rectangular array is determined by the positive or negative values given to the row and column distances.

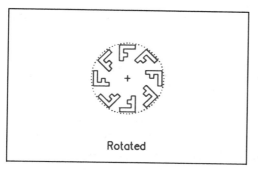

Rotated

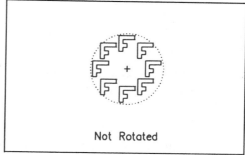

Not Rotated

In a polar array, you have the option of either rotating or not rotating objects as they are copied.

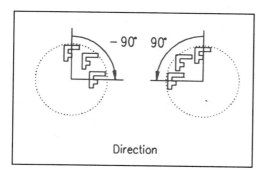

Direction

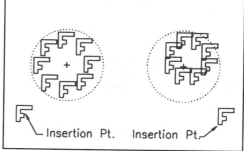

Insertion Pt. Insertion Pt.

The direction for a polar array is determined by assigning a positive or negative value to the angle. If the object you are arraying is complex, you should make a block out of it so that it will be arrayed as a unit. The insertion point of the block should be at the center of the block. If the insertion point is not centered, your array could be off-center.

◆ Array Notes

There are many uses for the Array command:

- You can put a regular pattern of columns on a plan. (Nontypical columns could then be erased and inserted individually.)
- You can do seating layouts for restaurants and workstation clusters for offices. You can array lines in the z direction for items such as bookshelves.
- If you set your snap to a specific angle, you can array at an angle other than orthogonal.

The objects placed by the Array command can be edited individually. If you are creating an array where you will not need to alter any of the objects, the Minsert command produces arrays that use less memory. The Minsert command requires a block as the item to array.

◆ EXTEND

Extends lines, plines, and arcs to meet specified boundary edges. You can select more than one boundary at a time, but you must pick individually with your cursor each object you want to extend.

Command Finder

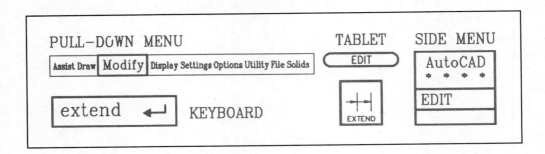

```
PULL-DOWN MENU                                    TABLET      SIDE MENU
┌────────┬────────┬──────────────────────────────────────┐  ┌──────────┐   ┌──────────┐
│Assist Draw│ Modify │Display Settings Options Utility File Solids│  │  EDIT  │   │ AutoCAD  │
                                                             ╰──────────╯   │ * * * *  │
┌──────────────────────┐                              ┌──────────┐   ├──────────┤
│ extend      ↵        │  KEYBOARD                     │   ┼─┤    │   │   EDIT   │
└──────────────────────┘                              │  EXTEND  │   └──────────┘
                                                      └──────────┘
```

✦ Using the Extend Command

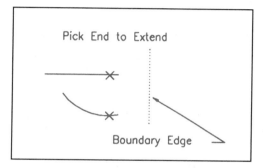
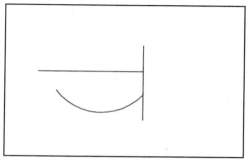

Pick the boundary edge, press ⏎, and select the objects you want to extend.

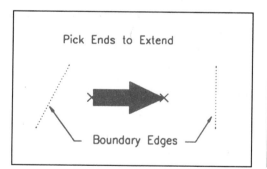
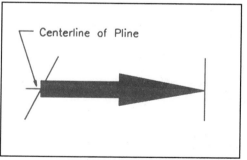

You may have more than one boundary edge. You must pick each of the ends you want to extend. Wide plines are extended to their centerlines. Tapered plines have their points extended to meet the boundary line.

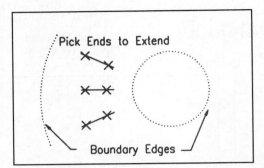 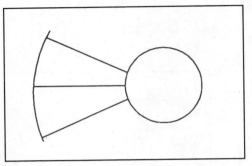

Arcs and circles can act as boundary lines. Again, you must individually select each end you want to extend.

✦   **Tip**

One common error is forgetting to press ⏎ after making a boundary selection (it is also a common error with the Trim command). Boundary edges and objects you want to extend must be separated by pressing ⏎. You don't have to pick endpoints when selecting the objects you want to extend, just the side of the line that is closest to the boundary edge.

✦ STRETCH

Stretches or shrinks that portion of a drawing cut by a crossing window. Arcs, lines, plines, solids, and 3-D faces can be stretched; circles, text, and blocks cannot.

Command Finder

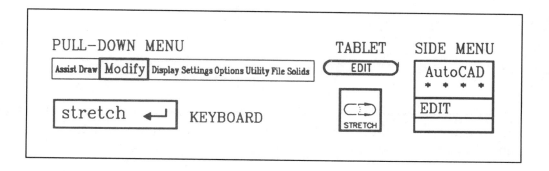

◆ Using the Stretch Command

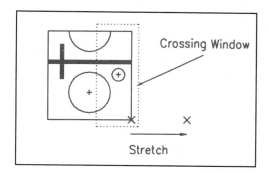

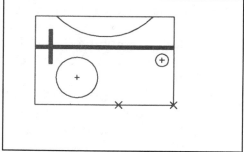

When you use the Stretch command, ends of lines and objects that are outside the crossing window are not moved. Objects completely inside the crossing window are moved along with the stretched items. Circles are considered to be inside if their centers are inside the crossing window.

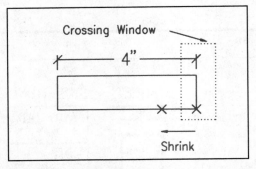
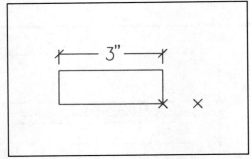

Changing the size of the object also changes the dimension if associative dimensioning is turned on (see Chapter 15).

♦ Stretch Notes

- The Stretch command is used to alter size in one direction only. If you want to change both the x and y dimensions, use the Scale command.

- Only the crossing window works in specifying what objects are to be stretched. If you are typing in the command, you must type **C** when AutoCAD prompts, *Select objects to stretch by window:*. The crossing box is supplied automatically when you pick the command from the screen or tablet.

- You can enter the amount you want an object stretched by typing in **0,0** when asked for a base point and the amount of displacement when asked for the new point. As an example, a base point 0,0 and new point 2,0 stretches a line 2 inches in the x direction; −2,0 shrinks the line 2 inches.

- When you are stretching an object that has dimensioning, do not include the dimension text in your box; this way, the new dimension text will be centered on the new dimension line. If your new dimension text happens to be inserted off-center, use the Hometext option in the Dim command (see Chapter 15).

✦ **Tip**

When stretching, keep Ortho mode turned on to keep your lines straight.

✦ SCALE

Changes the size of the items selected to whatever new size you specify. Changes in x and y will be identical. You can indicate the amount to be scaled by typing in a number, or you can use the screen cursor to show the amount.

Command Finder

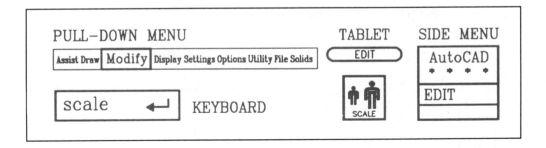

✦ Scale Options

- Scale factor
- Reference

✦ Using the Scale Command

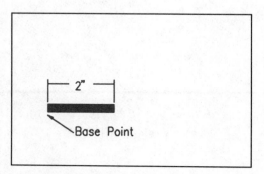
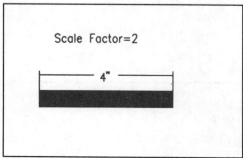

The default option asks for a scale factor. This is a single number indicating how much the item should be scaled: 2 indicates that the object should be enlarged two times. You can also move your cursor on the screen to scale dynamically: 1 unit produces an object the same size, 2 units enlarges the object two times.

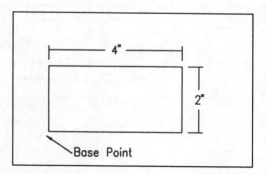
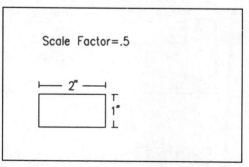

A scale factor of .5 reduces the object to one-half size.

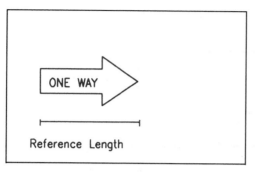
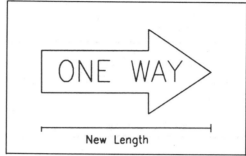

The Reference option asks for the original length (the reference length) and the new length. You can type these lengths in, or you can show the two lengths on the screen by pointing with your cursor.

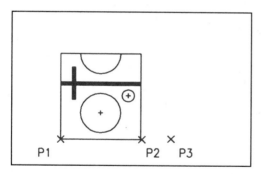
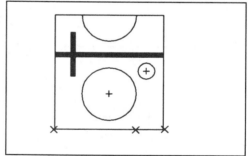

If you are using the pointing method, the first and second points indicate the reference length, and the third point indicates the endpoint of the new length.

✦ **Note**

The Scale command also changes the sizes of blocks. Notice that, when scaling up a drawing, plines with width are also enlarged.

✦ MEASURE

Measures out specified lengths along lines, plines, circles, and arcs. These segments can be marked off with regular points, complex points, or blocks.

Command Finder

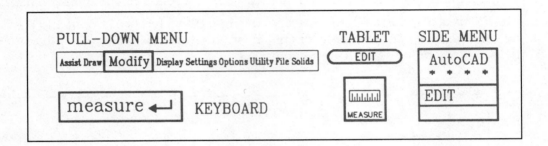

✦ Measure Options
- Segment length
- Block

✦ Using the Measure Command

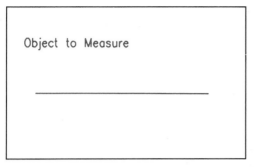

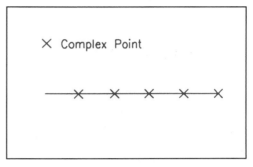

After selecting the object, you are asked for a segment length. Measuring starts nearest to the end you specify. The segments will be marked with points. These points are difficult to see, though you can use the Osnap mode *Node* to snap to them. A solution is to redefine the standard point as a complex point (see Chapter 5).

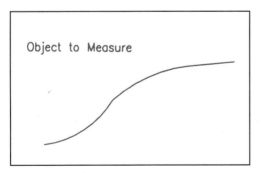

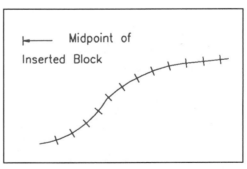

You can also use a block as a measuring marker. This block *must* be in the drawing. Generally, you will want to accept the option to align the block with the object being measured, but you also have the option not to.

✦ Note

The command forms for Measure and Divide are almost identical, except that Measure measures out specific lengths, and Divide divides an object into a specific number of segments.

✦ Tip

You can make railroad lines by using a block for the ties, or you can indicate different utility lines by using a letter as a block.

✦ DIVIDE

Divides lines, plines, circles, and arcs into the number of segments specified. These segments can be marked off with regular points, complex points, or blocks.

Command Finder

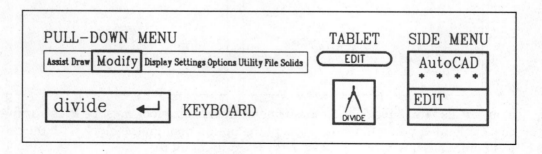

PULL–DOWN MENU		TABLET	SIDE MENU

Assist Draw | Modify | Display Settings Options Utility File Solids

divide ↵   KEYBOARD

TABLET: EDIT / DIVIDE

SIDE MENU: AutoCAD * * * * / EDIT

✦ Divide Options

- Segment length
- Block

✦ Using the Divide Command

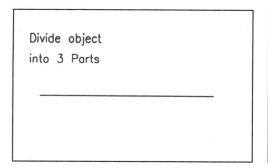

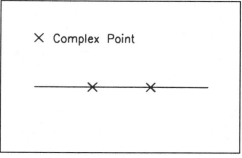

After selecting the object to be divided, you are asked for the number of segments. The segments will be marked off with points, though these are difficult to see. As in the Measure command, you can use the Osnap mode *Node* to snap to them and can use complex points to make the standard points more visible.

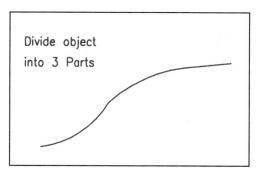

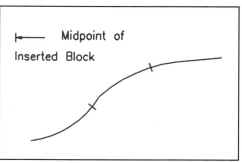

You can also use a block as the dividing marker. This block *must* be in the drawing. Generally, you will want to accept the option to align the block with the object being divided, but you also have the option not to.

✦ FILLET

Draws a user-specified radius curve between two lines. If the specified radius is 0, the lines chosen will automatically be trimmed or extended to meet each other.

Command Finder

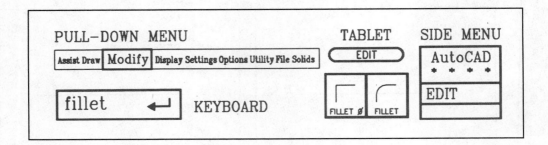

✦ Fillet Options

- Select two objects
- Polyline
- Radius

✦ Using the Fillet Command

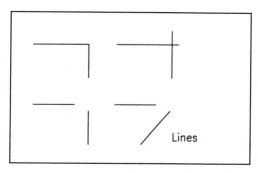

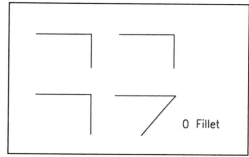

The default option asks you to select two lines you want to fillet; point to the side of the line you want to fillet. The Fillet command will work even if the lines selected intersect each other or do not meet. When you specify a 0 radius, the lines are trimmed at their intersection.

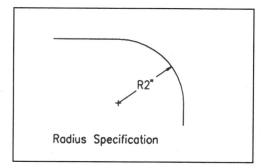

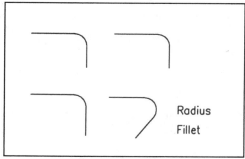

The curve for filleting is determined by the actual radius of the fillet. AutoCAD's default option is 0, so to draw a radius curve, you must first set the radius with the Radius option and then enter the Fillet command *again* to select the two lines.

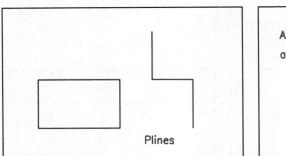

Plines

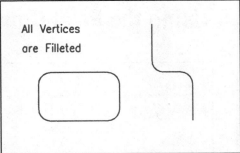

All Vertices
are Filleted

To fillet plines, select the Polyline option. Because plines are single entities, you only have to select one point to fillet all the vertices.

✦ Fillet Notes

- You can use the Crossing option to select the ends of lines you want to fillet.
- The Fillet command also works on arcs and circles. To avoid unexpected results, the points you pick should be closest to the ends you want to fillet.
- You cannot fillet lines parallel to each other.
- If you want to undo a fillet you have made, use the U command.

✦ **Tip**

Use the Fillet command to make radius curves on driveways and radius edges on furniture. With a 0 radius, it will clean up wall intersections.

✦ CHAMFER

Bevels corners; similar to the Fillet command, except that Chamfer asks for two distances and Fillet asks for a single radius. As with Fillet, if the distance specified is 0, the lines will automatically be trimmed or extended to meet each other.

Command Finder

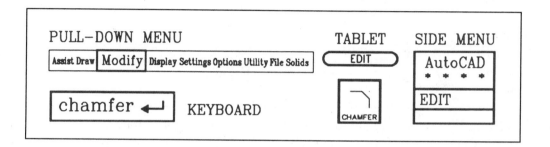

✦ Chamfer Options

- Select two objects
- Polyline
- Distance

✦ Using the Chamfer Command

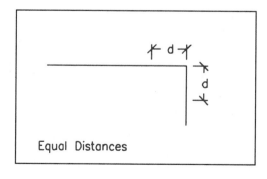

Equal Distances

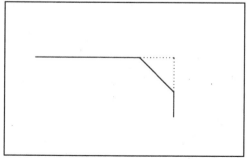

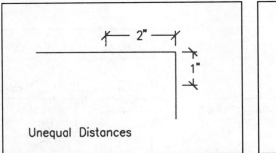

Unequal Distances

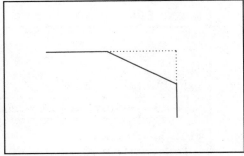

Because the AutoCAD default distance is set to 0, to get a chamfer, you first have to use the Distance option to set the amount for each side you want to trim back. You then reenter the Chamfer command, and pick the first and second lines to correspond with the distances you have specified. Distances can have the same or different dimensions.

✦ Chamfer Notes

- Chamfer works the same on plines as the Fillet command. To chamfer plines, select the Polyline option. Because plines are single entities, you only have to select one point to chamfer all the vertices.
- If you want to undo a bevel you have made, use the U command.

✦ TUTORIAL: CONTINUING WORK ON THE OFFICE PLAN

In this lesson you will use some of the new editing commands you have learned about to continue refining your office plan. First, load the PLAN drawing.

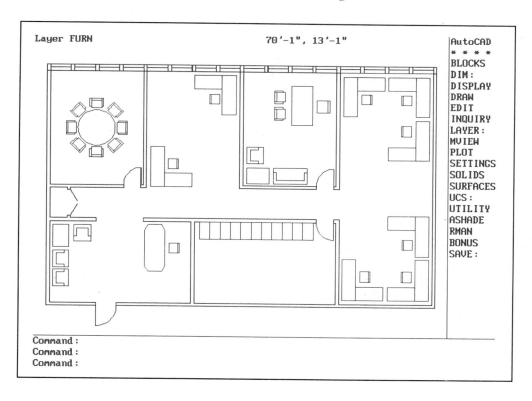

◆**1** Start by constructing the window wall at the upper wall line. Insert the window block that you made in Chapter 10. You will use the ID command to set "last point" to be the intersection of the inside wall in the upper-left-side corner.

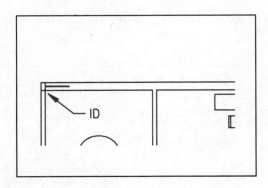

Command: **ID**
Point: END
of   *Select intersection of inside wall at upper-left-side corner*
(X=12'-6"   Y=52'-0"   Z=0'-0"; it is OK if your numbers are different)

Command: **INSERT**
Block name (or ?): **B-WINDOW**
Insertion point: @–3,6
X scale factor <1>/Corner /XYZ: ⏎
X scale factor <1>/Corner: ⏎
Y scale factor (default=X):
Rotation angle <0>: ⏎

◆**2** Array the block to make the window wall.

Command: **ARRAY**
Select objects: **L** (This picks the window block)
Rectangular or Polar array (R/P): **R**
Number of rows (---) <1>: ⏎
Number of columns (⌗) <1>: **17**
Distance between columns (⌗): **42**

✦ **3**   Explode the last window block, and erase the two glass lines.

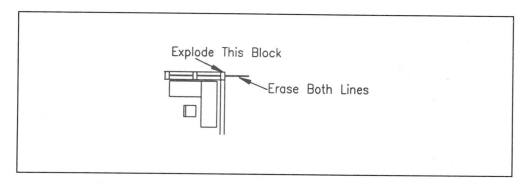

✦ **4**   Insert the side chair, B-CHS, as shown. Use the polar array to place chairs around the conference table.

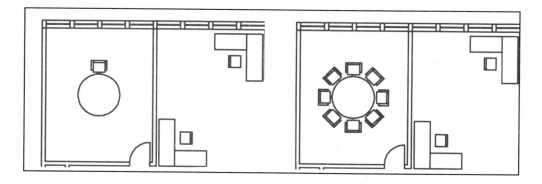

```
Command: ARRAY
Select object: L
Rectangular or Polar Array (R/P): P
Center point of array: Use CEN Osnap
Number of items: 8
Angle to fill (+=ccw, -=cw) <360>: ↵
Rotate objects as they are copied? <Y> ↵
```

✦**5**   Scale up the desk chair in the executive office.

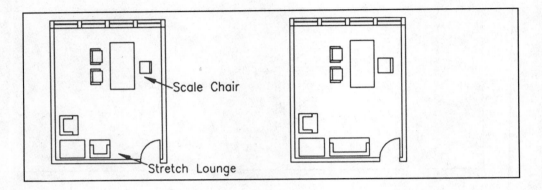

Command: **SCALE**
Select object: *Pick the chair*
Base point: *Pick the center of the chair*
<Scale factor>/Reference: **1.25**

✦**6**   Before you can stretch the lounge chair into a sofa, you will first have to explode the lounge block. The block will change color because it reverts to layer 0. You can change it back to the FURN layer later.

✦**7**   Stretch the lounge chair.

Command: **STRETCH**
Select objects to stretch by window
Select objects: **C** (With keyboard entry, Crossing must be specified)
Base point: *Select right corner of lounge chair*
New point: *Move cursor 2'6" in the 0 direction* (it helps to have Ortho on)

✦   **Note**

It would be more efficient to *insert* the chair block with a scale of 1.25 and the lounge with an X scale of 2 and a Y scale of 1; however, doing it the way we have done it gives you the opportunity to use the new editing commands you learned in this chapter.

✦**8**   You will now use the Stretch command to move a wall.

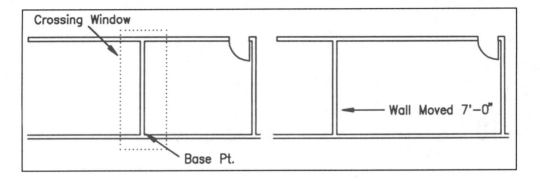

Command: **STRETCH**
Select objects to stretch by window
Select objects: **C**
Base point: *Select right corner of lounge chair*
New point: *Move cursor 2'6" in the 180° direction* (it helps to have Ortho on)

✦**9**   To make the row of files in the file room, you will first make a block for the files, using the dimensions in the drawing. Name it **b-file**.

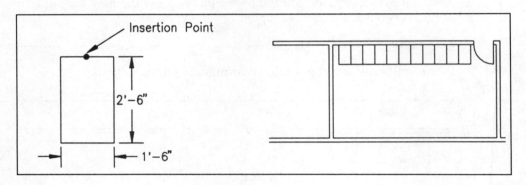

✦**10**   Use the Block option of the Measure command to specify the file block.

> Command: **MEASURE**
> Select object to measure: *Pick the upper wall*
> <Segment length>/Block: **B**
> Block name to insert: **B-FILE**
> Align block with object? <Y>: ⏎
> Segment length: **1'6** (width of file cabinet)

✦ **11** The last task remaining is to make the receptionist desk. Follow
the dimensions in the drawing, and chamfer the corners as shown.

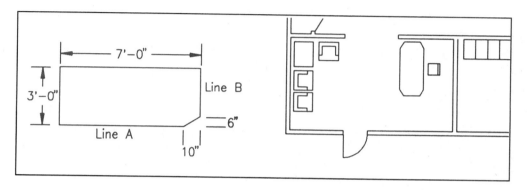

Command: **CHAMFER**
Polyline/Distances/<Select first line>: **D**
Select first chamfer distance: **10**
Enter second chamfer distance: **6**

Start the Chamfer command again.

Command: **CHAMFER**
Polyline/Distances/<Select first line>: *Pick line A*
Select second line: *Pick line B*

Finish off the other three corners, following the same procedure. At this point
you have a complete 2-D office plan. Only two objects, the doors and windows,
are in 3-D; the rest will be redrawn in 3-D in Chapter 16.

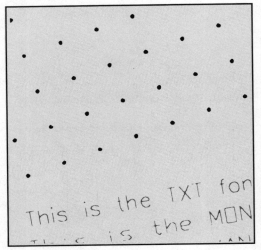

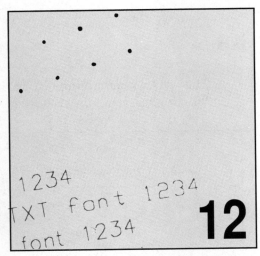

12

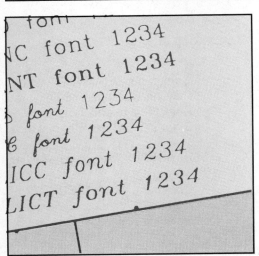

ADDING TEXT TO YOUR DRAWINGS

No more lettering guides, Leroy pens, and ink smudges—AutoCAD provides a wide variety of fonts, sizes, and spacings for you to use with text in your drawings. If there aren't enough typefaces to suit you, there is a large assortment provided by third-party software vendors, from Helvetica to simulated hand lettering.

- Dtext/Text
- Style
- Quicktext

✦ DTEXT/TEXT

Allows you to letter and place notes on drawings. Dtext has almost completely replaced the older command Text.

Command Finder

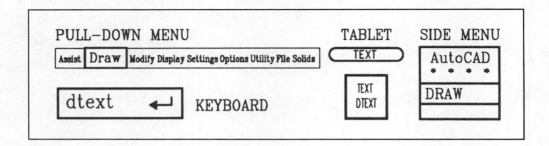

```
PULL-DOWN MENU                              TABLE        SIDE MENU
Assist  Draw  Modify Display Settings Options Utility File Solids   TEXT      AutoCAD
                                                                    * * * *
dtext        ↵    KEYBOARD                   TEXT       DRAW
                                             DTEXT
```

✦ Dtext Options
- Start point
- Justify
- Style

✦ Using the Dtext Command

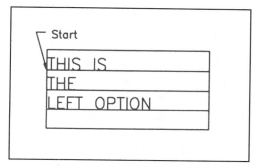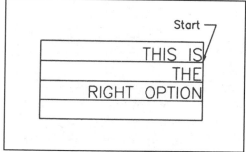

The default option is left-justified text; you start it by responding to the *Start point* prompt by indicating where you want the text to begin. You will be prompted for a height, unless the text style you are using already has the height specified (see "Style"), and rotation. The square marker on the screen indicates your letter size. For all other types of justification, you must first select the Justify option. The Right option places text so that the right-hand margin is aligned.

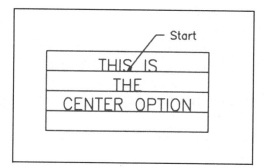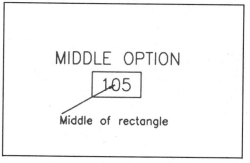

The Center option centers each line of text after you have selected the center point. The Middle option places the midpoint of a single line of text at the point you specify. This is particularly useful for placing numbers and letters inside of callouts for items such as room numbers and column indicators.

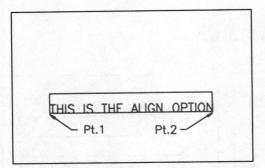 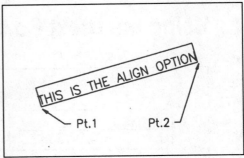

The Align option places text within two specified points, using the proportions of the current text style. Height is not constrained and as such is not required for the placement. The points specified also determine the angle for text placement.

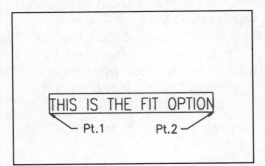 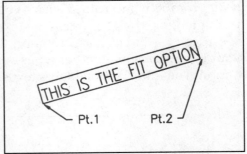

The Fit option also places text within two specified points, but in this case the text height is constrained, and the text is expanded or compressed to fit within the space. As with the Align option, the points specified also determine the angle for text placement.

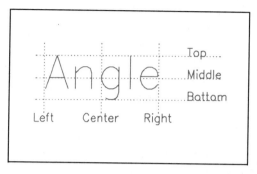

The alphabet soup—TL/TC/TR/ML/MC/MR/BL/BC/BR—lists the new justification options available in Release 11, which allow for greater precision in placing text. The letters indicate top, middle, or bottom horizontal placement and right, center, or left vertical placement.

The double percent sign (%%) allows you to insert some special notations in your text:

%%u	Underscore—you must indicate both on and off
%%o	Overscore—you must indicate both on and off
%%d	Degree symbol
%%p	Plus and minus tolerance symbol
%%c	Circle diameter symbol
%%%	A single % symbol

The Style option allows you to select a style for your text from those styles already designed (see "Style"). If you are going to change styles, you should select this option before picking the Justify option. If you don't remember the names of the styles you have made, respond with a ? to get a list of the styles in your drawing.

✦ Dtext Notes

Text is entered the same way as you normally do when you type.

- The Backspace key erases a letter at a time up to the start of the current entry.

- The ⏎ key terminates a text line and starts another one directly under the previous line. You can change this by moving your cursor and picking another location.

The type of justification you specify remains in effect until you reenter the Dtext command. Because a single ⏎ is the indication for a new line, two ⏎'s are necessary to indicate the end of text entry.

If you have chosen anything else except the left-justified default option, the actual text placement, such as centered or right-justified, will not occur until you have finished the command.

In both the Aligned and Fit options, the points picked indicate the rotation, so you will not get a rotation prompt for either of these commands. The right-, center-, and left-justified options are used for multiple lines of text, and the Align, Fit, and Middle options are used to place single lines of text.

The Text command is the older command for placing text and has almost been supplanted by Dtext, because Dtext is easier to use. Text is now mainly used in LISP programs to import script files from text editors.

You can pick Text Alignment under Dtext Options on the Options pull-down menu. You should have the style specified before using the Dtext command from the Draw pull-down, because you will not be prompted for it. The options you set on the pull-down work only if you pick the related command from the pull-down.

Text height and rotation can also be set this way; again you must use the Dtext command on the Draw pull-down menu. To unset any of the settings on the Options menu, type a period when prompted for a default.

✦ **Tips**

You only have to specify the first letter of the option when making your selection.

You usually pick the starting point for text with your screen cursor, but you can also type in absolute coordinates.

Although you usually type in the text height, you can also specify it on the screen by entering two points.

✦ Making Changes to Text in a Drawing

The ability to change text is important, because text is frequently entered in the wrong size or with spelling or other errors.

The Change command alters text location, height, spelling, or style type. Changes, however, cannot be made globally; each line of text must be handled individually. To change a single character in a line, you must retype the entire line. In Release 11 a more efficient mode of editing text has been added with the Ddedit command.

Editing Text Changes

To change characters in a line of text, it is easier to use a dialog box. You can access Ddedit on the Edit side menu or on the tablet under *Text Edit Dialogue.* (Of course, you can always type it in.) The text you select for editing appears in the dialog box. Move the arrow to the place on the text string you want to edit, and press the pick button to activate editing. Type in the changes.

If you highlight the box and begin typing, without first picking a point, the old line of text will be erased and the new text you type will be substituted.

Changing Text with a LISP Program

There are many LISP programs that deal with text modifications—some from Autodesk, many from third-party vendors. Autodesk provides one called *Chtext* on the Release 11 BONUS/SAMPLE disk. It can change the height, width, justification, location, or style of multiple lines of text, or replace a string of text globally.

Although using LISP programs is beyond the scope of this book, they can be very useful, so a brief example of how to access Chtext is covered here:

- Locate chtext.lsp. If you do not want to specify a path for its location, move it into your current directory.

- When you are inside the drawing where you want to use chtext.lsp, type **(load "chtext")**. Or, if you need to specify a path (for example, if it is on the C drive in a directory called *sample*), you type **(load "C:/sample/chtext")**.

- Once it is loaded, select Chtext under Bonus on the side menu, or type **CHT**. The program will prompt you for changes. You will have to reload this program each time you want to use it.

For more information on the use of LISP programs, see *Mastering AutoCAD Release 11*, George Omura, SYBEX, 1991.

Changing Text Size

Text size, along with hatches, dimension components, and linetypes, is sensitive to final plotting size. Because plotting reduces the drawing by the scale amount, text size has to be increased by the same amount. For example, the architectural scale 1/8"=1' translated into inches is 1"=96". This number, *96*, is the scale factor—the multiplier used to multiply text to compensate for the plotting scale reduction.

The chart below shows how to specify the appropriate text heights in AutoCAD for the three sizes of text commonly used in architectural drawings:

Drawing Scale	Scale Factor	Plotted Text Size	AutoCAD Text Height
1/8"=1'	96	3/32"	6"
		1/8"	12"
		1/4"	24"
1/4"=1'	48	3/32"	4.5"

Drawing Scale	Scale Factor	Plotted Text Size	AutoCAD Text Height
		1/8"	6"
		1/4"	12"

In Release 11 there are new options for sizing text by using *paper space* (this is covered in Chapter 17).

✦ STYLE

Lets you design how your text will look. The font, width, and obliquing options are used to style text.

Command Finder

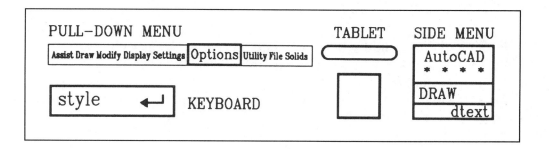

✦ Style Options

- Text style name
- Font file
- Width factor
- Height
- Obliquing factor

- Backwards
- Upside-down
- Vertical

✦ Using the Style Command

This is the TXT font 1234
This is the MONOTXT font 1234
This is the ROMANS font 1234
This is the ROMAND font 1234
This is the ROMANC font 1234
This is the ROMANT font 1234
This is the SCRIPTS font 1234
This is the SCRIPTC font 1234
This is the ITALICC font 1234
This is the ITALICT font 1234

Text width set to 1.
Text width set to .75
Text width set to 2.
Obliquing angle −20°
Obliquing angle 20°

When creating a style, give it an identifying name, such as *Big*, *Title*, *Fancy*, to remind you what it looks like or where it will be used. Once you type in a name, a dialog box appears with a list of font names. Select a name from the dialog box. There are twenty-two fonts available. The ten most useful are listed in the left-hand drawing. Seven of the others are from non-English and Gothic alphabets, and five are sets of symbols. The Text Font icon menu, which displays all the font styles, can be found under Dtext Options on the Options pull-down menu.

By modifying the width factor, you can give text an expanded or condensed look.

When you specify a height for a style, you will not get a height prompt when using the Dtext command. If you specify a 0 height, you will be prompted for the height each time you enter the Dtext command.

The obliquing angle affects the forward or backward slant of the lettering.

There are three lesser-used options that you may like to explore: Backwards, Upside-down, and Vertical. They modify the orientation of text.

✦ Style Notes

Beginners often confuse the Style command with the Style option in the Dtext command. The Style command designs how text will look. The Style option in the Dtext command only *selects* an existing style.

The style that is set in the prototype drawing is called *Standard*. It uses TXT as its font, which because of its simplicity, is the most efficient one for AutoCAD to draw. Many users find the square zeros that this font produces unaesthetic and substitute it with the Romans text font.

You can globally change the font in a style already used in your drawing by re-defining the style and selecting a different font. At the next regeneration, all the text with that style name will be changed to reflect the newly defined style. Height, width, and obliquing angle cannot be globally changed this way.

You can use this technique to "style up" a drawing before plotting: Define styles using the TXT font (because it is more efficient) and then redefine them with a more complex font when the drawing is completed.

The AutoCAD prompt *New style* is actually asking you for a font file. After you select a font from the dialog box, the selection has been made, even though no style name appears in the prompt area.

✦ Tip

If you make your font selection from the icon menu in the Options pull-down menu, your style will automatically be given the same name as the font you chose. This can pose a problem if you want to make more than one style using a specific font. You can work around this by renaming the style, but it is simpler to just use the Text Font dialog box to see what the fonts look like.

✦ QTEXT

Temporarily replaces text in a drawing with rectangular boxes.

Command Finder

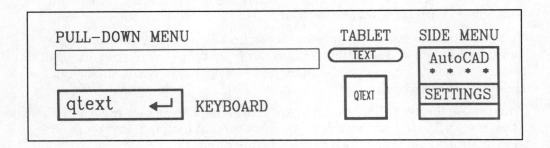

✦ Qtext Options

- On
- Off

✦ Using the Qtext Command

```
THIS  IS
THE
QTEXT  EFFECT
```

Text slows down the time it takes for AutoCAD to display your drawing. The Qtext command offers a way to deal with this by temporarily replacing text with rectangular boxes, allowing you to see the text location without actually drawing in the text. You must use the Regen command before the effects of Qtext can be seen.

✦ TUTORIAL: MAKING A TITLE BLOCK

In this lesson you will use the Text and Style commands to design a title block. Use the dimensions and the grid to help place lines and text. You can personalize your own title block by substituting your own name, office, and projects.

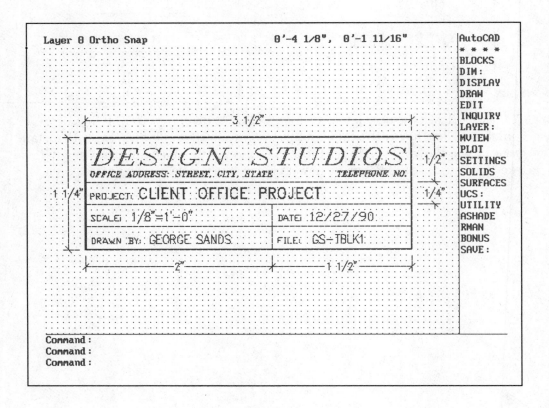

✦**1**   Start a new drawing called TBLOCK, and use the following settings:

Units: **4** (Architectural)
Denominator: **16**

Limits: **0,0**; **6,3**
Snap: **1/16** and set to On
Grid: **0** and set to On
Ortho: On
Coords: On

+ **2**   Using the dimensions shown in the lesson drawing, draw a border for the title block with a pline width of .01.

+ **3**   Use the Line command to draw the other divisions inside the border.

The chart that follows gives the settings for all the text in the title block. As you become familiar with the operation of the Style and Dtext commands, you may find this chart easier to use than the step-by-step directions.

TEXT	STYLE OPTIONS	DTEXT OPTIONS
DESIGN	Style = Fancy Font = Italic Width = .9 Height = 0	Justified = Fit Height = 3/16
OFFICE ADDRESS	Same as above	Height = 1/16
TELEPHONE NO.	Same as above	Height = 1/16 Justified = Right
CLIENT	Style = Project Font = Romand Width = .85 Height = 1/8	
DRAWN BY:	Style = Standard Font = txt Width = 1 Height = 0	Height = 1/16
GS—TBLK1	Style = Note Font = Simplex Width = .8 Height = 3/32	

All text is left justified unless indicated otherwise.
Allow 1/16 minimum allowance above and below text.

✦**4**   Create the style for *Design Studios.* Leave the height at 0, because you will want to vary it using the Dtext command.

> Command: **STYLE**
> Text style name (or ?) <STANDARD>: **FANCY**
> New style.(a dialog box appears)
> Font file <txt>: **ITALIC**
> Height <0'-0">: ⏎
> Width factor <1.00>: **.90**
> Obliquing angle <0>: ⏎
> Backwards? <N> ⏎
> Upside-down? <N> ⏎
> Vertical? <N> ⏎

FANCY is now the current text style.

✦**5**   Create a style for the project name. The height will be set because it will only be used at that size.

> Command: **STYLE**
> Text style name (or ?) <FANCY>: **PROJECT**
> New style. (a dialog box appears)
> Font file <txt>: **ROMAND**
> Height <0'-0">: **1/8**
> Width factor <1.00>: **.85**
> Obliquing angle <0>: ⏎
> Backwards? <N> ⏎
> Backwards? <N> ⏎
> Upside-down? <N> ⏎
> Vertical? <N> ⏎

PROJECT is now the current text style.

✦**6**   Create a style for the text you will use to fill in the information about the drawing.

> Command: **STYLE**
> Text style name (or ?) <PROJECT>: **NOTE**

New style.(a dialog box appears)
Font file <txt>: **SIMPLEX**
Height <0'-0">: ⏎
Width factor <1.00>: **.80**
Obliquing angle <0>: ⏎
Backwards? <N> ⏎
Backwards? <N> ⏎
Upside-down? <N> ⏎
Vertical? <N> ⏎

NOTE is now the current text style.

✦ **7** For the labels in the title block, use the existing default style, Standard.

✦ **8** Use the Dtext command to place the labels for the title block.

Command: **DTEXT**
Justify/Style/<Start point>: **S**
Style name (or ?) <NOTE>: **STANDARD**
Justify/Style/<Start point>: *Indicate starting point for "Drawn by:"*
Height <0'-0 1/8">: **1/16**
Rotation angle <0>: ⏎

Text: **DRAWN BY**: *Move cursor over to the next location*
Text: **FILE**: *Continue to move cursor and place text*
Text: **DATE**:
Text: **SCALE**:
Text: **PROJECT**:
Text: ⏎ ⏎

✦ **9** Place the office name, *DESIGN STUDIOS,* using the Fancy style. Use the Fit justification option in Dtext. The text will be expanded to fit the space.

Command: **DTEXT**
Justify/Style/<Start point>: **S**

Style name (or ?) <STANDARD>: **FANCY**
Justify/Style/<Start point>: **J**
Align/Fit/Center/Middle/Right/TL/…: **F**
First text line point: *Inside upper left of title block*
Second text line point: *Inside upper right of title block*
Height: **3/16**
Text: **DESIGN STUDIOS** ⏎
Text: ⏎

✦ **10** Use the same style to place *OFFICE ADDRESS.* Reenter the Dtext command, and set the height to 1/16. By picking a starting point for the text, the text will be left-justified automatically, because it is the default option. To place *TELEPHONE,* right-justify the text.

✦ **11** Continue using the Dtext command to place text using the style and height, following the settings as indicated in the chart.

✦ **12** Before ending the drawing, use the Base command to set the lower right-hand corner of the title box as the new base point. This way, when you insert the title block into a drawing, the corner of the title block will be lined up with your cursor, making it easier to place the block.

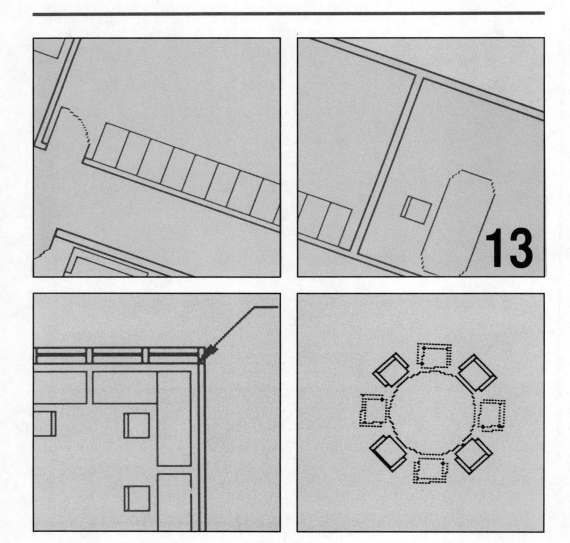

GETTING INFORMATION
ABOUT A DRAWING

13

AutoCAD has a number of inquiry commands that provide information on the entities in your drawing and information about your drawing environment. If something doesn't seem to work, these commands are a good place to start troubleshooting.

- List
- Status
- ID
- Dist
- Area
- Time

◆ LIST

Provides information specific to the entity selected.

Command Finder

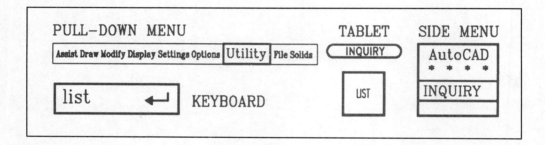

◆ Using the List Command

The List command provides all the vital statistics about the object selected: what the entity is, what layer it is on, its dimensions, and its location. If the entity is a block, it provides the object's name, scale, and rotation.

◆ STATUS

Gives you information about the drawing environment.

Command Finder

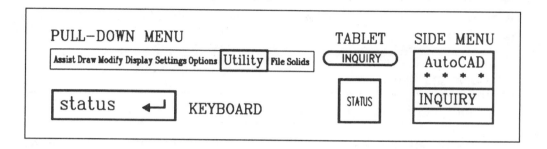

✦ Using the Status Command

The Status command gives you a lot of information all in one place. The information that you will find most useful is the following:

- The limits of your drawing
- The current status of Snap, Grid, and Osnap
- The settings of your current layer, linetype, and color
- The name of your drawing

✦   **Tip**

When odd things happen in your drawing, using Status is a good way to start checking. For instance, if your cursor is behaving funny, you might have an Osnap on, or you may have set your Snap to 1' with your limits set to 0,0 and 1',9 (the result is that your cursor won't move). If you seem to have lost your drawing, check to see that the numbers after the *Display shows* prompt are somewhere near those specified in your limits; otherwise, you have wildly exceeded your limits and are in outer space.

♦ ID

Gives the coordinates of a point you select or places a blip at a coordinate location you specify.

Command Finder

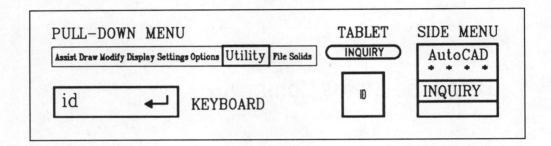

♦ Using the ID Command

If you pick a point on the drawing, ID will print the x, y, and z coordinates. The reverse is also true: If you specify coordinates, ID will place a blip there.

♦ DIST

Gives you the distance between two points you select.

Command Finder

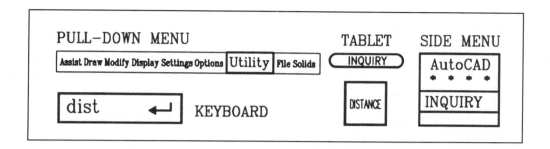

✦ Using the Dist Command

To use the Dist command, pick two points that encompass the distance you want to know. If the line is continuous, you can use the List command, but if the line is in segments or you want to find the distance between two points, you must use the Dist command.

✦   **Note**

The command is *Dist,* not *Distance.* Distance is a variable that is an internal AutoCAD value.

✦ AREA

Gives the area, both in inches and feet, and the perimeter of the space enclosed by the points you select.

Command Finder

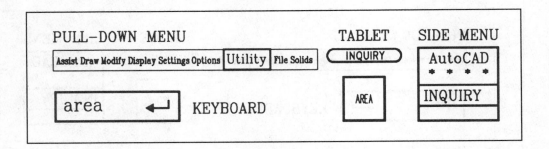

✦ Area Options

- First point
- Add
- Subtract
- Entity

✦ Using the Area Command

If you want to find the area of a space, respond to the *First point* and *Next point* prompts by selecting points on the perimeter.

If you plan to subtract spaces from a total area, select the Add option first to get the total area, then select the Subtract option and pick the area to subtract. If you want to find the areas enclosed by polylines and entities such as circles and polygons, select the Entity option of the command.

✦   **Tip**

In calculating area and perimeter, AutoCAD assumes the polygon to be closed by an imaginary line from the first point to the last; therefore, it is not necessary for you to close the polygon when specifying the perimeter.

✦ TIME

A useful command that shows the start date for the drawing and how much time has been spent in the drawing.

Command Finder

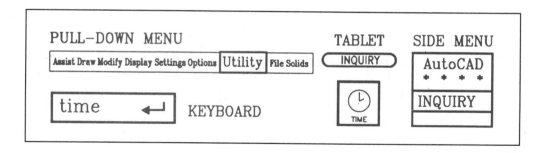

✦ Time Options

- ON: Turning Display to ON sets the Elapsed timer to recording time if it has been set previously to OFF.
- OFF: Turning Display to OFF turns off the Elapsed timer.
- Reset: allows you to reset the Elapsed timer.

✦ Using the Time Command

The Time command provides the following information:

Current Time	Today's date and time
Drawing Created	The date and time you first created the drawing; these are set when you select option 1 on the Main Menu or Save to create a new drawing or Wblock
Drawing Last Updated	The last time you were in the drawing editor
Time in Drawing Editor	The total time you have spent in the drawing; this timer cannot be turned off
Elapsed Timer	An additional timer that can be reset, and turned off or on (you can use it like a stopwatch to keep track of how long some procedures take)

✦ **Note**

The Time display uses the 24-hour clock. The timer is set to On as soon as you enter the drawing editor. Time is not accumulated if you quit a drawing or while you are plotting or printer-plotting.

✦ TUTORIAL: FINDING THE AREA OF THE OFFICE

In this lesson you will use the Area command to find the area of the office, and then subtract the corridor area from the total area. Select the PLAN drawing for editing, and set an INTersection Osnap to help you make accurate picks.

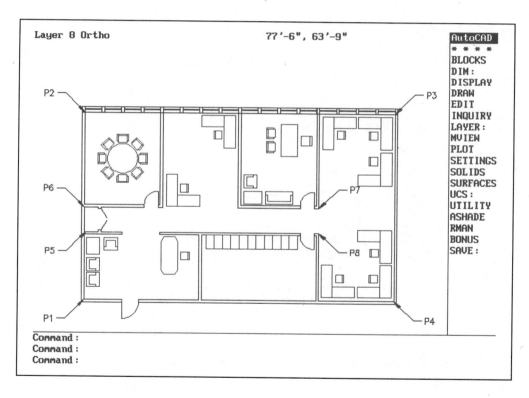

✦**1**   Because you plan to subtract an area from a total, your first
response will be *A* for *Add*. Refer to the drawing for the locations
of the points.

> Command: **AREA**
> <First point>/Entity/Add/Subtract: **A**
> <First point>/Entity/Subtract: ⏎
> (ADD mode) Next point: **P1**
> (ADD mode) Next point: **P2**
> (ADD mode) Next point: **P3**
> (ADD mode) Next point: **P4** ⏎
>
> Area=275724 square in. (1914.75 square ft.), Perimeter=180'-0"
> Total area=275724 square in. (1914.75 square ft.)

✦**2**   Remain in the Area command, and enter *S* for *Subtract* to subtract
the corridor area.

> <First point>/Entity/Subtract: **S**
> <First point>/Entity/Add: ⏎
> (SUBTRACT mode) Next point: **P5**
> (SUBTRACT mode) Next point: **P6**
> (SUBTRACT mode) Next point: **P7**
> (SUBTRACT mode) Next point: **P8** ⏎
>
> Area=27216 square in. (189.00 square ft.), Perimeter=93'-0"
> Total area=28508 square in. (1725.75 square ft.)
>
> <First point>/Entity/Add: ⏎

If you want, you can continue to find the areas of other spaces. When you have
finished, end the drawing.

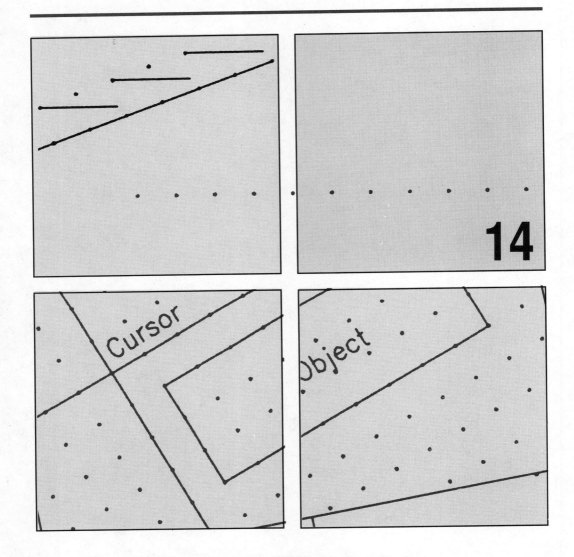

14

FINE-TUNING YOUR
DRAWING ENVIRONMENT

The commands covered in this chapter provide additional control over your drawing environment. Although many of these are not used in this book, a knowledge of them will make various drawing tasks easier, provide you with additional linetypes, and allow you to change some of the variables to better suit your needs, such as target and pickbox size.

+ System variables (Setvar)

+ Ucsicon

+ Linetype

+ Ltscale

+ Snap (Rotate and Isometric)

+ Isoplane

+ Elev

+ Tablet

✦ SYSTEM VARIABLES—SETVAR

The system variables are the values that control some of the functions of AutoCAD. Many of these can be set by the user; some are "read-only" and cannot be changed.

Command Finder

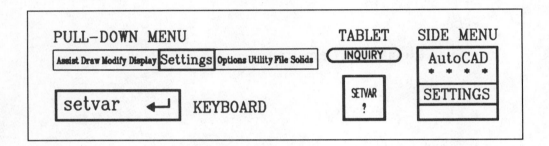

✦ Using the System Variables

To access the system variables, type in the name of the one you want to change at the command prompt. In prior versions of AutoCAD, you had to access them through the Setvar command. When picked from the tablet or screen menus, they operate transparently.

Most of these variables are stored in the current drawings; a few, such as Aperture and Pickbox, are saved in the configuration file, which means that their values carry over to your other drawings.

The following list of variables will give you some idea of their usefulness. (For a full description of system variables, refer to the AutoCAD reference manual.)

Aperture	Size, in pixels, of the Osnap target box (pixels are the smallest visible picture element)
Pickbox	Size, in pixels, of the box used for object selection

Blipmode	0=no blips; 1=blips enabled
Dwgname	Current drawing name
Mirrtext	0=text mirrored; 1=text not mirrored
Unitmode	0=displays feet and inches with a dash between feet and inches, as in *1'-3 3/4"*; 1=displays feet and inches as required for input with the dash used to separate whole from fractional inches, as in 1'3-3/4" (remember, leading zeros and the inch mark are not required for input)

♦ **Note**

Aperture and Pickbox are so useful that they are specifically listed on the side and tablet menus.

♦ UCSICON

The orientation of the UCS icon provides clues to where you are in 3-D space. The x and y on the icon point to the positive direction of the x and y axes in the current user coordinate system. There is also an icon that lets you know when you are in paper space, which is the space you use when setting up your drawing for plotting.

Command Finder

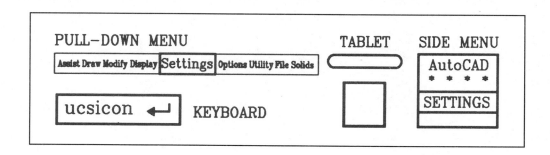

PULL–DOWN MENU   TABLET   SIDE MENU

Assist Draw Modify Display | Settings | Options Utility File Solids

AutoCAD

* * * *

ucsicon ↵   KEYBOARD

SETTINGS

✦ Ucsicon Options

On	Turns UCS icon on
Off	Turns UCS icon off
A (All)	Effects icon changes in all viewports instead of just the current one
N (Noorigin)	Default setting; when on, the icon is located at the lower-left corner of the viewport
OR (Origin)	Places the UCS icon at the 0,0,0 origin; if the origin is off the screen, the icon is placed at the default location

✦ Using the Ucsicon Command

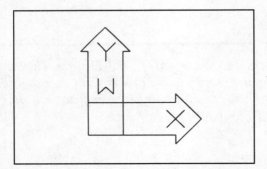 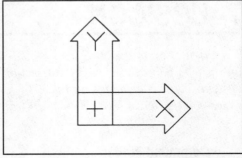

When you are in the world coordinate system, there is a *W* on the icon. When the icon is displayed at the UCS origin, there is a plus mark (+) in the corner of the icon.

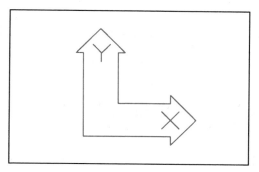
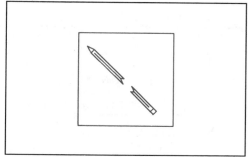

When your view is from below, the corner box does not appear in the icon. When your view is edge-on (or within one degree of edge-on), the icon is replaced with the image of a broken pencil. This alerts you that you may have difficulty placing points in that view.

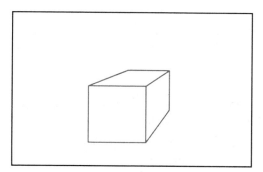
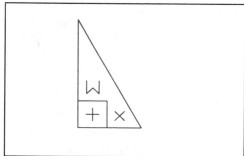

When you activate the Distance option, perspective is turned on and the perspective icon appears on the screen. When you are in paper space, the triangle appears on the screen.

◆ LINETYPE

Drawing standards require the use of various types of lines to indicate items such as hidden objects, property lines, and centerlines. The Linetype command provides access to an assortment of linetypes.

Command Finder

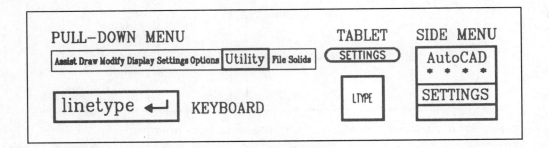

✦ Linetype Options

?   Lists the linetypes available in the linetype file; the standard linetypes are stored in ACAD.LIN. There are three varieties for each of the following types: Border, Center, Dashdot, Dashed, Divide, Dot, Hidden, Phantom.

Load   Asks for the name of the linetype to load. If you type an asterisk (*), AutoCAD will load all the linetypes.

Create   Prompts you in creating a custom linetype. (For explicit directions, consult the AutoCAD reference manual.)

Set   Sets the linetype for all subsequent entities. It is strongly recommended that this option not be used; instead, use the "by layer" procedure when assigning linetypes. This way, items that have special linetypes assigned to them can be managed using the Layer command.

✦ Linetype Notes

- To see a display of available linetypes, it is easiest to simply type in **linetype**, then **?**, and then press ⏎ (or select OK in the dialog box). If you don't like using the keyboard, you can select the ? option from Linetype on the Settings side menu (you still have to pick OK in the dialog box).

- The Load Ltypes option on the Utility pull-down menu is not really designed to view linetypes. If you insist on seeing samples of linetypes, type **?**, cancel the dialog box, type **?**, press ⏎ to get the Select Linetype File dialog box, and press ⏎ again (or select OK).

- When assigning linetypes to layers from the dialog box, the linetypes must already have been loaded; however, if you select the Layer command from the keyboard or from the side or tablet menus, you can type in the linetype you want.

♦ LTSCALE

Modifies the scale of the linetype to fit the scale of the drawing.

Command Finder

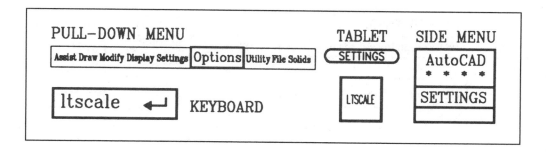

♦ Using the Ltscale Command

The scales of linetypes (except for Continuous) are affected by the scale at which you will be plotting your drawing. The "magic" number is about one-third of the scale factor. You can fine-tune how the linetype looks by adjusting the linetype scale, but one-third is a good place to start. (Example: Plot scale: 1/8=1'; Scale factor: 96; Ltscale: 32.)

If one of the noncontinuous linetypes looks continuous, check the Ltscale. The chances are that it is too small.

Changes to linetypes require a regeneration of the drawing. If you have turned Regenauto off, you must manually request a regen before the changes will appear on-screen.

✦ SNAP—ROTATE AND ISOMETRIC

The Snap command provides two additional options that are useful to know about: the ability to rotate the grid from 90 through −90 degrees and an isometric grid to use when doing isometric drawing.

Command Finder

✦ Snap Options

- Rotate
- Style

✦ Using the Snap Command

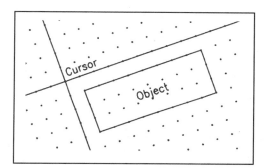
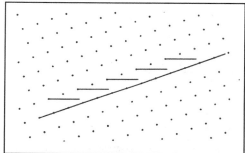

The Rotate option rotates both the grid and cursor at any angle from 90 through – 90 degrees. When set in this mode, Ortho is orthogonal to the angle set. This option also allows you to relocate the grid to line up with a point in your drawing when you specify a new base point. The drawing on the right shows how arrays done with a rotated snap will follow the rotation angle.

Although the Style option is generally set to Standard, which is orthographic, the other choice is the Isometric grid. Refer to "Isoplane" for information on how the grid is used in isometric drawing.

✦ Tip

Rotating the snap is extremely useful when drawing anything that is not oriented at right angles. You can align the grid with an existing object by responding to the *Base point* and *Rotation angle* prompts by picking two points on the object.

✦ ISOPLANE

Cycles through the three different isoplanes. The isometric grid must be set to Isometric, and Ortho mode must be set to On.

Command Finder

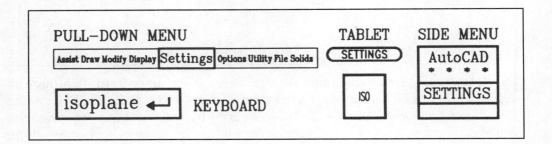

✦ Isoplane Options

- Left
- Top
- Right

✦ Using the Isoplane Command

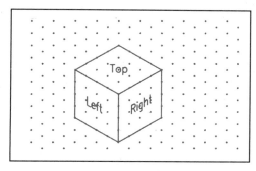 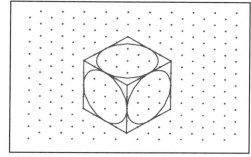

When doing an isometric drawing, it is helpful to be able to move into a different isoplane without getting out of a drawing command. Because it is important to be able to toggle between the planes transparently, there are various ways to do this:

- Press Ctrl-E (to cycle through the planes).
- Pick Iso from the tablet menu.
- Pick Left, Top, or Right in the Drawing Tools dialog box under the Settings pull-down menu.

Iso circles can be drawn using the Iso option Ellipse. When inserting circles, you must make sure that the appropriate Iso plane is activated.

Isometric drawings are 2-D representations of 3-D objects using set drawing angles: 30, 90, 150, 210, 270, and 330. They have no 3-D view because they have no z component.

✦ Tip

You can do isometric drawings without using the Isoplane command if you turn Ortho off and use just the grid to place points.

✦ ELEV

Sets the elevation and thickness of subsequent entities that you draw.

Command Finder

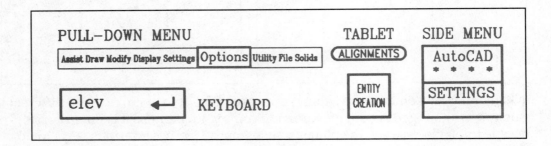

✦ Using the Elev Command

The Elev command sets the elevation so that drawing commands and block insertions will be done at the elavation set instead of at 0.

In earlier versions of AutoCAD, elevation could be changed through the Change command. If you want to change the elevation of *existing* entities, you now use the Move command and change the z-coordinate.

Here is an example:

```
Command: MOVE
Select object: Pick the object
Base point of displacement: 0,0,–6 (Moves the object 6 inches down)
Second point of displacement: ⏎
```

✦ **Note**

Another way of setting elevation and thickness is by selecting Entity Creation on the Options pull-down menu.

✦ TABLET

*The **digitizing tablet** is one kind of input device you can use with AutoCAD. AutoCAD provides a standard menu and template for the tablet. The Tablet command provides ways of using the tablet for menu selection or as a digitizing tablet to trace a drawing electronically.*

Command Finder

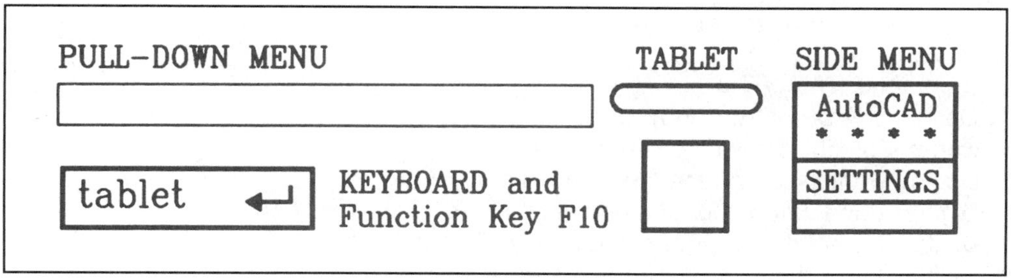

PULL–DOWN MENU	TABLET	SIDE MENU
		AutoCAD
		* * * *
tablet ⏎ KEYBOARD and Function Key F10		SETTINGS

✦ Tablet Options

- CFG
- CAL
- On
- Off

✦ Using the Tablet Command

Before you can use the tablet, you have to configure and calibrate it.

Configuring the Tablet

Configuring the tablet is aligning it with the template so that you can access commands by picking a box on the template. When you select CFG, AutoCAD prompts you to pick the four areas on the overlay and to give the numbers corresponding to the numbers and rows in that tablet area. Each area is defined by three points that form a right angle and includes the gray space between the command boxes. The points are indicated by the donuts on the overlay.

The easiest way to configure the tablet is to do it from the side menu under Settings, Tablet, Config: AutoCAD provides the column and rows information, and you only have to pick the menu areas. When configuring the tablet after the first time, use the Re-Cfg. option.

To configure your tablet, refer to the drawing to locate the points.

Answer the prompts as follows:

```
Command: TABLET
Option (ON/OFF/CAL/CFG): CFG
Number of tablet menus desired: (4 is the standard number)
Do you want to realign the tablet menu area: Y
Digitize upper left corner of menu area 1: Pick point 1
Digitize lower left corner of menu area 1: Pick point 2
Digitize lower right corner of menu area 1: Pick point 3
```

Continue as shown for all four areas:

```
Do you want to respecify the screen pointing area: Y
Digitize lower left of screen pointing area: Pick point 13
Digitize upper right of screen pointing area: Pick point 14
```

Your tablet is now configured; you can select commands from the template.

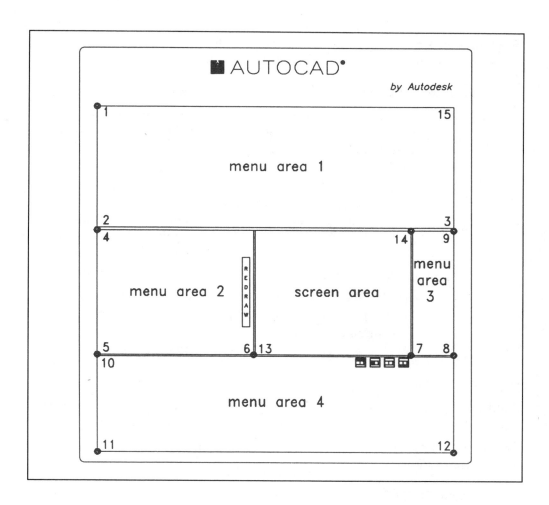

Using Swap Menus

A swap menu provides alternative functions for the commands under the same tablet icon. There are four swap menus in Release 11; their locations are indicated in the four tablet icons on the tablet menu. When you activate them, one of the four stars under AutoCAD on the root menu changes to a number indicating the tablet area has been swapped. They swap the following:

Menu Area	Regular	Swapped
1	Reserved for AME (Advanced Modeling Extension) and AutoShade tablet menus	Alternate or third-party applications and menu items
2	Transparent commands operate as such; Vpoint and Dview in Worldview mode	Zoom and other commands that are normally transparent are not transparent; Vpoint and Dview are in current UCS mode
3	Units are in feet/inches and decimal	Units are in metric
4	Osnap is in override mode; commands do not repeat	Osnap is in a permanent running mode; commands repeat

Calibrating the Tablet

Calibrating the tablet is done when you want to use the surface of the tablet to trace a drawing electronically by picking points on an existing paper drawing.

To use the whole tablet, you must first flush out the existing tablet configuration. Follow these steps:

```
Command: TABLET
Option (ON/OFF/CAL/CFG): CFG
Number of tablet menus desired: 0
Do you want to respecify the screen pointing area: Y
Digitize lower left of screen pointing area: Pick point 11
Digitize upper right of screen pointing area: Pick point 15
```

Tape down your paper drawing to the tablet to calibrate the tablet to the drawing:

```
Command: TABLET
Option (ON/OFF/CAL/CFG): CAL
Digitize first known point: (Any point will do)
Enter coordinates for first point: (Generally in feet and inches)
Digitize second known point: (Some distance away from the first point)
Enter coordinates for second point: (The distance in coordinates from the first point)
```

You are now ready to "trace" over your drawing with the puck, picking the points you want to enter.

✦ Tablet Notes

When calibrating a tablet, the coordinates must be given in the scale of the drawing. AutoCAD converts these values; the drawing in the computer will be in full scale.

The On option switches the tablet from template mode to digitizing mode. With this option, commands must be entered from the keyboard.

The Off option switches the tablet from digitizing mode to template mode so that the tablet/puck can be used to pick menu items from the screen. The function key F10 can be used as a toggle switch to switch between On and Off.

Picking in the unmarked gray area is the same as pressing ⏎.

If for some reason, your tablet configuration is not working from the side menu, the row and column numbers are as follows:

Menu Area	Columns	Rows
1	25	9
2	11	9
3	9	13
4	25	7

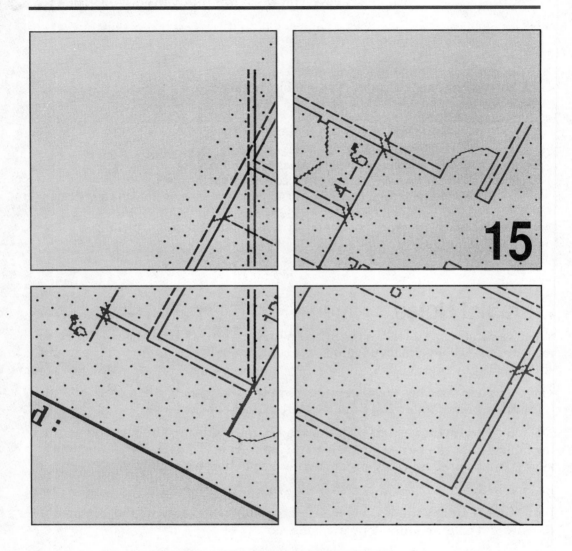

ADDING DIMENSIONS
TO YOUR DRAWINGS

AutoCAD has a very rich dimensioning palette. The task of dimensioning is easy because AutoCAD already knows the lengths, angles, and radii of the objects you have drawn. It involves letting AutoCAD know what you want dimensioned and where you want the dimensions placed. Although AutoCAD starts out with certain dimension variables set, you can create a dimensioning style specifically designed for your office by changing the settings of the variables.

The Dim command accesses a separate subsystem in AutoCAD. The Command prompt changes to Dim, and only a select group of standard AutoCAD commands (the transparent ones) are active. (For example, if you want to use Erase, you must first exit Dim.) The Dim1 command allows you only one dimensioning command before returning you to the drawing editor.

The extensive commands and variables that control dimension styles can be organized into four groups:

- ✦ Dimension types

- ✦ Dimension editing

- ✦ Dimension utilities

- ✦ Dimension variables

✦ DIMENSION TYPES

The general format for using the dimensioning commands is to indicate the item you want dimensioned, specify where you want the dimension line to be drawn, and approve the dimension value that AutoCAD displays by pressing ⏎. In addition, each type of dimension offers options relating to the object being dimensioned. When entering dimension commands from the keyboard, you only have to enter the first three letters.

Command Finder

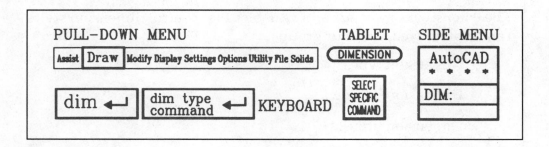

✦ Dimension Type Commands

HORizontal   ANGular

VERtical   DIAmeter

CONtinue   RADius

BASeline   ORDinate

ALIgned   CENter

ROTated   LEAder

✦ Using Dimension Types

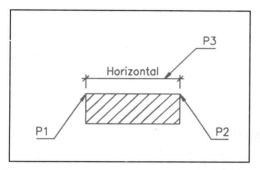
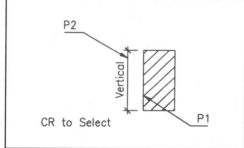

The Horizontal and Vertical commands handle dimensions in the same way. One or the other must be specified before you start your dimensions. The examples shown here work equally well for Horizontal and Vertical. Specify the first point (P1) and second point (P2) on the distance to be dimensioned, and then indicate the location of the dimension line (P3). Alternatively, you can press ⏎ at the first prompt and select the line to be dimensioned.

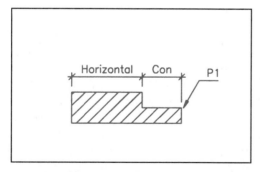
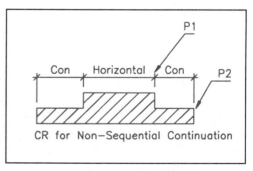

The Continue command continues a string of dimensions from an existing Vertical or Horizontal dimension by selecting the next point (P1) to be dimensioned. If the Continue dimension does not immediately follow the previous Horizontal or Vertical dimension, press ⏎ to select a point on or near the extension line from which you want to continue dimensioning. Then pick the point you want to dimension to. The Continue command works in any direction.

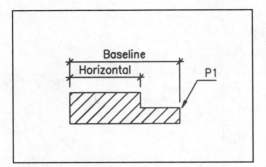

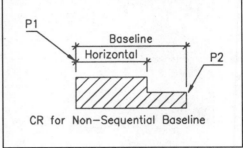

The Baseline command works the same way as Continue except that all dimensions begin at the same baseline. As with the Continue dimension, if the Baseline dimension does not immediately follow the previous Horizontal or Vertical dimension, press ⏎ to select a point on or near the baseline, and then pick the next point to be dimensioned.

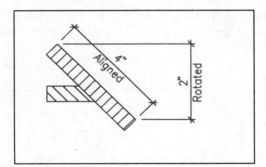

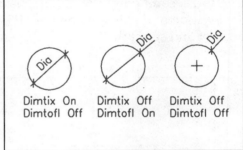

With the Align command, you can either pick the line to which you want to align the dimension or specifically pick the endpoints of that line. The Rotate command allows you to specify the angle for the dimension line. The Diameter command has three styles, depending on how the dimension variables are set. The point at which you select the circle determines the location of the dimension.

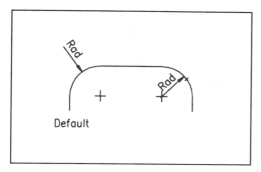

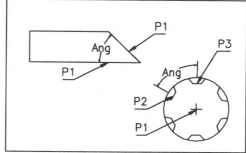

The Radius command also depends upon how the dimension variables are set. Select the arc to be dimensioned; as with circles, the point you pick determines the placement of the dimension. The default leader line is drawn on the outside of the arc. If you want the leader drawn on the inside, pick the point with your cursor. You can add the center mark with the CEN command.

With the Angle command, you can select two lines forming the angle. If you respond by pressing ⏎, you can pick a vertex and a first and second endpoint defining the angle. The vertex can be the center of the circle, but it need not be. A third command (not shown) allows you to pick a circle or an arc plus another point for the angle dimension.

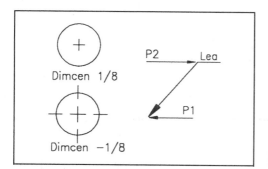

Default	Type	Effect
<4'–2">	CR	4'–2"
<4'–2">	14'–0"	14'–0"
<4'–2">	<>max	4'–2" max
<4'–2">	verify	verify
<4'–2">	Space+CR	

The Center command draws center marks or centerlines for circles or arcs, depending on the setting of the dimension variable Dimcen. The Leader command draws leader lines. It works like the Line command, starts with an arrowhead, and ends with the shoulder and dimension text. A space plus a ⏎ suppresses the dimension default. A *U* at the *2nd point* prompt suppresses the shoulder. Leaders are not associative dimension entities (covered later in this chapter) and cannot be modified or changed after insertion.

The term *dimension text* refers to both numerical and text entries for dimensions. There are a variety of responses to the default prompt, *Dimension text <Default>* (see the right-hand drawing):

- Press ⏎ to accept the default.
- Type in a new value.
- Type text before or after <> to add text to dimensions.
- Type in text (particularly useful with leaders).
- Press the spacebar and then ⏎ to produce a blank.

Ordinate dimensioning is specific to machine tooling. It specifies x and y dimensions from a 0,0 base point. (Refer to the Release 11 reference manual for more information on dimensioning commands related to mechanical drawing.)

◆ EDITING—ASSOCIATIVE DIMENSIONS

The associative dimension commands (available as an AutoCAD default) will work on all your dimensions unless you are working with a version earlier than 2.6, or you have turned off Dimaso, or you have exploded the dimension, or the entity is a leader. Associative dimensions are changed automatically when the features that they are associated with change. These editing commands offer tools to modify and manage dimensions.

Command Finder

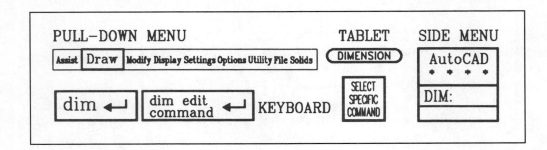

✦ Editing Commands

OBLique	DIMstyle
TEDit	SAVe
TROtate	REStore
UPDate	OVErride
HOMetext	VARiables
NEWtext	

✦ Using the Editing Commands

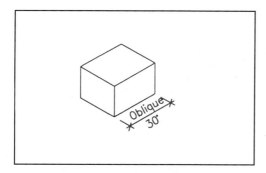

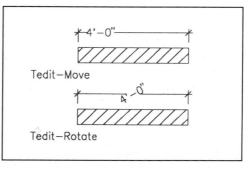

Oblique modifies an existing dimension so that the extension lines are perpendicular to the direction of the dimension. This command is very useful when dimensioning isometric drawings. Tedit rotates a single line of dimension text or relocates it to the left or right. This command is used to make crowded dimensions more readable.

The other commands do the following:

- *Trotate* rotates more than one line of dimension text.
- *Update* updates an existing dimension to the current dimension style, dimension variables, current text style, and units setting.

- *Hometext* returns dimension text to its default position.
- *Newtext* changes the content of the text on dimensions.
- *Dimstyle* gives the name of the current style.
- *Save* saves the current settings of the dimension variables with the name you specify so that you can retrieve them. The ? produces a list of existing styles and compares the current dimension style with the one named when the name is preceded by a tilde (~).
- *Restore* restores a dimension style when you type in the name or when you press ⏎ and then select a dimension with that style. As with Save, the ? produces a list of existing styles; the name of a style preceded by a tilde (~) is compared with the existing style.
- *Override* allows you to override an existing dimension without altering the existing dimension style. This command also provides the option of modifying the dimension style.
- *Variables* lists the dimension variables for the style name selected.

♦ DIMENSION UTILITIES

The dimension utility commands assist you with dimensioning. They can be used without exiting the dimensioning subsystem.

Command Finder

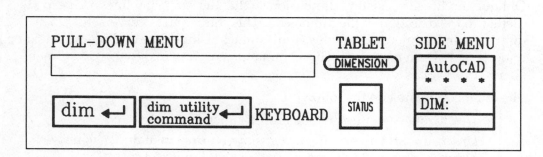

✦ Utility Commands

STAtus   Lists all the dimension variables with their current values.

STYle   Switches to a different existing text style.

UNDo   Undoes the effect of the last dimension command. It can be used instead of Erase, which can't be used when you are in the dimensioning subsystem.

EXIt   Exits you from the dimensioning subsystem and returns you to the drawing editor (as does the Cancel command). If you want to cancel a dimension command without exiting Dim, press CTRL C .

✦   **Note**

Remember, all the transparent commands work in dimensioning.

✦ DIMENSION VARIABLES

Because AutoCAD is used in different disciplines—architecture, mechanical engineering, interior design—the dimensions require different styling. For example, a part that is being machined to a – 0.002 tolerance requires a very different dimensioning format from a site plan being dimensioned in miles or meters. By changing the values of the dimension variables, you can set up these kinds of formats.

Command Finder

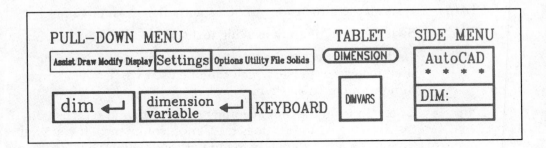

✦ Using Dimension Variables

All dimension variables start with the three letters *DIM*, as in *DIMALT*. The second part of the name, *ALT*, represents AutoCAD's attempt at an acronym to give some hint about what the variable stands for. You can access the variables (42 in all, organized alphabetically) by selecting Status when you are in Dim. Refer to Appendix B for a list of the variables organized by the types of dimensioning components they affect.

✦ **Tip**

Release 11 provides graphic aids for the dimension variables, which make them much easier to use, under Set Dim Vars on the Settings pull-down menu.

✦ TUTORIAL: DIMENSIONING THE OFFICE PLAN

In this lesson you will dimension your PLAN drawing in the architectural format. You will have to change a number of dimension variables before you begin, because most of them are set for the mechanical style of dimensioning. You will also change some variables while you are dimensioning.

To place your dimension points, make use of the various transparent Zoom options, such as Vmax, Previous, and Dynamic, which you can pick from the screen or tablet menus.

Remember that while you are working in dimensions, the only standard AutoCAD commands that can be used (without exiting the Dim subprogram) are the transparent ones. Erase will not work, but you can use Undo if you make a mistake.

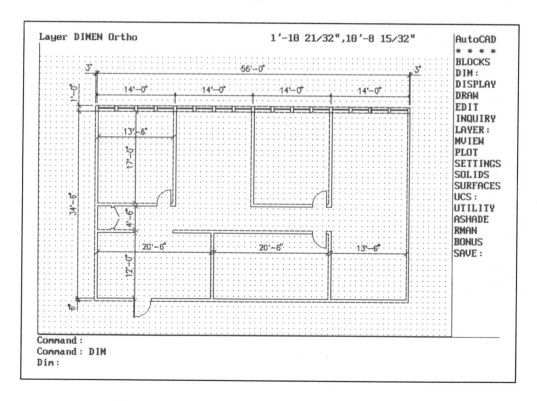

✦**1**   Edit the PLAN drawing; before you get into the dimensioning commands, establish these settings:

> Snap: Off
> Grid: **1'** and set to On
> Ortho: On
> Aperture: **3**

✦**2**   Increase your limits to make more room for dimensions: LL **0,0**; UR **75',62'**

✦**3**   For units, stay in Architectural but set Denominator to *64* so that you will be able to see the changes that you make to the dimension variables.

✦**4**   Make a new text style to be used for dimensions.

> Text Style Name: **DIMS**
> Font: **Romans**
> Ht: **0**
> Width: **.85**

✦**5**   You will be using a combination of NEA, MID, and END Osnaps to place dimension points. Because you will be using NEArest most frequently, set it to On with the Osnap command and use the others in override mode.

✦**6**   You don't need furniture in the dimension plan, so freeze the FURN layer, and set the current layer to DIMEN.

✦**7**   Get into dimensions and save the current standard AutoCAD dimension settings under the name *Standard* should you want to restore them. Notice that the Command prompt has changed to the Dim prompt.

> Command: **DIM**
> Dim: **SAVE**
> ?/Name for new dimension style: **STANDARD**

✦ **8**   Change the settings of the variables by typing their names and the new values. Do not type the explanations of what they are or the inch marks.

> Dim: **DIMASZ** (Arrow size)
> Current value <3/16"> New value: **3/64**

Continue changing these dimension variables to the following settings:

> DIMBLK1: **DOT** (First arrow substitute)
> DIMBLK2: **DOT** (Second arrow substitute)
> DIMEXE: **1/16"** (Shortens extension above dimension line)
> DIMGAP: **0"** (Minimizes gap between text and dimension line)
> DIMRND: **1"** (Rounds any fraction to a whole number)
> DIMSAH: On (Activates arrow substitute)
> DIMTAD: On (Text above dimension line)
> DIMTIH: Off (Text between extensions oriented to dimension line)
> DIMTOH: Off (Text outside of extensions oriented to dimension line)
> DIMTXT: **1/8"** (Text height)
> DIMZIN: **3** (Produces 0-inch notation as 2'-0")

✦ **9**   You will first dimension the midpoints of columns. Because you have specified *DOT* as a substitute for arrows and have activated the substitution by turning on DIMSAH, you will get dots instead of arrows. Specify a Horizontal dimension. Use a midpoint Osnap override.

> Dim: **HOR**
> First extension line origin or RETURN to select: *Pick midpoint of first column*

Second extension line origin: *Pick midpoint of second column*
Dimension line location: *Pick a point about 2' above building line*
Dimension text <14'-0">: ⏎ (Accepts dimension)

Dim: **CON** (Continued dimension)
Second extension line origin or RETURN to select: *Pick midpoint of third column*
Dimension text <14'-0">: ⏎

Dim: ⏎ (Repeats Continued dimension)
CON
Second extension line origin or RETURN to select: *Pick midpoint of fourth column*
Dimension text <14'-0">: ⏎

Dim: ⏎
CON
Second extension line origin or RETURN to select: *Pick midpoint of fifth column*
Dimension text <14'-0">: ⏎

♦ **10** You are now finished using the dots as markers. To set up ticks, you have to specify the size in the variable Dimtsz. Any value other than 0 will enable ticks and suppress arrows or dots.

Dim: **DIMTSZ**
Current value <0"> New value: **3/64**

♦ **11** Now dimension the overall window line. First dimension the 56' length, then use Continue for the 3" dimension on the right-hand side. The leftmost 3" dimension will be dimensioned last with the Continue command. The reason that it is done this way is to force the left-hand number to come out on the left side of the dimension. When numbers don't fit between extension lines, they are placed next to the second extension line, so by dimensioning that section from right to left, the 3" comes out on the side you want. Use the MID and END Osnap overrides.

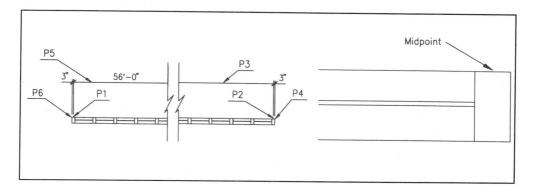

Dim: **HOR**
First extension line origin or RETURN to select: *Pick P1*
Second extension line origin: *Pick P2*
Dimension line location: *Pick P3*
Dimension text <56′-0">: ⏎

Dim: **CON**
Second extension line origin or RETURN to select: *Pick P4*
Dimension text <3">: ⏎

Dim: **CON**
Second extension line origin or RETURN to select: ⏎
Select continued dimension: *Pick P5 to continue an existing dimension*
Second extension line origin or RETURN to select: *Pick P6*
Dimension text <3">: ⏎

✦**12** Use the same technique for the outside dimension on the left side of the drawing. Continue using Osnaps and Zooms as needed. Refer to the PLAN drawing for dimension locations.

Indicate that you will be doing vertical dimensioning: **VER**
The dimension text should be: **34′-6"**

Continue with Dim: **CON**
The dimension text should be: **1′-0"**

Continue from the 34'-6" dimension line
with Dim: **CON**
The dimension text should be: **6"**

✦ **13**   You will now dimension the interior spaces. Your dimension place-
ments can vary from those in the book, because you can place
them at various points along the wall. Because the dimensions are
from wall to wall, drawing extension lines would be redundant.
Suppress them by setting the dimension variables Dimse1 and
Dimse2 to On. The remaining dimensions are simple Horizontal
or Vertical dimensions. The Nearest Osnap, which you have already set, will ensure that the dimension lines touch the walls.

Dimension the conference room using Horizontal
The dimension text should be: **13'-6"**

Dimension the office space from window line to entrance door using Vertical
The dimension text should be: **17'-6"**
The dimension text should be: **4'-6"**
The dimension text should be: **12'-0"**

Dimension the long dimension of the office space using Horizontal
The dimension text should be: **20'-6"**
The dimension text should be: **20'-6"**
The dimension text should be: **13'-6"**

✦ **14**   You have finished dimensioning your plan. You can exit from the
dimensioning subprogram by typing **Exit** or pressing CTRL C .
Remove any Osnaps you have, reset the Units denominator to 1,
thaw the FURN layer, freeze the DIMEN layer, and end your
drawing.

AutoCAD offers numerous options for dimensioning, so you can develop a style
for your specific needs. Take the time to set up dimensioning procedures and
styles—it will enable you to quickly produce clear and unambiguous dimensions.

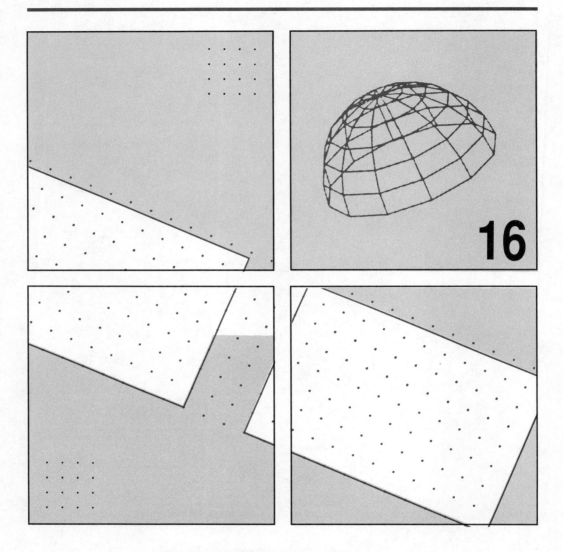

WORKING IN 3-D

In this chapter you begin to explore some of AutoCAD's capabilities for working in three dimensions. The commands you'll learn provide split-screen viewing, construct both simple extruded shapes and actual 3-D objects, and create perspective views.

- 3Dface

- 3D Objects

- Vports

- Vpoint

- Plan

- Hide

- Dview

- Shade

◆ 3DFACE

Draws a surface that appears as a wire frame but will be opaque when the Hide command is used. The 3Dface command is similar to the Solid command, but the points are entered in a clockwise or counterclockwise order.

Command Finder

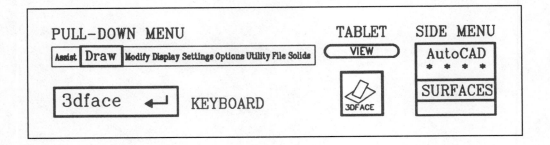

◆ Using the 3Dface Command

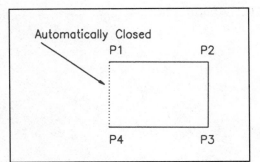

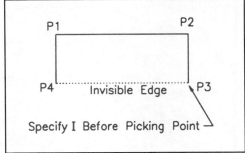

3Dfaces are built of three or four points. After you draw four points, AutoCAD closes the figure and prompts for additional third and fourth points. The Invisible (I) option makes an edge of a 3Dface invisible. This is used to hide the lines between faces when constructing shapes made up of more than one face. You must specify the I before beginning the first point of the edge you want to make invisible. Also, the I must precede any Osnap or filter.

✦ 3Dface Notes

- 3Dfaces cannot be extruded.
- Points defining a 3Dface need not be in the same plane.
- Continuing a shape by drawing the third and fourth points can produce unexpected results. Sometimes it is easier to begin the command for each section.
- Lines that are extruded do not have "tops" on them (a table made from extruded lines appears to have a glass top). 3Dfaces are useful for putting tops on things so they won't appear transparent. Solids can also be used for this purpose (see "Hide" in this chapter).
- When you make the edges of a 3Dface invisible, it can present a problem in editing. To make the edges visible, set the variable Splframe to 1 or select ShowEdge from the side menu under 3Dface.

✦ 3D OBJECTS

3D Objects is not a command but a series of some basic forms made from polygon meshes. AutoCAD has set up the formulas in AutoLISP; all you have to do is supply some size parameters. Although the selection includes the sphere, torus, and cone, this book covers the shapes more useful in architecture: the box, wedge, pyramid, and dome.

Command Finder

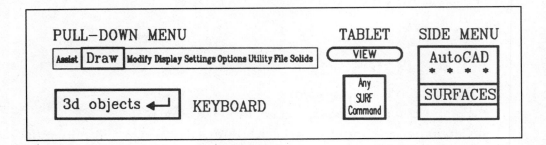

✦ Using 3D Objects

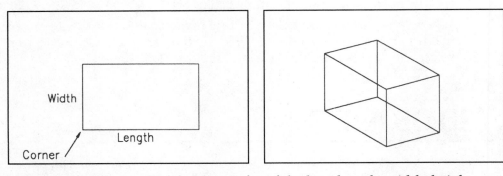

To form the box you are asked for the corner of the box, length, width, height, and the rotation angle about Z (you must specify 0 for no rotation). You can show the length and width on the screen; the dimensions start from the corner of the box. The height is easier to enter from the keyboard, but you can enter it on-screen if you are in a 3-D view. If you are drawing a cube, you only have to specify one side and then pick C.

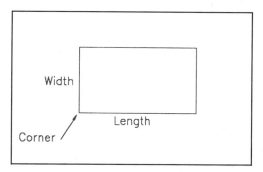
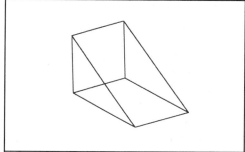

The prompts are the same for the wedge as for the box. The height for the wedge is always drawn from the corner originally specified.

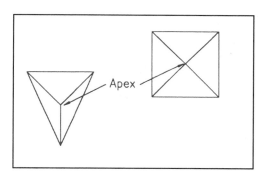
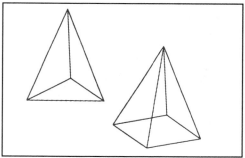

Pyramids can be constructed with three- or four-sided bases; you are prompted to specify lengths for the three or four (tetrahedron) sides. The sides of the base need not be equal. Specification for the apex must have x, y, and z coordinates. The easiest way to do this is to use filters and pick the x-y point from the screen and specify z from the keyboard.

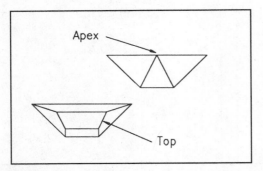

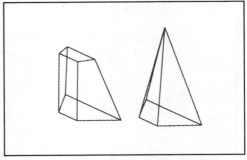

The apex of the pyramid can be placed off to one side. If you want a flat-topped pyramid, specify Top (T). The x,y,z coordinates must be specified for each point on the top face. (The Ridge option is not as useful, so it is not dealt with in this book).

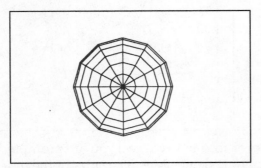

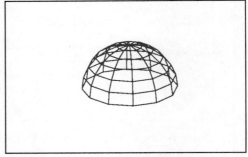

The dome is constructed by first specifying the center and then the radius. The number of segments determines how smooth the dome will be. Start by accepting the defaults and adjust them if necessary. You can modify these shapes but first they have to be exploded. The dome can then be flattened by removing the bottom segments, or an opening (like the oculus in the Pantheon) can be placed in the top by erasing the center section.

✦ VPORTS

It is sometimes useful to see more than one view of your drawing. The Vports command allows you to divide your screen into different ports, each able to have a separate view. Although only one viewport can be active at a time, commands can be started in one viewport and carried over into another one, enabling you to work in multiple views.

Command Finder

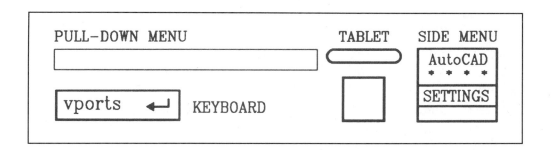

✦ Vports Options

2,3,4	*See explanation in "Using the Vports Command."*
Join	Ports can be joined as long as they are adjacent and their joining forms a rectangle. With Join you can design various types of viewport configurations.
SIngle	Returns your monitor to the full screen; the resulting image is the one from the last current viewport.
Save	Saves a configuration with a given name so that you can retrieve it later. The view and settings in each port are saved.
Restore	Brings back a previously saved viewport configuration.
Delete	Removes viewport configurations that you no longer need.

✦ Using the Vports Command

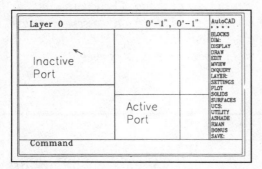
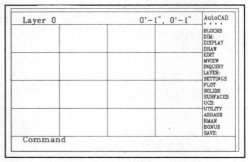

The default setting is 3, with the largest port to the right, but you can have up to 16 ports. Each viewport will be divided by the number that you pick, after you have specified whether the division is to be horizontal or vertical.

You can distinguish the active port by the cross-hair cursor. In nonactive ports the cross hair changes to an arrow. Ports are activated by moving the cursor into the port and pressing the pick button.

✦ Tip

Each viewport can have its own settings, such as snap, grid, 3-D view, and pan and zoomed orientation. You can set up your prototype drawing with a viewport configuration.

✦ VPOINT

Lets you pick the orientation for viewing your drawing in 3-D. The visual method provides a circle and a tripod to help you orient your view; the other methods are combinations of picking views and entering angles or coordinates.

Command Finder

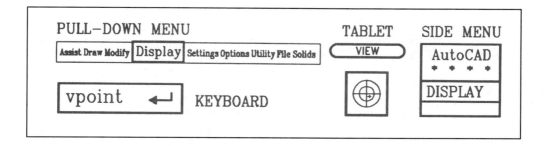

✦ Using the Vpoint Command

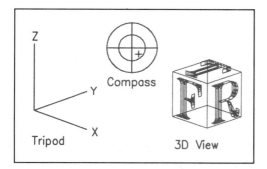

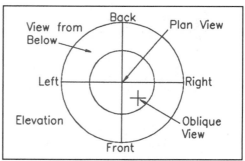

If you respond to the Vpoint command by pressing ⏎, the compass and tripod will appear on your screen. As you move your cursor, the tripod moves to simulate the orientation of your drawing.

You choose your view by moving your cursor within the small circle. The small circle represents the view of the top of the object; the larger circle is the view from below the object. For most purposes, you will only be working in the small circle. Where the cross hairs intersect is the plan view. The small circle itself represents elevations at ground level. The space in between increases the viewing angle from ground to plan to produce an oblique view.

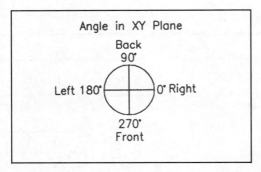

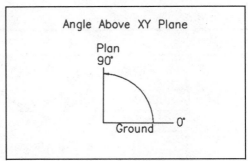

The Rotate option requires you to specify two angles: an angle *in* the x-y plane and an angle *above* the x-y plane. The view of the cube in the first drawing in this section is 315 degrees in the x-y plane and 20 degrees from (above) the x-y plane. You can respond to the View point option by entering x, y, and z coordinates, but the previous two options are more intuitive.

✦ Vpoint Notes

- Vpoint lets you specify a view direction but not distance. You can use Zoom to change the magnification.
- The views you get by using Vpoint are parallel (axonometric) projections. To get a perspective view, use the Dview command.
- Selecting Vpoint 3D from the Display pull-down menu provides a screen of Vpoint orientation choices. You still must specify the angle from the x-y plane (height).

✦ PLAN

Restores your 3-D image to a plan view.

Command Finder

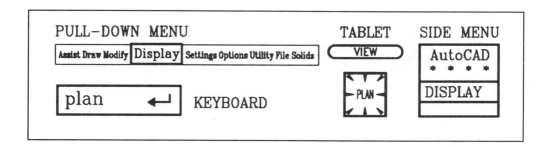

PULL–DOWN MENU

| Assist Draw Modify | Display | Settings Options Utility File Solids |

TABLET
VIEW
PLAN

SIDE MENU
AutoCAD
✶ ✶ ✶ ✶
DISPLAY

plan   ↵   KEYBOARD

✦ Using the Plan Command

A simple ↵ will bring back your plan view when you are in the 3-D view.

UCS stands for *user coordinate system*, which is a reorientation of the x, y, and z coordinates by the user. (This book uses the *world coordinate system*.) Because some users work in more than one coordinate system, the Plan command provides the option of returning to the plan view of a specific coordinate system.

✦ HIDE

Obscures lines and planes that lie behind other objects. The Hide command has different effects on different entities. Depending on the size of your drawing, removing hidden lines can take from a few minutes to hours.

Command Finder

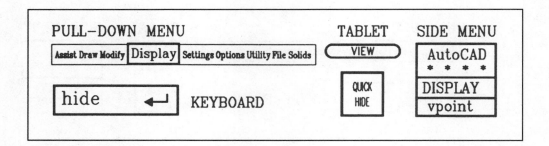

✦ Using the Hide Command

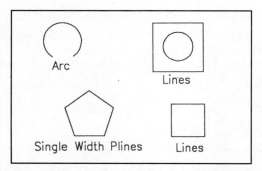

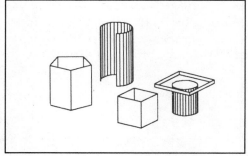

The Hide command works automatically to produce views with hidden lines removed. Vertical surfaces of extruded lines, single-width polylines, and arcs will be rendered opaque. However, these entities have no top or bottom and as a result, horizontal surfaces appear transparent. Hide used in the plan view with these entities has no effect.

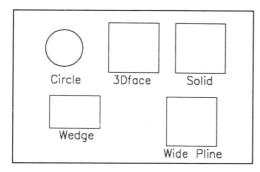

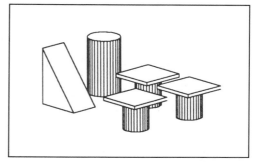

All the surfaces of circles, 3-D solids, and wide polylines and those surfaces produced by 3Dface and Solid look opaque when hidden. These objects will appear to have closed tops and bottoms. Hide used in the plan view obscures objects that lie under these entities.

✦ Hide Notes

- Wide Plines and surfaces produced with the Solid command will hide objects even when Fill is off.

- The hidden-line effect is only temporary. Objects revert to wire-frame mode as soon as you use a command that requires a regeneration or you use Zoom or Pan.

- A saved view will not save your drawing with the hidden lines removed, but you can make a slide showing the lines hidden.

- When you want to plot a drawing with the hidden lines removed, you have to use the Hide option of the Plot command—and yes, it takes a long time.

- Every so often, some lines that should be hidden won't be. This is caused by minute round-off errors in calculating the position of two objects that touch.

✦ **Tip**

You can shorten the time it takes to hide a view by zooming in to a smaller portion of the drawing. Hide works on the number of lines displayed on your screen—the fewer the lines, the shorter the time.

✦ DVIEW

*Stands for **dynamic viewing**. This is the command that makes perspective views. It also enables you to work interactively to get the views you want instead of using the static View command.*

Command Finder

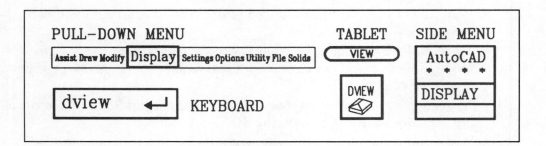

```
PULL-DOWN MENU                              TABLET      SIDE MENU
┌───────────────────────────────────────┐  ┌─────────┐ ┌──────────┐
│ Assist Draw Modify │Display│ Settings   │  │  VIEW   │ │ AutoCAD  │
│                            Options      │  └─────────┘ │ ✦ ✦ ✦ ✦  │
│                            Utility File │  ┌─────────┐ ├──────────┤
│                            Solids       │  │ DVIEW   │ │ DISPLAY  │
│ ┌─────────────────┐                     │  │  ▱      │ │          │
│ │ dview      ↵    │  KEYBOARD           │  └─────────┘ └──────────┘
│ └─────────────────┘                     │
└───────────────────────────────────────┘
```

✦ Dview Options

POints	Hide
CAmera	PAn
TArget	Zoom
Distance	TWist

Off   Undo
CLip   eXit

✦ Using the Dview Command

The first prompt, which you have to respond to before you can use any of the options, asks you to select the object. If it is a complicated drawing, limit the parts you choose to those that define the boundary edges or show the identifying features. The fewer entities you pick, the quicker your view will be displayed. The side menu offers the option of selecting entities by layer.

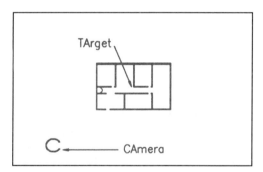

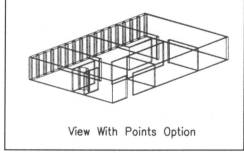

View With Points Option

The Points option is a good starting place for manipulating 3-D views. You are asked to enter the target point and then the camera point. The default starting point for the target is the center of the screen. A rubber-banding line extends from the target point and follows the movement of your cursor to help you visualize the sight line when you pick the camera location.

Pick the points on the screen using .xy filters, and give the height when prompted for the z-coordinate. Alternatively, you can just pick points on the screen and set heights later with the Camera and Target options.

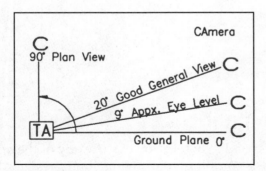
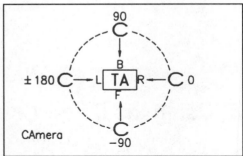

With Camera you can fine-tune your view. You are first prompted for the angle from the x-y plane and then the angle in the x-y plane. You can think of the angle *from* the x-y plane as height above the ground plane (excluding below for this example) and the angle *in* the x-y plane as rotation on the ground plane. You can pick the points using x-y filters, or you can specify rotation and elevation by using slider bars. The slider end is fixed at the value representing your current view; you move the diamond shape to the new location.

The vertical slider adjusts height and is very intuitive. Plan view is 90 degrees and 0 is at the horizon or in line with the target. When using the horizontal slider to pick the angle in the x-y plane, the drawing pivots as though it were on a turntable. Front view is –90 degrees. As you move the slider to the right, the object rotates clockwise (left). The views are as though you were walking around the object in a counterclockwise direction. Actually, it may seem more natural to move the camera than the target, but you do have the option to move the target while the camera is stationary.

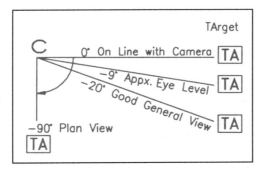

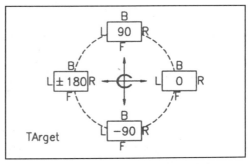

In the Target option, the numbers have the opposite sign from those for Camera: Plan view is −90 and front view is +90 degrees. As with the sliders in the Camera option, the vertical slider affects elevation, and the horizontal slider affects movement in the x-y plane. As you move the horizontal slider to the right, the target revolves around a center point in a counterclockwise direction.

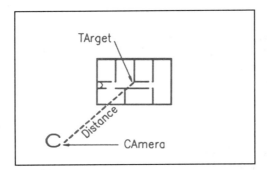

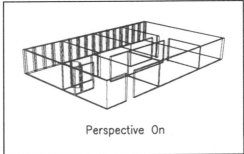

Perspective On

The Distance option turns on perspective, which is determined by the distance between the target and camera. Although you may have set the distance with the Points option, you will again be prompted for distance; the default is the original distance you specified. If you have not previously set the camera to target distance, the default is 1 *inch*. The slider bar on the top of the screen is a multiplier of the default number in the prompt area.

The Off option turns perspective viewing off. The Clip option removes portions of your drawing that are obscuring portions you want to show. The target is considered to be at 0. A negative distance places a clipping plane behind the target, and a positive distance places it in front. Using the slider and watching the effect is the easiest way to perform this function.

Clipping works best with straight-on views: left, right, front, and back. Oblique views result in walls with odd diagonal sections clipped out. You can achieve better results by placing unwanted walls on a separate layer and freezing that layer.

The Hide option in Dview provides only a temporary hide, useful in helping you set up your view. To actually get a view with hidden lines removed, you have to use the Hide command outside the Dview command.

The Pan option repositions the image on the screen. Once you exit Dview, the standard Pan command will not work on a perspective view. The Zoom option operates as the standard zoom function when you are *not* in perspective. When you are working in perspective, Zoom changes to the camera-lens specification. Standard is 55, wide is approximately 35 and widens the view, and narrow is about 155 and produces a telephoto view. A wide-angle lens is a good choice for buildings.

✦   **Note**

Zoom doesn't affect the perspective view, because the distance for perspective depends on the distance you set between the camera and the target point, not on AutoCAD's zoom function, which is based on the drawing extents. Once you exit Dview, the standard Zoom command will not work on a perspective view.

The Twist option rotates the ground plane (this is more appropriate, for example, for views of planes taking off or landing). The Undo option reverses the effect of the last thing you did in Dview. You can step back and undo successive operations. The Exit option takes you out of Dview with the view you have made. An extra ⏎ does the same.

✦ Dview Tips

- When you use the Distance option to get perspective and have not previously set the distance for the camera with the Points option, the default distance for the camera is 1". This ant's-eye view of your space generally results in a blank screen. Depending upon the size of your building or space, this distance should range from 30 to 300 feet.

- Use the house icon to try out the different options. Zoom out so the house is quite small to avoid the common problem of being so close to your image that you can't see it.

- By setting your coordinate readout to On, you can use the numbers to provide information when placing camera and target points.

- If you get disoriented, exit Dview, get a plan view, and start again.

- If you press ⏎ after the options, the default settings are those of the existing view. You can use these numbers to make adjustments to your view.

- Distances can only be set with the Points and Distance options. Camera and Target change the orientation between Camera and Target only.

- Zoom affects the wide or narrow angle aspect of your perspective and should not be substituted for Distance.

- Use Undo alot if what you get is not what you want.

✦ SHADE

The Shade command is a sample from another AutoCAD program called AutoShade and is beyond the scope of this book. It produces shaded images of drawings and has a single, fixed light source (modifying the variable Shadedge produces different effects). You can make slides of, but cannot plot, these images.

✦ TUTORIAL: TRANSFORMING 2-D INTO 3-D

In your use of AutoCAD so far, you have been drawing mostly in two dimensions. In this lesson you will complete the transition from 2-D to 3-D. Although working drawings are done in 2-D, the third dimension contributes greatly to the understanding of a space—both for the architect and designer and for their clients. New techniques using animation, rendering, sound, and video are all being explored as tools for producing more effective presentations. But it all begins with 3-D.

*Drawing an item in 3-D is similar to actually constructing it. Each part must be made, and the sequence of putting together all the parts is important. In this lesson, you will draw new 3-D furniture and replace 2-D furniture by updating the office plan with **oldblock=new block.** You also will modify some 2-D blocks directly by giving them height/thickness.*

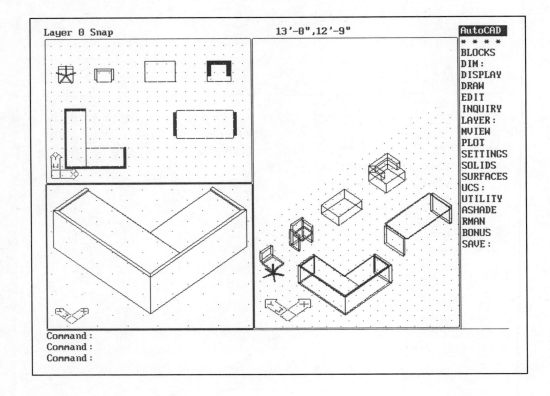

This lesson uses a variety of entities to make 3-D furniture; in this way you can see the effect the Hide command has on the various entities. Start by editing the PLAN drawing.

✦1   We can finally use the UCS icon. Use the Ucsicon command to turn it on.

✦2   Divide the screen into three viewports using the Vports default configuration. Your screen will look like the one at the beginning of the tutorial, except that the plan view will be in all the viewports.

> Command: **VPORTS**
> Save/Restore/Delete/Join/SIngle/?/2/<3>/4: ⏎
> Horizontal/Vertical/Above/Below/Left/<Right>: ⏎

✦3   Leave the plan view in the upper-left port, but change the view in the large port to a 3-D view. Remember, to activate a port, you move your cursor into that port and press the pick button; the arrow will change to cross hairs, indicating that this is the active port.

> Command: **VPOINT**
> Rotate/<View point> <0'-0",0'-0",0'-1">: **R**
> Enter angle in X-Y plane from X axis <270>: **225**
> Enter angle from X-Y plane <90>: **45**

If you want to access Vpoint from the pull-down menu by picking Display and Vpoint 3D, it is the box to the left of the Front button and below the Left Side button on the icon screen; you still have to specify the angle from the x-y plane.

✦4   As you can see, only the doors and windows have vertical dimensions. Before you go on to the furniture, change the height/thickness of the walls. If 0 is not the current layer, make it so and then turn off all the other layers. This way, it is easier to change only the walls. When you are finished, turn the layers back on and make FURN the active layer.

```
Command: CHANGE
Select objects: W (Window the entire plan)
Properties/<Change point>: P
Change what property (Color/LAyer/LType/Thickness)?   T
New thickness <0'-0">: 8'
```

◆ **5**   Change the elevation and thickness of the conference table. You must explode the block first to be able to change it. When the block is exploded, the drawing will revert to layer 0. Change it back to layer FURN.

It is not necessary to draw a base, because the chairs around the table will hide it. Use the Change command to give the top thickness and the Move command to raise the top 27" from the floor.

Activate the lower left-hand port and use it to zoom in and get close-up views of the objects you are working on. You can observe the changes taking place in 3-D in the large viewport.

```
Command: CHANGE
Select objects: Select conference table edge
Properties/<Change point>: P
Change what property (Color/LAyer/LType/Thickness)?   T
New thickness <0'-0">: 1-1/2
```

```
Command: MOVE
Select objects: P
Previous Base point or displacement: 0,0,27 (Raises the top 27" in z)
Second point of displacement: ⏎
```

◆ **6**   To make a 3-D file, you will modify the old block to give it height and then redefine the original File block. First, insert another file, explode it, and change the height to 3'. Then remake the block with the same name. Remember that the insertion point is the midpoint of the line at the back of the file.

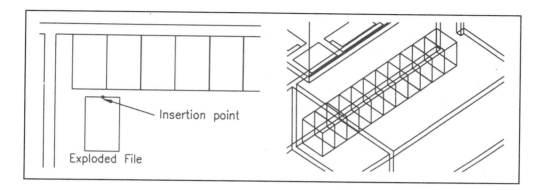

Insertion point

Exploded File

Command: **BLOCK**
Block name (or ?): **FILE**
Block FILE already exists.
Redefine it? <N> **Y**
Insertion base point: MID of   *Pick back of file*
Select objects: **W**
Block FILE redefined.

✦ **7**   The receptionist's desk is lying on the floor. You will make the
panel legs by using plines and will offset the desk ends as
guidelines. (It is difficult to line up the edges of wide plines.) The
desk top will be given thickness and raised from the floor—it's
just like actually building it. Zoom as you need to.

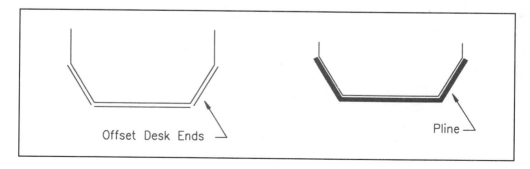

Offset Desk Ends

Pline

Command: **OFFSET**
Offset distance or Through <Through>: **1**
Select object to offset: *Pick one of the edges*
Side to offset: *Pick outside of desk edge*

Repeat for the other two edges. Then, use Fillet with a radius of 0
to join the three sections into a continuous line.

Command: **FILLET**
Polyline/Radius/<Select first object>: *Join first two sections*
Polyline/Radius/<Select first object>: *Join remaining sections*

Draw a panel leg by using Pline with a width of 1", and draw over
the guidelines.

Command: **PLINE**
From point: *Use END Osnap*
Arc/Close/Halfwidth/Length/Undo/Width/<Endpoint of line>: **W**
Starting width <0'-0">: **1** (Sets width to 1")
Ending width <0'-1">: ⏎

✦8 Give the panel leg height/thickness.

Command: **CHANGE**
Select objects: **L**
Properties/<Change point>: **P**
Change what property (Color/LAyer/LType/Thickness)?   **T**
New thickness <0'-0">: **30**

✦9 Mirror the leg to the other side of the desk using the midpoint of
the desk as the mirror line.

Command: **MIRROR**
Select objects: *Pick the panel leg*
First point of mirror line: MID of   *Desk top*
Second point: <Ortho on> ⏎
Delete old objects? <N> ⏎

✦ **10**   Raise and give thickness to the desk top.

> Command: **CHANGE**
> Select objects: **W** (Window the whole desk)
> Select objects: **R** (Remove the two panel legs)
> Properties/<Change point>: **P**
> Change what property (Color/LAyer/LType/Thickness)?   **T**
> New thickness <0'-0">: **1-1/2**
>
> Command: **MOVE**
> Select objects: **P**
> Previous Base point or displacement: **0,0,29**
> Second point of displacement: ⏎

✦ **11**   Now go on to more serious 3-D dimensioning. End this drawing.
Start a new one called *Furn3D=A24*. This uses the old prototype
drawing to set up a new one.

Because there are many steps to perform in 3-D drawing, the command prompts in
the following part of the tutorial have been abstracted to provide just the information
needed for your input. Your drawing layout does not have to look like the drawing
at the beginning of the tutorial. This drawing is used as a workspace to make blocks
of 3-D furniture. You will first make the drawings and then Wblock them.

✦ **1**   Divide the screen into two ports. Make one a plan view and the
other a 3-D view. The technique is to work in plan view and watch
the results in 3-D view.

> Command: **VPORTS**
> Save/Restore/Delete/Join/SIngle/?/2/<3>/4: **2**
> Horizontal/<Vertical>: **H** (You may prefer V)
>
> Command: **VPOINT**
> Rotate/<View point> <0.0000,0.0000,1.0000>: **R**
> Enter angle in X-Y plane from X axis <270>: **225**
> Enter angle from X-Y plane <90>: **45**

.2 You will draw the side table using the 3D Object called Box. From the pull-down menus, select Draw and then 3D Construction. These objects are created using a AutoLISP routine that is automatically loaded when you request 3D Objects. It takes a while, so AutoCAD asks you to wait.

> 3D Objects **BOX**
> Please wait...Loading 3D Objects. nil (loaded with no error)
> Corner of box: *Place anywhere*
> Length: **3'2**
> Cube/<Width>: **2'4**
> Height: **15**
> Rotation angle about Z axis: **0** (You must specify something to get out of the command)

.3 When drawing the three-dimensional side chair, using Pline makes it easier to select the different sections when you are changing elevation or thickness. The technique is to draw each part—seat, back, and arms—and change their thickness and elevation immediately after you draw them. This allows you to use the Previous (P) and Last (L) options as selections when working with the editing commands.

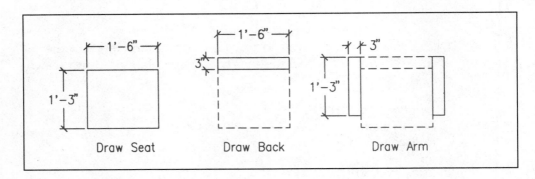

Command: **PLINE**

+4   Draw the seat of the side chair.

+5   Change the thickness of the seat to 2 inches, and then move the
           seat up 15 inches.

> Command: **CHANGE**
> Select objects: **L**
> Change what property (Color/LAyer/LType/Thickness)?   **T**
> New thickness <0'-0">: **2**
>
> Command: **MOVE**
> Select objects: **P**
> Base point or displacement: **0,0,15**
> Second point of displacement: ⏎

+6   Draw the back of the chair. Drawing in 3-D is different from draw-
           ing in two dimensions, because you have to draw all the planes.

> Command: **PLINE** (Draw all four sides)

+7   Change the back thickness to 32". The back and arms of this chair
           have been designed as panels and go to the floor.

> Command: **CHANGE**
> Select objects: **L**
> Change what property (Color/LAyer/LType/Thickness)?   **T**
> New thickness <0'-0">: **32**

+8   Draw one of the arms.

> Command: **PLINE** (Draw all four sides)

✦**9**   Change the arm thickness to 26".

Command: **CHANGE**
Select objects: **L**
Change what property (Color/LAyer/LType/Thickness)?   **T**
New thickness <0'-0">: **26**

✦**10**   Mirror the other arm to the other side of the chair.

Command: **MIRROR** (Use the midpoint of the chair seat as the mirror line)

✦**11**   You will draw the lounge chair using a combination of 3D Objects and wide plines.

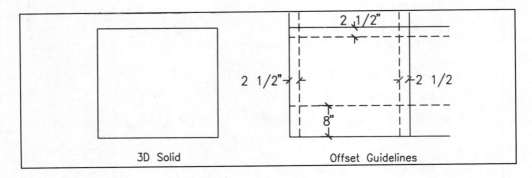

3D Objects **BOX**
Corner of box:
Length: **30**
Cube/<Width>: **28**
Height: **15**
Rotation angle about Z axis: **0**

◆ **12**   Make guidelines for the centerlines of the plines.

> Command: **LINE** (Draw four construction lines marking the ends of all four sides)
>
> Command: **OFFSET** (Offset the front side 8" inward)
> Command: **OFFSET** (Offset the other three sides 2-1/2" inward)

◆ **13**   Using the guidelines, draw the back and side of the lounge with a pline, with a width of 5". Turn on Fill if it is not already on.

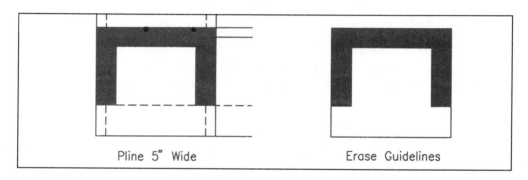

Pline 5" Wide   Erase Guidelines

> Command: **PLINE** (Use INT Osnap)
> Command: **ERASE** (Turn Osnap off and erase the construction lines)

◆ **14**   Change the thickness and height of the pline you just drew.

> Command: **CHANGE**
> Select objects: **L**
> Change what property (Color/LAyer/LType/Thickness)?   **T**
> New thickness <0'-0">: **10**
>
> Command: **MOVE**
> Select objects: **P**
> Base point or displacement: **0,0,15**
> Second point of displacement: ⏎

✦ **15** To make the executive desk, you will use plines for the legs and a 3Dface to make the top opaque.

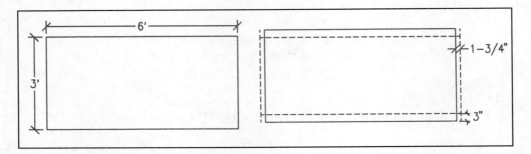

First, draw the outline of the desk top using the dimensions shown. Then, make guidelines for the panel leg using the lines from the desk.

Command: **OFFSET** (Offset the sides of the desk outward 1-3/4")
Command: **OFFSET** (Offset the front and back edges of the desk inward 3")
Command: **EXTEND** (Extend the lines to get intersections)

✦ **16** Draw the side panel legs with a width of 3".

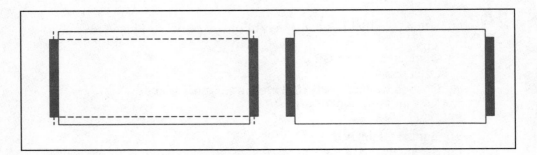

Command: **PLINE** (Use INT Osnap)
Command: **ERASE** (Turn Osnap off and erase the guidelines)

✦**17** Change the height/thickness of the two legs.

Command: **CHANGE**
Select objects: *Pick both legs*
Change what property (Color/LAyer/LType/Thickness)? **T**
New thickness <0'-0">: **30**

✦**18** Put a 3Dface on the desk top. Use an END Osnap to make sure
that the face edges match the top exactly. Remember to pick the
points by going sequentially around the perimeter (not like Solid).

Command: **3DFACE**
First point:
Second point:
Third point:
Fourth point: (Specify only four corners; do not duplicate first point)
Third point: ⏎

✦**19** Window the desk top and move it to an elevation of 29". It is
easier to window the entire desk and remove the two side panels
with the Remove (R) option than to try to pick only the desk top.
This will move both the desk top and the 3Dface.

Command: **MOVE**
Select objects: **W** (Window whole desk)
Select objects: **R** (Remove legs)
Base point or displacement: **0,0,29**
Second point of displacement: ⏎

♦ **20**   To get a top with thickness, specify a thickness of –1-1/2". Because 3Dfaces cannot have thickness, this gives the top an extrusion thickness while leaving the face on the desk top. 3Dfaces are difficult to separate from the lines they are drawn upon, so workarounds like this one have been developed.

Command: **CHANGE**
Select objects: *Select the desk top*
Change what property (Color/LAyer/LType/Thickness)?   **T**
New thickness <0'-0">: **–1-1/2**
Change what property (Color/LAyer/LType/Thickness)?   ⏎
Cannot change thickness of 3dFaces *(OK by us)*

♦ **21**   The process for the workstation is similar to the one used for the executive desk.

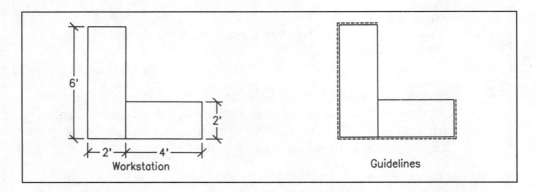

Draw the workstation using the dimensions shown. Make guidelines for the panel using the lines from the desk.

Command: **OFFSET** (Offset outside edges 1-1/4")
Command: **FILLET** (Use 0 radius to make corners intersect)

✦ **22**   Put a 3Dface on the desk top. Do each section separately.

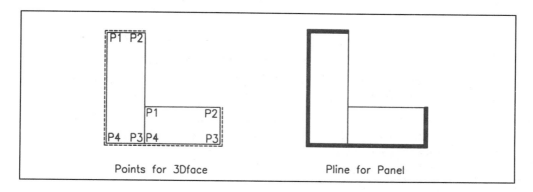

Points for 3Dface   Pline for Panel

Command: **3DFACE**
First point: (Use End Osnap to place points at desk corners)
Second point:
Third point:
Fourth point: (When you specify this point, AutoCAD closes the polygon)
Third point: ⏎

Command: **3DFACE** (Do the same for the other section)

Draw the panel around the desk with a 2" wide pline.

Command: **PLINE** (Use End Osnap to draw pline)

✦ **23**   Give the panel thickness/height.

Command: **CHANGE**
Change what property (Color/LAyer/LType/Thickness)?   **T**
New thickness <0'-0">: **30**

✦ **24**   Elevate the desk top and 3Dface. As in the executive desk, window the entire workstation and remove the panels from the selection.

> Command: **MOVE**
> Select objects: **W** (Window the whole workstation)
> Select objects: **R** (Remove panels)
> Base point or displacement: **0,0,29**
> Second point of displacement: ⏎

✦ **25**   Once again you will fool AutoCAD, as you did when you made the executive desk and gave the top thickness while leaving the face on the desk top.

> Command: **CHANGE**
> Select objects: *Select both sections of the desk top*
> Change what property (Color/LAyer/LType/Thickness)?   **T**
> New thickness <0'-0">: **–1-1/2** (remember the minus sign)
> Change what property (Color/LAyer/LType/Thickness)?   ⏎
> Cannot change thickness of 3dFaces *(AutoCAD fooled again)*

✦ **26**   The best is for last—the desk chair. Start by constructing the base, which is made up of a wedge that is one of the 3D Objects.

> 3D Objects **WEDGE**
> Corner of wedge: *Place anywhere*
> Length: **12**
> Width: **1**
> Height: **2**
> Rotation angle about Z axis: **90**

◆**27** Draw a circle for the post and give it thickness/height.

> Command: **CIRCLE**
> 3P/2P/TTR/<Center point>: *Select a Point*
> Diameter/<Radius>: **D**
> Diameter: **1.5**
>
> Command: **CHANGE**
> Select objects: **L**
> Change what property (Color/Elev/LAyer/LType/Thickness)?   **T**
> New thickness <0'-0">: **19**

◆**28** Move the circle to the edge of the wedge using Osnap overrides

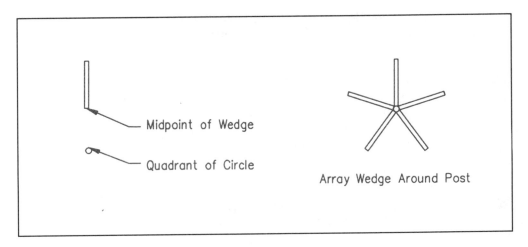

Midpoint of Wedge

Quadrant of Circle

Array Wedge Around Post

for exact placement.

> Command: **MOVE**
> Select objects: *Pick the circle*
> Base point or displacement: **QUA** (Pick upper quadrant of circle)
> of Second point of displacement: **MID**
> of   *Pick midpoint on width of wedge*

Array the wedge around the circle.

> Command: **ARRAY**
> Select objects: *Select the wedge*
> Rectangular or Polar array (R/P): **P**
> Center point of array: **CEN**
> of *Pick a point on the circle*
> Number of items: **5**
> Angle to fill (+=ccw, −=cw) <360>: ⏎
> Rotate objects as they are copied? <Y> ⏎

✦ **29** Draw the chair seat and back with Pline. Draw all four sides of both parts.

> Command: **PLINE** (Draw a seat 18" × 18")
> Command: **PLINE** (Draw a back 18" × 3")

✦ **30** Change the thickness of the seat and its elevation.

> Command: **CHANGE**
> Change what property (Color/Elev/LAyer/LType/Thickness)?   **T**
> New thickness <0'-0">: **3**
>
> Command: **MOVE**
> Select objects: **P** (Pick seat)
> Base point or displacement: **0,0,16**
> Second point of displacement: ⏎

✦ **31** Change the thickness of the back and its elevation.

> Command: **CHANGE**
> Change what property (Color/Elev/LAyer/LType/Thickness)?   **T**
> New thickness <0'-0">: **15**

Command: **MOVE**
Select objects: **P** (Pick seat back)
Base point or displacement: **0,0,19**
Second point of displacement: ⏎

✦ **32**   Move the seat and back onto the base.

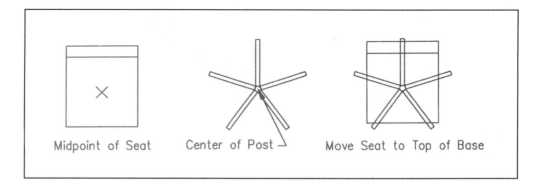

Midpoint of Seat   Center of Post ⌐   Move Seat to Top of Base

Command: **MOVE**
Select objects: *Select both seat and back*
(Use filters to select the center of the seat)
Base point or displacement: **.X**
of MID
of (need YZ): **MID**
of Second point of displacement: **CEN** (Select edge of circle)

✦**33**   To make the seat and back of the chair appear opaque so that the base will not show through, put a 3Dface on them. Use the END Osnap to pick the points in one direction around the perimeter.

   Command: **3DFACE** (Pick the four corners of the seat)

✦**34**   Change the elevation of the 3Dface to the top of the seat.

   Command: **MOVE**
   Select objects: **L** (This selects the 3Dface)
   Base point or displacement: **0,0,3**
   Second point of displacement: [↵]

✦**35**   Follow the same procedure for the back, making the 3Dface and then moving it up.

   Command: **3DFACE** (Pick the four corners of the seat back)

✦**36**   Change the elevation of the 3Dface to the top of the seat back.

   Command: **MOVE**
   Select objects: **L** (This selects the 3Dface)
   Base point or displacement: **0,0,15**
   Second point of displacement: [↵]

You have finished making all the furniture in 3-D. The next step is to Wblock these pieces and to replace the 2-D pieces in the PLAN drawing with the ones you just made. Keeping the correct names for the blocks is important and will make the instructions easier to follow.

✦**1** Wblock the items you have drawn, giving them the insertion points and names shown in the drawing.

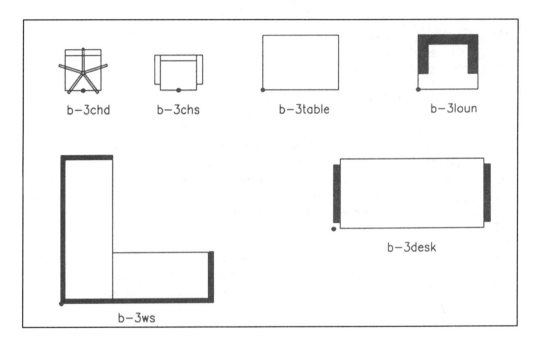

✦**2** Edit the PLAN drawing, use the existing 3-D view or make a new one, and redefine the blocks. When asked for the insertion point, press CTRL C . If you have Regenauto turned off, you must regenerate the drawing after the block is redefined.

Command: **INSERT**

Insert the following:

b-chd=b-3chd
b-chs=b-3chs
b-table=b-3table
b-loun=b-3loun
b-ws=b-3ws
b-desk=b-3desk

✦**3**   You will notice that the sofa that you made by stretching the lounge chair was not updated. That is because you exploded it so you could stretch it. To make a new sofa, erase the old block and insert the new one, explode it, and stretch it again. You will have to change it back to the FURN layer.

✦**4**   If you want the files to have a top so that you do not see through them, put a 3Dface on them. Use a height of 36-1/4". Adding the little extra ensures that there is no round-off error between the files and the top.

✦**5**   Now it's time to take a look at the plan in both axonometric and perspective views. To get a view of the reception area and the conference room, put the left outside wall and conference wall on a separate layer. Call it *HIDE* and freeze it. In doing drawings for presentations, it is often necessary to hide walls and objects that obscure views.

◆ **6**   Although a 45-degree angle from the X-Y plane is good for working, for a presentation 20 degrees is a more pleasing angle. The
drawing has been slightly rotated to give a better view.

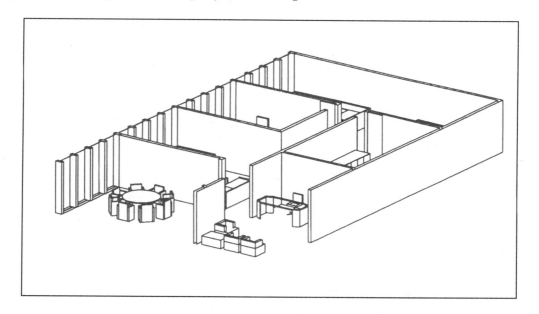

This axonometric view was made with the following settings:

```
Command: VPOINT
Rotate/<View point>: R8
Enter angle in X-Y plane from X axis: 210
Enter angle from X-Y plane <20>: ↵
```

✦ **7**

To get a perspective of the office, start with the viewport where you have the plan view. Zoom out so that you have room to place the camera.

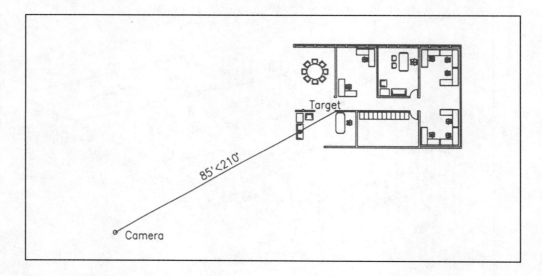

Command: **DVIEW**
Select objects: *Select the reception area*
CAmera/TArget/Distance/POints/PAn/Zoom/
TWist/CLip/Hide/Off/Undo/<eXit>: **PO**
Enter target point: **.XY** *(Use filters and END Osnap to pick wall next to reception desk)*
of (need Z): **5'** (Target height)
Enter camera point .XY *(Use filters and coordinate readout to place camera at 85' and 210 degrees from the target point)*
(need Z): **10'6** (Camera height)
CAmera/TArget/Distance/POints/PAn/Zoom/
TWist/CLip/Hide/Off/Undo/<eXit>: **D**
New camera/target distance <85'-0">: ⏎ (Distance already specified)
CAmera/TArget/Distance/POints/PAn/Zoom/
TWist/CLip/Hide/Off/Undo/<eXit>: **X**

Your plan is now in perspective and should look like this after the
hidden lines have been removed:

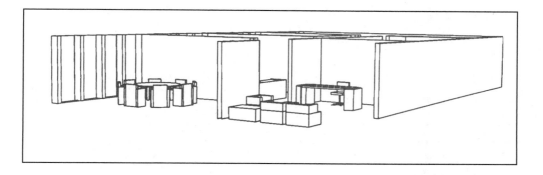

♦ **8** Before you end the session, save the perspective view, because
you will need it in the next lesson.

Command: **VIEW**
Save: **PERSP**

You have experimented with a number of different techniques to produce 3-D objects. Some are more successful than others, and some are easier to use. Extruded
forms are the easiest to use, but as you can see from the receptionist's desk, although their vertical surfaces are opaque, their top surfaces are not. Circles are
opaque on top. Plines are also opaque (as you can see from the lounge chair and
the desk), but in plan view they are filled and can produce a heavy appearance
on the plan if used excessively. 3Dfaces are opaque but are trickier to use. 3D Objects are meshes and are opaque, but they increase the size of your drawing.
Sometimes a simple extrusion will do; at other times, the presentation will require you to use all the 3-D tools available.

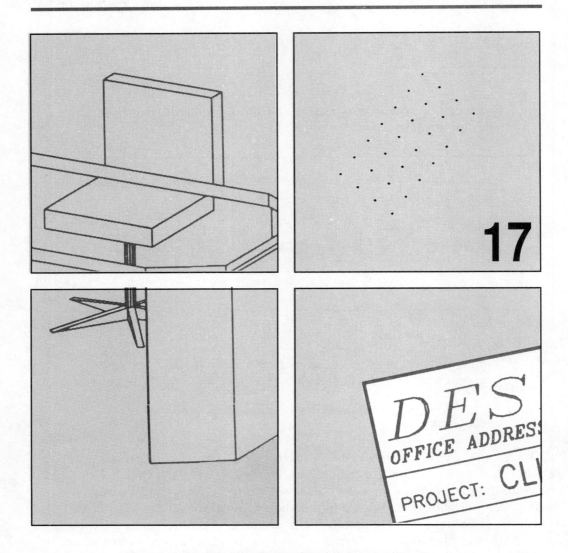

PLOTTING DRAWINGS

CAD doesn't seem real until you hold hard copy in your hands. This chapter steps you through the plotting commands and introduces you to Release 11's boon to plotting—paper space.

Before Release 11, if you wanted to plot a drawing that had various scales or had a 3-D view and plan view on a single sheet, you had to go through complex gyrations. All this can now be easily done through paper space.

- ✦ Plot
- ✦ Prplot
- ✦ Pspace
- ✦ Mspace
- ✦ Tilemode
- ✦ Mview
- ✦ Vplayer
- ✦ Zoom—XP

♦ PLOT

Controls the process by which you transfer your drawings to paper. Specific sizes of plots and numbers of pens are governed by the type of plotter you have.

Command Finder

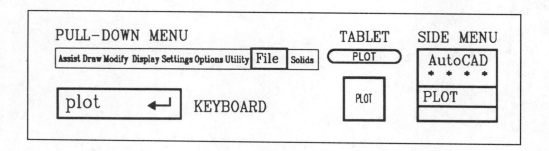

♦ Using the Plot Command

After you issue the Plot command, there are a number of AutoCAD prompts you must respond to:

> **What to plot—Display, Extents, Limits, View or Window:** Select the appropriate method.
>
> **Write the plot to file?:** Some systems allow you to write a plot to a file so that you can continue to draw while another station plots or so that you can plot the drawing later. Plots are not usually written to the file.
>
> **Size units (Inches or Millimeters):** Inches is more common.
>
> **Plot origin <0.00,0.00>:** A point in the lower left of the paper.
>
> **Standard values for plotting size (Size, Width, Height):** Lists the plot sizes available (depends upon your plotter).

Rotate plot 0/90/180/270: For plotters, 0 is a horizontal (landscape) orientation.

Pen width <0.010>: Generally, you can accept the default. Change it if you are dissatisfied with how your solid and wide plines plot. If you are using a PostScript printer as a plotter, this number controls the widths of the lines.

Area fill will NOT be adjusted for pen width: Use only when you need extremely accurate solid-filled areas. AutoCAD makes the adjustment based upon pen width. This is not an option for printers.

Remove hidden lines?: For 3-D drawings, responding Yes removes hidden lines.

Specify scale by entering: (Plotted Inches = Drawing Units or Fit): For architecture, you can enter the scale for the plot in actual architectural units (1/8" = 1'). The Fit option plots the drawing to fit the available paper space.

To pick pen assignments, you have to answer Y when the list appears that shows entity colors, pen numbers, and line types. The list contains seven color names; the additional colors will have numbers 8 through 15. To assign a pen to a color, enter a pen slot number next to the color.

AutoCAD strongly recommends that you leave the linetype setting at 0 and use the Linetype command to draw linetypes. The linetype setting in Plot uses the plotter's hardware to draw linetypes, which can lead to a lot of confusion.

✦ **Tip**

The Plot command is accessible from the Main Menu, allowing you to plot a drawing without having to bring it up on the screen. If your drawing is large, this saves time.

✦ PRPLOT

Uses a printer as a plotting device. PostScript printers, however, use the Plotter menu. As with the Plot command, the choices are machine-dependent.

Command Finder

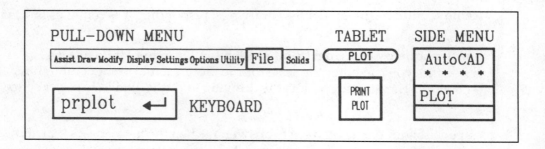

✦ Using the Prplot Command

Generally, the questions asked in Prplot are the same as in Plot, with these notable exceptions:

Plot origin <0.00,0.00>: A point in the upper left of the page.

Rotate plot 0/90/180/270: For printers, 0 is a vertical (portrait) orientation.

Pen width <0.010>: For laser printers, this number controls the widths of the lines; 0.003 is the thinnest.

Area fill will NOT be adjusted for pen width: Not applicable to printers.

Pen assignments: Not applicable to printers.

Prplot is also accessible from the Main Menu.

✦ PSPACE

*Stands for **paper space**; allows you unlimited ways to design your drawing sheet. You can produce plots with different scales and views on the same sheet.*

Command Finder

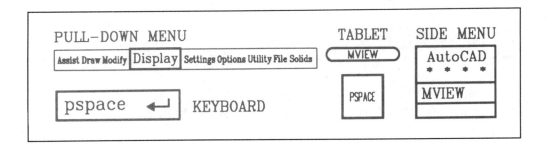

✦ Using the Pspace Command

In paper space you open up views of your actual drawing, now called *model space*. You actually manipulate two separate spaces: Mspace and Pspace, each with its own grid, scale limits, and layers.

When you are in paper space, a *P* appears on the status line, and the triangle icon appears in the lower-left part of your screen. You must set Tilemode to 0 before you can access paper space.

Vplayer and Mview work only in paper space. You can insert text in paper space and modify the size and location of the viewports with some of the editing commands: Copy, Scale, Move, Stretch, and Erase. Zoom XP and the standard Vports command do not work in paper space.

✦ Tip

If you become confused in paper space, reset Tilemode to 1. Once in model space, you will find your old drawing just as you left it. If necessary, you can start constructing paper space again—it's only paper, it's not the drawing.

When you plot your drawing, make sure that you issue the Plot command from Pspace.

✦ MSPACE

*Stands for **model space** (MS); it is a convenient way to get back into your original drawing once you have set Tilemode to 0. The standard AutoCAD commands work when you are in Mspace; the commands that are specific to paper space, Mview and Vplayer, do not.*

Command Finder

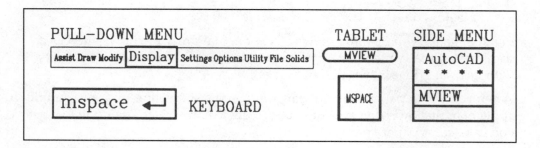

PULL-DOWN MENU	TABLET	SIDE MENU

PULL-DOWN MENU

Assist Draw Modify | Display | Settings Options Utility File Solids

mspace ↵   KEYBOARD

TABLET

MVIEW

MSPACE

SIDE MENU

AutoCAD
* * * *
MVIEW

✦ Using the Mspace Command

It is easier to work in Mspace, because you are switched to Pspace automatically for those commands that work only in Pspace. When fitting your view into the paper-space viewports, you are in Mspace. Take care that you use Zoom and Pan to manipulate the view. The Move command actually *moves* things in your drawing.

◆ TILEMODE

The variable that switches you from model space to paper space. When Tilemode is set to 1, you are in model space; when Tilemode is 0, you are in paper space.

Command Finder

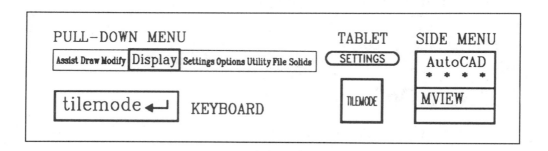

◆ MVIEW

The main command by which you manipulate paper space (Mview is the paper-space version of Vports). This command makes and controls paper viewports. Mview doesn't deal with the content of the ports, only the viewport frames. It will also remove hidden lines from selective viewports when you plot.

Command Finder

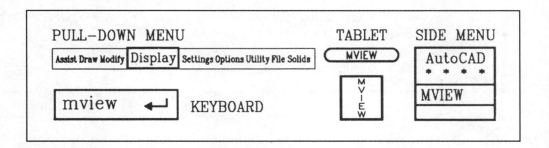

✦ Mview Options

First Point
Makes a custom-size paper viewport. When the port is drawn, the view that was current in model space fills the paper viewport. Subsequent paper viewports will automatically have the current paper viewport view.

Fit
Produces a paper viewport that fills the zoomed area of your screen (the maximum size is the limits of your paper space).

Restore
Copies a viewport configuration from model space into paper space. The Fit suboption asks you the size of the screen area for the configuration. The ? lists saved viewports in model space.

2/3/4
Similar to the 2/3/4 option in the Vports command in model space. It divides your screen into the specified number of paper ports in horizontal or vertical orientation. The Fit suboption sizes the configuration and moves it to the window area you specify.

On/Off
Turns selected paper viewports on or off by picking edges of the frame. Turning ports off saves regeneration time.

Hideplot   Removes hidden lines from the selected paper ports when plotting; Tilemode must be 0. Selections are made while in Pspace mode. The Plot command is issued from paper space. These settings will override the standard Plot command.

To change views inside paper viewports, go into Mspace and activate the paper port you want to change by pressing the pick button inside the port. Use any of the AutoCAD commands, such as Pan, Zoom, View, Viewpoint, and Dview, to get the view you want.

◆   **Note**

All the paper viewports can be moved and sized independently of one another.

◆ VPLAYER

Selectively controls layer visibility in paper viewports.

Command Finder

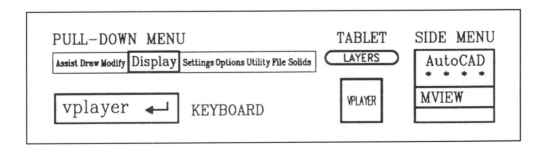

✦ Vplayer Options

Freeze/Thaw	Can be used by first making your choice to freeze or thaw, selecting the layers, and selecting whether this should apply to the current paper viewport (the default), all the paper viewports (A), or only those ports selected (S).
Vpvisdflt	Sets the layer visibility defaults for *subsequent* paper viewports.
Reset	Restores the Vpvisdflt settings in all (A) or only selected (S) paper viewports. You first specify the layers you want reset and then select the viewports that should be affected.
Newfrz	Creates new layers that are frozen in all paper viewports; this makes it simpler to thaw those layers you want to appear in selective paper viewports. (Vplayer does not override the frozen conditions set by the standard Layer command.)

The current viewport is wherever your cursor appears full-screen. In paper space, it is the whole page; in model space, it extends across the port you have picked.

✦ ZOOM—XP

Special option in the Zoom command, which is specifically used to scale images from model space into paper-space viewports. The option must be accessed from Mspace.

Command Finder

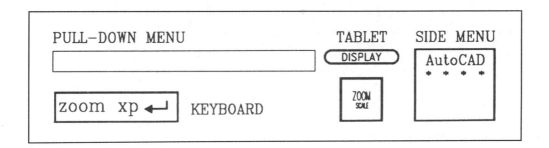

+ Using the XP Option

Select the paper viewport first, then use the Zoom command with the XP option
to specify what scale the image should be zoomed to. This number is the recipro-
cal of the scale factor. For example,

3′ = 1′	Zoom to 1/4 XP
1/2" = 1′	Zoom to 1/24 XP
1/4" = 1′	Zoom to 1/48 XP
1/8" = 1′	Zoom to 1/96 XP

✦ TUTORIAL: PLOTTING YOUR OFFICE PLAN

In this lesson you will plot your drawing of the office using standard plotting and plotting with paper space. Using the standard techniques, you will plot a plan view with the title block you drew in Chapter 12. Using paper space, you will plot the office drawing, showing plan view, perspective view, and an axonometric view of the receptionist's desk.

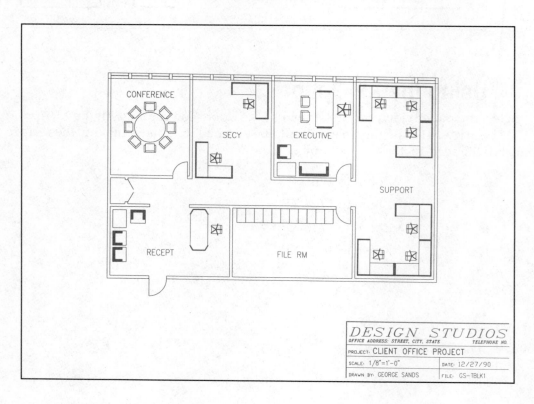

.1 Edit the Plan drawing. Get a plan view of the drawing, thaw the Hide layer you froze to get objects out of the way, and set Text as the current layer.

.2 Now you are ready to label the spaces in the drawing. Remember that the size of text, at least in model space, is dependent on the scale at which the drawing will be plotted. You will plot this drawing at 1/8"= 1′. For text to appear 1/8" high on the drawing, you will have to use a Dtext height of 12" (96 × 1/8). Make a new style, and label the spaces on the plan according to the drawing.

> Command: **STYLE**
> Text style name: **LABEL**
> Font file: **ROMANS**
> Height: **0**
> Set height with Dtext Width factor: **.85**

.3 You will plot the drawing on an A-size sheet. Draw a border of 82′ × 61′ with a Pline width of 1". These numbers may differ depending upon the plotter you are using. Essentially, the numbers represent the paper size (8 1/2 × 11) multiplied by 8 to get the plotting extents in feet. Plotters can never utilize the entire sheet, so the extents are always smaller than the actual paper size. Place the border on a layer called *Border*.

.4 Bring your title block into the drawing. Instead of inserting it as a block, bring it in as an Xref, because you will use the title block differently when you use paper space to plot a drawing.

```
Command: XREF
?/Bind/Detach/Path/Reload/<Attach>: A
Xref to Attach: TBLOCK
Attach Xref TBLOCK: TBLOCK
17TBLOCK loaded.
Insertion point: Lower-right corner
X scale factor<1>/Corner/XYZ: 96 (Scale factor for 1/8")
Y scale factor (default = X): 96
Rotation angle <0>:
```

◆**5**   Select the plan and border to be plotted.

```
Command: PLOT
Remove hidden lines? (No—there aren't any in plan view)
Plot scale: 1/8 = 1'
```

◆**6**   Detach the Xref.

```
Command: XREF
?/Bind/Detach/Path/Reload/<Attach>: D
Xref to Detach: TBLOCK
```

You will now set up and plot a drawing using paper space. With paper space, you can develop much more sophisticated plots. Arranging views on the final plot is more an art than a science. The plot you will do here only offers a hint of what you can do.

◆**7**   Set up three viewports, the largest one on top and the two smaller ones on the bottom. This is not a standard configuration, so you first have to divide the viewport in half horizontally and then divide the bottom half in two vertically.

```
Command: VPORTS
Save/Restore/Delete/Join/SIngle/?/2/<3>/4: 2
Horizontal/<Vertical>: H
```

Command: **VPORTS** (Pick the bottom viewport)
Save/Restore/Delete/Join/SIngle/?/2/<3>/4: **2**
Horizontal/<Vertical>: **V**

✦**8**   Restore the perspective view in the upper port. Keep the plan
view in the lower-left viewport, and use Vpoint to get an
axonometric view of the receptionist's desk in the lower-right
viewport. Zoom the desk so it looks similar to the drawing.

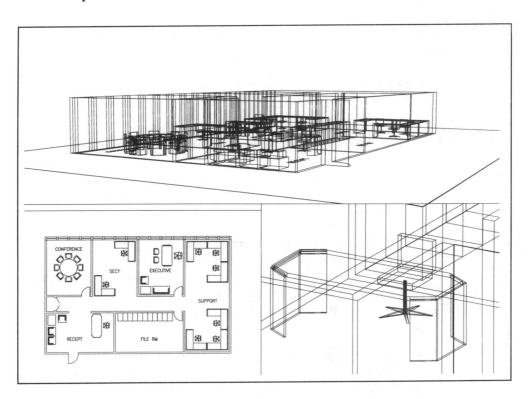

```
Command: VIEW
?/Delete/Restore/Save/Window: R
View name to restore: PERSP
```

```
Command: VPOINT
Rotate/<View point> <0'-0",0'-0",0'-1">: R
Enter angle in X-Y plane from X axis <270>: 210
Enter angle from X-Y plane <90>: 20
```

✦ **9** You are now ready to enter paper space, which you will do by setting the variable Tilemode. A triangle will appear in the lower left of a blank screen.

```
TILEMODE:
New value for TILEMODE <1>: 0
```

✦ **10** You will make a border for the paper space. Make two new layers, *P-frame* and *P-tb*. Make P-tb the current layer. Use Pline with a width of .01 to draw the border. The border should be less than A size. In this case, it is 10" × 7- 1/2". (Your plotter limits may vary.)

✦ **11** Insert your title block in the lower-right corner. Notice that in paper space you insert it at a scale of 1, while in model space you had to insert it at a scale of 96. This is because you are not reducing the paper sheet, so your 3 1/2" title block will be plotted at 3 1/2". Text will also be inserted at the size you want it to appear on the plot.

```
Command: INSERT
Block name (or ?): TBLOCK
X scale factor<1>/Corner/XYZ: ↵
Y scale factor (default = X):
```

✦**12** Use Mview to make views of your model space. In this case you will restore the Vports configuration you set up in model space. When asked for the size, window the area above the title block. First, make P-frame the current layer.

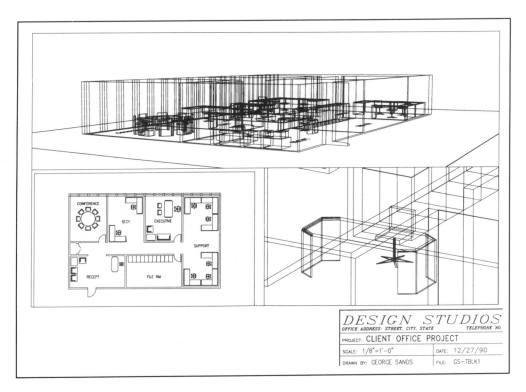

Command: **MVIEW**
ON/OFF/Hideplot/Fit/2/3/4/Restore/<First Point>: **R**
?/Name of window configuration to insert <*ACTIVE>: (Inserts the model-space viewport configuration)
Fit/<First Point>: *Window the area above the title block*

◆ **13**   Fix up the views by turning off layers.

> Command: **VPLAYER**

Freeze text in the perspective view.

> ?/Freeze/Thaw/Reset/Newfrz/Vpvisdflt: **F**
> Layer(s) to Freeze: **TEXT**
> All/Select/<Current>: **S**
> Switching to Paper space. *(So you can select the paper port)*
> Select objects: *Pick the perspective frame*

Freeze the border in all the viewpoints.

> ?/Freeze/Thaw/Reset/Newfrz/Vpvisdflt: **F**
> Layer(s) to Freeze: **BORDER**
> All/Select/<Current>: **A** (Selects all three)

Freeze the Hide layer in the perspective and desk views.

> ?/Freeze/Thaw/Reset/Newfrz/Vpvisdflt: **F**
> Layer(s) to Freeze: **HIDE**
> All/Select/<Current>: **S**
> Switching to Paper space.
> Select objects: *Pick the perspective and desk views*

◆ **14**   There are extraneous items in the paper ports showing the desk. Select these items and put them on the Hide layer; because Hide is frozen, they will disappear. If you are not already in Mspace, get there now. You can continue to manipulate the desk with Zoom and Pan until you are satisfied with how it looks.

> Command: **MS** (Mspace)
> Command: **CHANGE**
> Select objects: *Select walls and files*
> Properties/<Change point>: **P**
> Change what property (Color/LAyer/LType/Thickness)?   **LA**
> New layer: **HIDE**

✦**15** To size the plan view to exactly 1/16" = 1′, use the XP option of the Zoom command. Pick the plan view first.

> Command: **ZOOM**
> All/Center/Dynamic/Extents/Left/Previous/Vmax/Window/<Scale(X/XP)>: **1/192XP**

✦**16** Label the different views in paper space. Use the style Label and a height of 1/8".

> Command: **DTEXT**
> Justify/Style/<Start point>:

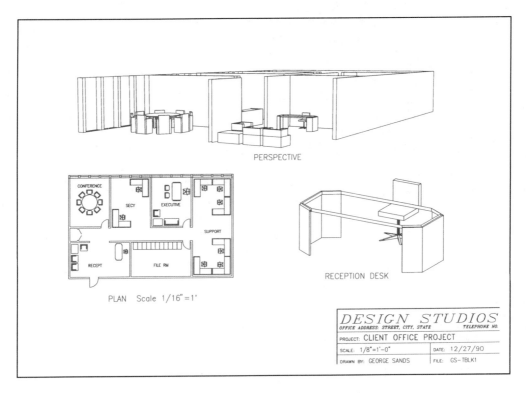

✦ **17** Use the Hideplot option of the Mview command to remove hidden lines from the perspective and desk views.

> Command: **MVIEW**
> ON/OFF/Hideplot/Fit/2/3/4/Restore/<First Point>: **H**
> ON/OFF: **ON**
> Select objects: *Pick the viewport frames of the desk and perspective views*

✦ **18** Remove the paper viewports before plotting by freezing them. Make sure that you are in paper space, and issue the Plot command.

> Command: **VPLAYER**
> ?/Freeze/Thaw/Reset/Newfrz/Vpvisdflt: **F**
> Layer(s) to Freeze: **P-frame**
> All/Select/<Current>: ⏎ (Turns off P·frame layer)

> Command: **PLOT**
> What to plot—Display, Extents, Limits, View or Window: **E**
> Hidden lines will NOT be removed. Hidden lines will be removed in selective viewports.
> Specify scale: **1 = 1** (Paper space is always plotted full-scale)

Before you end this drawing, return the objects you moved to the Hide layer to their appropriate layers.

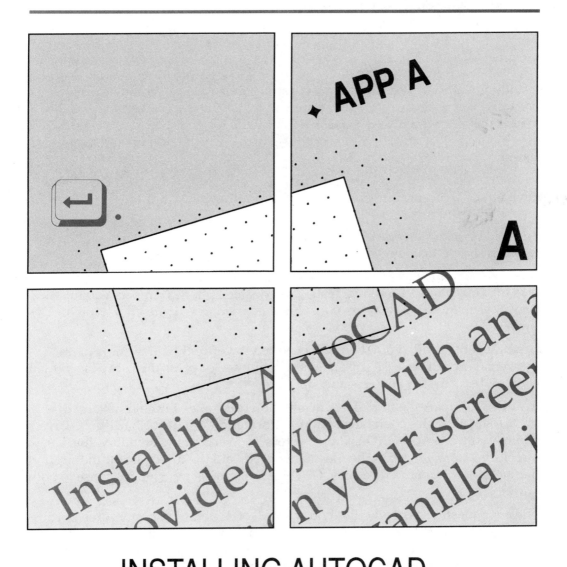

INSTALLING AUTOCAD

Installing AutoCAD Release 11 is quite straightforward, as Autodesk has provided you with an automated procedure. Just answer the questions as they appear on your screen, and the task will be done for you. The following describes the "plain-vanilla" installation procedure, which will get you up and running the fastest.

Place the first floppy disk, labeled *Executables 1*, in floppy-drive A. This disk must not be write-protected. At the DOS prompt, type **A:** and press ↵. Then type **install** and press ↵.

You will be asked several questions. In most cases, just accept the default answer, which is shown inside of angle brackets (< >), by pressing ↵.

After the introductory screen, you will be presented with a form to fill out, which asks for your name, company, dealer, and dealer's phone number. You must answer each question; your responses will be used to activate your copy of AutoCAD.

Once the form is filled out, you will be asked to verify the correctness of the answers (twice). Press Y if the answers are correct, or press the Escape key if you want to discard your answers and start over.

AutoCAD prepares your disk for installation (this takes a little time) and displays a screen with general installation information. Select the hard-disk drive where you want AutoCAD installed (press ↵ to accept the default value, C:), the directory where you want the files transferred, and the directory for the support files (accept the default directory, C:\ACAD, by pressing ↵ in response to both questions).

The next question asks whether you want all of AutoCAD or only some portions installed. Press ↵ to load the whole program (you must have over 9.5MB of disk space available on the C drive). Answer the questions about the Advanced Modeling Extensions and AutoShade, and you're off!

AutoCAD keeps you informed of what it's doing by listing file names on the screen as they are being processed, along with comments such as "Reading," "Writing," "Appending," "Making," "Decompressing," and "Verifying." You will be instructed to exchange disks as the installation proceeds. Each disk is clearly named; just follow the instructions.

After all the files are transferred from the collection of disks, you will be asked whether you want AutoCAD to create a batch file for you on the C drive. Answer Yes. This completes the installation; you will get a DOS prompt again.

Now go to the directory containing all the AutoCAD files, and start up AutoCAD. Type

    C: cd\acad acad

First you will see an AutoCAD screen displaying the licensing information for your copy and containing other messages from Autodesk. Press ⏎.

Then, you will get this message:

    AutoCAD is not yet configured. You must specify devices to which AutoCAD will interface. Press RETURN to continue.

Press ⏎.

At this point, you specify what kind of display you have, what kind of pointing device (for example, puck or mouse) you have, and what kind of printer or plotter you have (if any). When you are finished, you will have configured AutoCAD to run with your particular hardware, and you can start to work.

First, select your display from the list. The two most common ones are (7) IBM Enhanced Graphics Adapter (commonly known as EGA) and (8) IBM Video Graphics Array (commonly known as VGA).

You will then be asked whether you want to measure the screen, etc. Just accept the default answers by pressing ⏎.

After a while, you will get to choose your digitizer or pointing device. If the digitizer or mouse you own is not on the list, you will have to get help from your dealer.

Accept the default answers, and go on to the Plotter and the Printer Plotter selections. It is not necessary to have either to run AutoCAD, so you can select (1) None if you are in doubt.

Finally, you will be shown a summary of your selections for review. Press 0 to exit to the Main Menu, and press Y to keep your configuration changes.

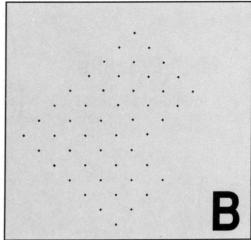

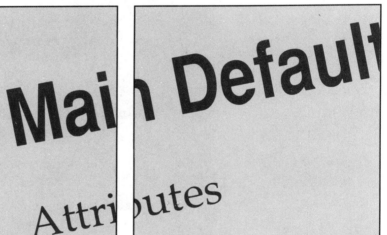

DEFAULT SETTINGS
IN THE PROTOTYPE DRAWING

✦ Main Defaults

Attributes	Visibility controlled individually; entry of values during Insert permitted (using prompts rather than a dialog box)
AXIS	Off, spacing (0.0, 0.0)
BASE	Insertion base point (0.0, 0.0, 0.0)
BLIPMODE	On
CHAMFER	Distance 0.0
COLOR	Current entity color BYLAYER
DRAGMODE	Auto
ELEVATION	Elevation 0.0, thickness 0.0
FILL	On
FILLET	Radius 0.0
GRID	Off, spacing (0.0, 0.0)
HANDLES	Off
Highlighting	Enabled
ISOPLANE	Left
LAYER	Current/only layer is 0, On, with color 7 (white) and linetype CONTINUOUS
LIMITS	Off, drawing limits (0.0, 0.0) to (12.0, 9.0)
LINETYPE	Current entity linetype BYLAYER; no loaded linetypes other than CONTINUOUS
LTSCALE	1.0
MENU	acad
MIRROR	Text mirrored same as other entities
ORTHO	Off
OSNAP	None

PLINE	Line width 0.0
POINT	Display mode 0, size 0.0
QTEXT	Off
REGENAUTO	On
SHADE	Rendering type 3, percent ambient 70
SKETCH	Record increment 0.10, producing lines
SNAP	Off, spacing (1.0, 1.0)
SNAP/GRID	Standard style, base point (0.0, 0.0), rotation 0.0 degrees
Space	Model
Spline curves	Frame off, segments 8, spline type = cubic
STYLE	Only defined text style is STANDARD, using font TXT with variable height, width factor 1.0, horizontal orientation, and no special modes
Surfaces	6 tabulations in M and N directions, 6 segments for smoothing in U and V directions, smooth surface type = cubic B-spline
TABLET	Off
TEXT	Style STANDARD, height 0.20, rotation 0.0 degrees
TILEMODE	On
TIME	User elapsed timer on
TRACE	Width 0.05
UCS	Current UCS same as World, origin at World (0.0.0), Auto plan view off, coordinate-system icon on (at origin)
UNITS (linear)	Decimal, 4 decimal places
UNITS (angular)	Decimal degrees, 0 decimal places; angle 0 direction is to the right; angles increase counterclockwise

Viewing modes	One active viewport, plan view, perspective off, target point (0,0,0), front and back clipping off, lens length 50mm, twist angle 0.0, fast zoom on, circle zoom percent 100, WORLDVIEW 0
ZOOM	To drawing limits

✦ Configuration File Defaults

Object snap	Aperture size 10 pixels
Object selection	Pick-box size 3 pixels
Dragging control	DRAGP1 10, DRAGP2 25
File dialog boxes	On
Sorting	On, 200 symbols maximum

✦ Dimension Variable Defaults

To make the dimension variables easier to understand, the DIM- prefix has been dropped, and they have been organized in groups roughly relating to what type of dimensioning component they affect. The values given are those that come with the prototype drawing.

Numerical Modifications

ALT	Off	On enables alternate units
ALTD	2	Alternate unit decimal places
ALTF	25.4	Alternate unit scale factor (mm/inch factor)
LFAC	1.0	Global multiplier for linear dimensions
RND	0	Rounding value (not unit places)

Graphic Elements: Markers

ASZ	0.1800	Arrow size
BLK		Arrow block name
BLK1		First arrow block name
BLK2		Second arrow block name
CEN	0.0900	Center mark size
SAH	Off	Separate arrow blocks
TSZ	0.0000	Tick size

Graphic Elements: Color

CLRD	BYBLOCK	Dimension line color
CLRE	BYBLOCK	Extension line and leader color
CLRT	BYBLOCK	Dimension text color

Graphic Elements: Dimension Line

DLE	0.0000	Dimension line extension
DLI	0.3800	Dimension line increment for continuation
GAP	0.0900	Gap from dimension line to text
TOFL	Off	Forces line inside extension lines
SOXD	Off	Suppresses outside extension dimension line

Graphic Elements: Extension Lines

EXE	0.1800	Extension above dimension line
EXO	0.0625	Extension-line origin offset
SE1	Off	Suppresses first extension line
SE2	Off	Suppresses second extension line

Text Placement

TAD	Off	Places text above dimension line
TIH	On	Horizontal text inside extensions
TIX	Off	Places text inside extensions
TOH	On	Horizontal text outside extensions
TVP	0.0000	Vertical text position
TXT	0.1800	Text height

Text Modifications

APOST		Suffix for alternate text
POST		Default suffix for dimension text
ZIN	0	Zero suppression

Here are some examples of measurements, given different values for zero suppression:

Value	Examples		
0	1/2"	6"	1'
1	0'-0 1/2"	0'-6"	1'-0"
2	0'-0 1/2"	0'-6"	1'
3	1/2"	6"	1' 0"

Associative Dimensions

ASO	On	Creates associative dimensions
SHO	On	Updates dimensions while dragging

Tolerance

LIM	Off	On generates limits from TM and TP values
TFAC	1.0000	Tolerance text-height scaling factor
TM	0.0000	Minus tolerance
TOL	Off	Generates dimension tolerances
TP	0.0000	Plus tolerance

Informational/General

| SCALE | 1.0000 | Overall scale factor |
| STYLE | *UNNAMED | Current dimension style (read-only) |

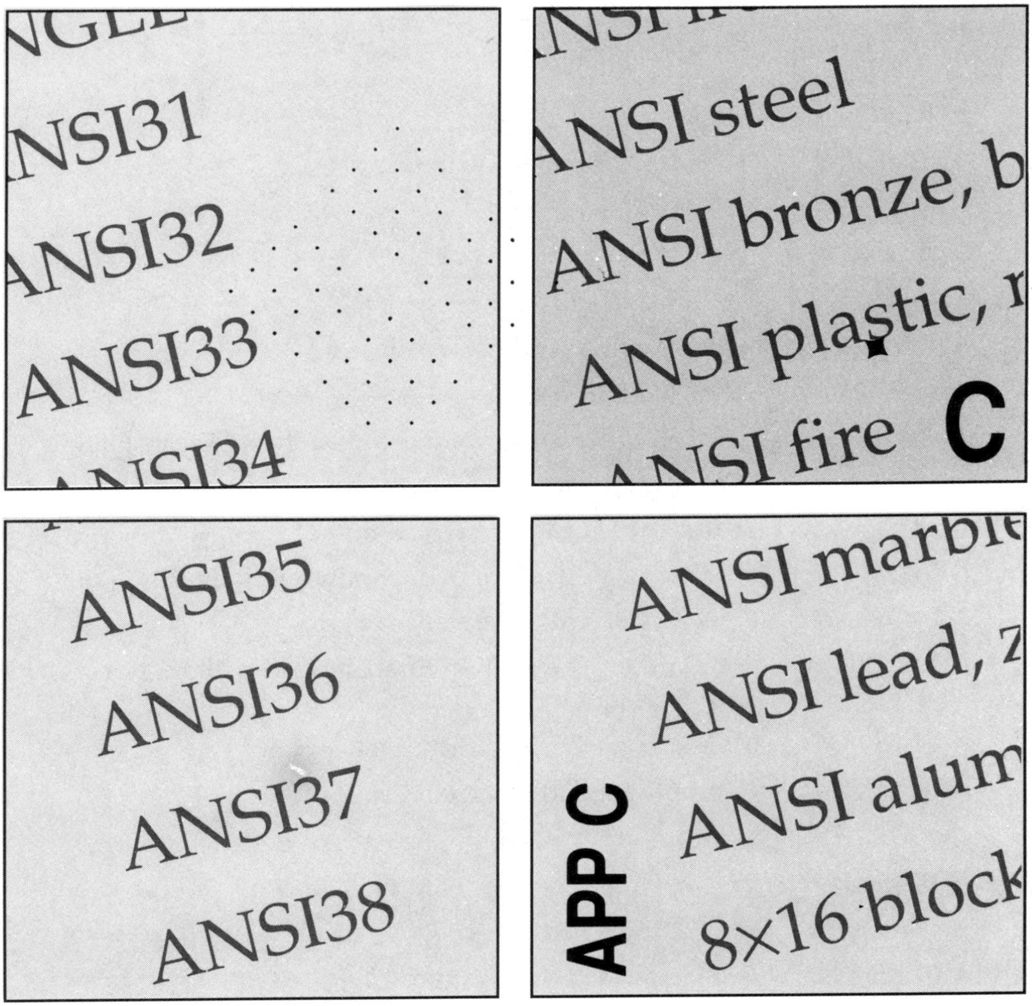

NGEL

NSI31

ANSI32

ANSI33

ANSI34

NSI

ANSI steel

ANSI bronze, b

ANSI plastic, r

ANSI fire **C**

ANSI35

ANSI36

ANSI37

ANSI38

ANSI marble

ANSI lead, z

APP C ANSI alum

8×16 block

HATCH PATTERNS

ANGLE	Angle steel
ANSI31	ANSI iron, brick, stone masonry
ANSI32	ANSI steel
ANSI33	ANSI bronze, brass, copper
ANSI34	ANSI plastic, rubber
ANSI35	ANSI fire brick, refractory material
ANSI36	ANSI marble, slate, glass
ANSI37	ANSI lead, zinc, magnesium, sound/heat/elec insulation
ANSI38	ANSI aluminum
AR-B816	8×16 block elevation stretcher bond
AR-B816C	8×16 block elevation stretcher bond with mortar joints
AR-B88	8×8 block elevation stretcher bond
AR-BRELM	Standard brick elevation English bond with mortar joints
AR-BRSTD	Standard brick elevation stretcher bond
AR-CONC	Random dot and stone pattern
AR-HBONE	Standard brick herringbone pattern @ 45 degrees
AR-PARQ1	2×12 parquet flooring: pattern of 12×12
AR-RROOF	Roof shingle texture
AR-RSHKE	Roof wood shake texture
AR-SAND	Random dot pattern
BOX	Box steel
BRASS	Brass material
BRICK	Brick or masonry-type surface
BRSTONE	Brick and stone

CLAY	Clay material
CORK	Cork material
CROSS	A series of crosses
DASH	Dashed lines
DOLMIT	Geological rock layering
DOTS	A series of dots
EARTH	Earth or ground (subterranean)
ESCHER	Escher pattern
FLEX	Flexible material
GRASS	Grass area
GRATE	Grated area
HEX	Hexagons
HONEY	Honeycomb pattern
HOUND	Houndstooth check
INSUL	Insulation material
LINE	Parallel horizontal lines
MUDST	Mud and sand
NET	Horizontal/vertical grid
NET3	Network pattern 0-60-120
PLAST	Plastic material
PLAST1	Plastic material
SACNCR	Concrete
SQUARE	Small, aligned squares
STARS	Star of David
STEEL	Steel material

SWAMP	Swampy area
TRANS	Heat transfer material
TRIANG	Equilateral triangles
ZIGZAG	Staircase effect

INDEX

drawings, 158
grids, 72
viewports, 341
views, 76
right justification of text, 269
roads, drawing, 93
root menu, 9, 11, 13–14
Rotate command, 173–175, 188
rotating
arrays of objects, 241
blocks, 213, 235
dimensions, 320, 323
with plotting, 381–382
snap grid, 306–307
text, 236, 269, 272
3-D drawings, 344

S

Save command, 54–55
saving
blocks, 208–211
dimension variable settings, 324
drawings, 54–55
viewports, 341, 347
views, 75–76
Scale command, 247–249
scaling
for blocks, 212
dynamic, 248
with exploding, 223
for hatch patterns, 144
for linetypes, 305–306
for paper space, 388–389
for plotting, 381
for tablets, 315
and text height, 274–275, 391

with zooming, 68–69
scroll bars and scroll boxes, 12–13
seating layouts, arrays for, 242
section identification symbol, 112–115
segments
dividing objects into, 252–253
measuring, 250–252
selection sets, 17–18
setup commands, 27
for axes, 37–38
for blips, 39
for constraining lines, 40
for drawing space, 30–31
function keys for, 40–43
for grids, 33–36
for layers, 43–46
for snap mode, 31–33
for units, 28–30
Setvar command, 300–301
Shade command, 353
ShowEdge command, 337
side chairs
drawing, 102–103, 261–262
3-D, 360–362
side menus, 8, 14
size
of doors, 199, 201
of drawing space, 30–31, 48–49
editing, 234–236
of object selection box, 300
for plotting, 380
of points, 97–98, 111
scaling for, 247–249
of target box, 133, 300
of text, 236, 269, 272–274, 282, 391
.SLD files, 59
slider bars, 350–351

Selections from The SYBEX Library

CAD

The ABC's of AutoCAD
(Second Edition)
Alan R. Miller
375pp. Ref. 584-0

This brief but effective introduction to AutoCAD quickly gets users drafting and designing with this complex CADD package. The essential operations and capabilities of AutoCAD are neatly detailed, using a proven, step-by-step method that is tailored to the results-oriented beginner.

The ABC's of AutoLISP
George Omura
300pp. Ref. 620-0

This book is for users who want to unleash the full power of AutoCAD through the AutoLISP programming language. In non-technical terms, the reader is shown how to store point locations, create new commands, and manipulate coordinates and text. Packed with tips on common coding errors.

The ABC's of Generic CADD
Alan R. Miller
278pp. Ref. 608-1

This outstanding guide to computer-aided design and drafting with Generic CADD assumes no previous experience with computers or CADD. This book will have users doing useful CADD work in record time, including basic drawing with the keyboard or a mouse, erasing and unerasing, making a copy of drawings on your printer, adding text and organizing your drawings using layers.

Advanced Techniques
in AutoCAD
(Second Edition)
Robert M. Thomas
425pp. Ref. 593-X

Develop custom applications using screen menus, command macros, and AutoLISP programming—no prior programming experience required. Topics include customizing the AutoCAD environment, advanced data extraction techniques, and much more.

AutoCAD Desktop Companion
SYBEX Ready Reference Series
Robert M. Thomas
1094pp. Ref. 590-5

This is a complete reference work covering all the features, commands, and user options available under AutoCAD Release 10, including drawing basic and complex entities, editing, displaying, printing, plotting, and customizing drawings, manipulating the drawing database, and AutoLISP programming. Through Release 10.

AutoCAD Instant Reference
SYBEX Prompter Series
George Omura
390pp. Ref. 548-4, 4 3/4" × 8"

This pocket-sized reference is a quick guide to all AutoCAD features. Designed for easy use, all commands are organized with exact syntax, a brief description, options, tips, and references. Through Release 10.

Mastering AutoCAD Release 11
George Omura
1150pp, Ref. 716-9
Even if you're just beginning, this comprehensive guide will help you to become an AutoCAD expert. Create your first drawing, then learn to use dimensions, enter pre-existing drawings, use advanced 3-D features, and more. Suitable for experienced users, too—includes tips and tricks you won't find elsewhere.

Mastering VersaCAD
David Bassett-Parkins
450pp. Ref. 617-0
For every level of VCAD user, this comprehensive tutorial treats each phase of project design including drawing, modifying, grouping, and filing. The reader will also learn VCAD project management and many tips, tricks, and shortcuts. Version 5.4.

OPERATING SYSTEMS

The ABC's of DOS 4
Alan R. Miller
275pp. Ref. 583-2
This step-by-step introduction to using DOS 4 is written especially for beginners. Filled with simple examples, *The ABC's of DOS 4* covers the basics of hardware, software, disks, the system editor EDLIN, DOS commands, and more.

ABC's of MS-DOS (Second Edition)
Alan R. Miller
233pp. Ref. 493-3
This handy guide to MS-DOS is all many PC users need to manage their computer files, organize floppy and hard disks, use EDLIN, and keep their computers organized. Additional information is given about utilities like Sidekick, and there is a DOS command and program summary. The second edition is fully updated for Version 3.3.

DOS Assembly Language Programming
Alan R. Miller
365pp. 487-9
This book covers PC-DOS through 3.3, and gives clear explanations of how to assemble, link, and debug 8086, 8088, 80286, and 80386 programs. The example assembly language routines are valuable for students and programmers alike.

DOS Instant Reference SYBEX Prompter Series
Greg Harvey
Kay Yarborough Nelson
220pp. Ref. 477-1, 4 ¾" × 8"
A complete fingertip reference for fast, easy on-line help:command summaries, syntax, usage and error messages. Organized by function—system commands, file commands, disk management, directories, batch files, I/O, networking, programming, and more. Through Version 3.3.

Encyclopedia DOS
Judd Robbins
1030pp. Ref. 699-5
A comprehensive reference and user's guide to all versions of DOS through 4.0. Offers complete information on every DOS command, with all possible switches and parameters—plus examples of effective usage. An invaluable tool.

Essential OS/2 (Second Edition)
Judd Robbins
445pp. Ref. 609-X
Written by an OS/2 expert, this is the guide to the powerful new resources of the OS/2 operating system standard edition 1.1 with presentation manager. Robbins introduces the standard edition, and details multitasking under OS/2, and the range of commands for installing, starting up, configuring, and running applications. For Version 1.1 Standard Edition.

Essential PC-DOS
(Second Edition)
Myril Clement Shaw
Susan Soltis Shaw
332pp. Ref. 413-5

An authoritative guide to PC-DOS, including version 3.2. Designed to make experts out of beginners, it explores everything from disk management to batch file programming. Includes an 85-page command summary. Through Version 3.2.

Graphics Programming
Under Windows
Brian Myers
Chris Doner
646pp. Ref. 448-8

Straightforward discussion, abundant examples, and a concise reference guide to graphics commands make this book a must for Windows programmers. Topics range from how Windows works to programming for business, animation, CAD, and desktop publishing. For Version 2.

Hard Disk Instant Reference
SYBEX Prompter Series
Judd Robbins
256pp. Ref. 587-5, 4 ¾" × 8"

Compact yet comprehensive, this pocket-sized reference presents the essential information on DOS commands used in managing directories and files, and in optimizing disk configuration. Includes a survey of third-party utility capabilities. Through DOS 4.0.

Inside DOS: A Programmer's
Guide
Michael J. Young
490pp. Ref. 710-X

A collection of practical techniques (with source code listings) designed to help you take advantage of the rich resources intrinsic to MS-DOS machines. Designed for the experienced programmer with a basic understanding of C and 8086 assembly language, and DOS fundamentals.

Mastering DOS
(Second Edition)
Judd Robbins
722pp. Ref. 555-7

"The most useful DOS book." This seven-part, in-depth tutorial addresses the needs of users at all levels. Topics range from running applications, to managing files and directories, configuring the system, batch file programming, and techniques for system developers. Through Version 4.

MS-DOS Power User's Guide,
Volume I
(Second Edition)
Jonathan Kamin
482pp. Ref. 473-9

A fully revised, expanded edition of our best-selling guide to high-performance DOS techniques and utilities—with details on Version 3.3. Configuration, I/O, directory structures, hard disks, RAM disks, batch file programming, the ANSI.SYS device driver, more. Through Version 3.3.

Understanding DOS 3.3
Judd Robbins
678pp. Ref. 648-0

This best selling, in-depth tutorial addresses the needs of users at all levels with many examples and hands-on exercises. Robbins discusses the fundamentals of DOS, then covers manipulating files and directories, using the DOS editor, printing, communicating, and finishes with a full section on batch files.

Understanding Hard Disk
Management on the PC
Jonathan Kamin
500pp. Ref. 561-1

This title is a key productivity tool for all hard disk users who want efficient, error-free file management and organization. Includes details on the best ways to conserve hard disk space when using several memory-guzzling programs. Through DOS 4.

Teach Yourself AutoCAD on Disk

In keeping with the visual approach of *Teach Yourself AutoCAD*, I have made the command drawings from the book available on disk. You can use them in going through the steps in the exercises. Students have found these exercises very useful in helping them get up to speed quickly with AutoCAD. The drawings come with layers and colors already set up, so you can actually experience the correct way to use each command by tracing over the steps in the drawings. These exercises are useful both as a teaching and a learning tool.

To introduce beginners to 3-D drawing, I have also included a prototype 3-D drawing on the disk. This drawing is set up with the viewports and the cube 3-D icon used in the book.

All lessons and drawings will work with AutoCAD versions 10 and 11.

To order, please fill out the form below, indicating the disk format you require. Make check or money order payable to *Metron Computerware, Ltd.*, and send to

Metron Computerware, Ltd. 3317 Brunell Drive Oakland CA 94602

	Price	Quantity	Subtotal
✦ Teach Yourself AutoCAD on Disk	$12.00	_____	_____
✦ California residents add 7% sales tax	$.84		_____
✦ Shipping	$2.00		_____
✦ Foreign orders add $12.00 for postage and handling			_____
✦ Total			_____

Name _____

Address _____

City/State/Zip _____

Country _____

Phone Number _____

Indicate disk size required: 3½" (1.44MB)_____   5¼" (1.2MB)_____   Apple Macintosh_____

Sorry, no credit-card orders. Please allow three weeks for stateside delivery.

A quantity discount is available to schools and AutoCAD training centers.

SYBEX ®

FREE CATALOG!

Mail us this form today, and we'll send you a full-color catalog of Sybex books.

Name _____

Street _____

City/State/Zip _____

Phone _____

Please supply the name of the Sybex book purchased.

_____

How would you rate it?

_____ Excellent   _____ Very Good   _____ Average   _____ Poor

Why did you select this particular book?

_____ Recommended to me by a friend

_____ Recommended to me by store personnel

_____ Saw an advertisement in _____

_____ Author's reputation

_____ Saw in Sybex catalog

_____ Required textbook

_____ Sybex reputation

_____ Read book review in _____

_____ In-store display

_____ Other _____

Where did you buy it?

_____ Bookstore

_____ Computer Store or Software Store

_____ Catalog (name: _____)

_____ Direct from Sybex

_____ Other: _____

Did you buy this book with your personal funds?

_____ Yes   _____ No

About how many computer books do you buy each year?

_____ 1-3   _____ 3-5   _____ 5-7   _____ 7-9   _____ 10+

About how many Sybex books do you own?

_____ 1-3   _____ 3-5   _____ 5-7   _____ 7-9   _____ 10+

Please indicate your level of experience with the software covered in this book:

_____ Beginner   _____ Intermediate   _____ Advanced

Which types of software packages do you use regularly?

_____ Accounting   _____ Databases   _____ Networks

_____ Amiga   _____ Desktop Publishing   _____ Operating Systems

_____ Apple/Mac   _____ File Utilities   _____ Spreadsheets

_____ CAD   _____ Money Management   _____ Word Processing

_____ Communications   _____ Languages   _____ Other _____
                                                                             (please specify)

Which of the following best describes your job title?

_____ Administrative/Secretarial   _____ President/CEO

_____ Director   _____ Manager/Supervisor

_____ Engineer/Technician   _____ Other _____
                                                                            (please specify)

Comments on the weaknesses/strengths of this book: _____

_____

_____

_____

_____

PLEASE FOLD, SEAL, AND MAIL TO SYBEX

- -

SYBEX, INC.
Department M
2021 CHALLENGER DR.
ALAMEDA, CALIFORNIA USA
94501

SYBEX ®

SEAL

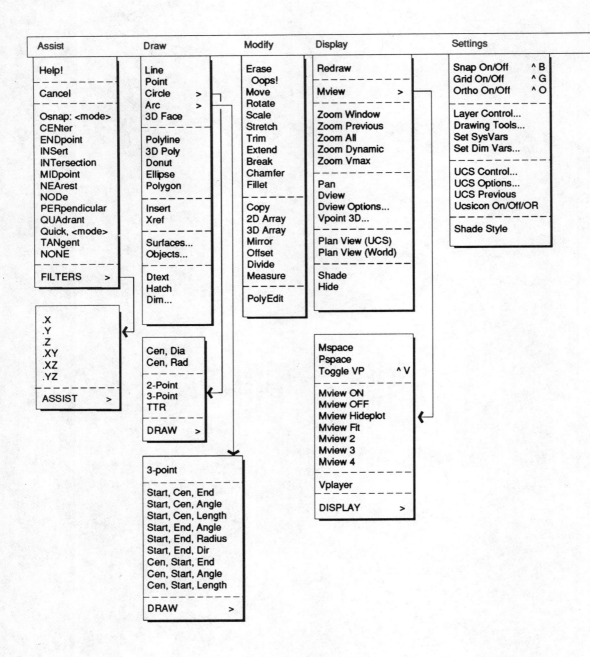

Assist

Help!

Cancel

Osnap: <mode>
CENter
ENDpoint
INSert
INTersection
MIDpoint
NEArest
NODe
PERpendicular
QUAdrant
Quick, <mode>
TANgent
NONE

FILTERS   >

.X
.Y
.Z
.XY
.XZ
.YZ

ASSIST   >

Draw

Line
Point
Circle   >
Arc   >
3D Face

Polyline
3D Poly
Donut
Ellipse
Polygon

Insert
Xref

Surfaces...
Objects...

Dtext
Hatch
Dim...

Cen, Dia
Cen, Rad

2-Point
3-Point
TTR

DRAW   >

3-point

Start, Cen, End
Start, Cen, Angle
Start, Cen, Length
Start, End, Angle
Start, End, Radius
Start, End, Dir
Cen, Start, End
Cen, Start, Angle
Cen, Start, Length

DRAW   >

Modify

Erase
Oops!
Move
Rotate
Scale
Stretch
Trim
Extend
Break
Chamfer
Fillet

Copy
2D Array
3D Array
Mirror
Offset
Divide
Measure

PolyEdit

Display

Redraw

Mview   >

Zoom Window
Zoom Previous
Zoom All
Zoom Dynamic
Zoom Vmax

Pan
Dview
Dview Options...
Vpoint 3D...

Plan View (UCS)
Plan View (World)

Shade
Hide

Mspace
Pspace
Toggle VP   ^ V

Mview ON
Mview OFF
Mview Hideplot
Mview Fit
Mview 2
Mview 3
Mview 4

Vplayer

DISPLAY   >

Settings

Snap On/Off   ^ B
Grid On/Off   ^ G
Ortho On/Off   ^ O

Layer Control...
Drawing Tools...
Set SysVars
Set Dim Vars...

UCS Control...
UCS Options...
UCS Previous
Ucsicon On/Off/OR

Shade Style